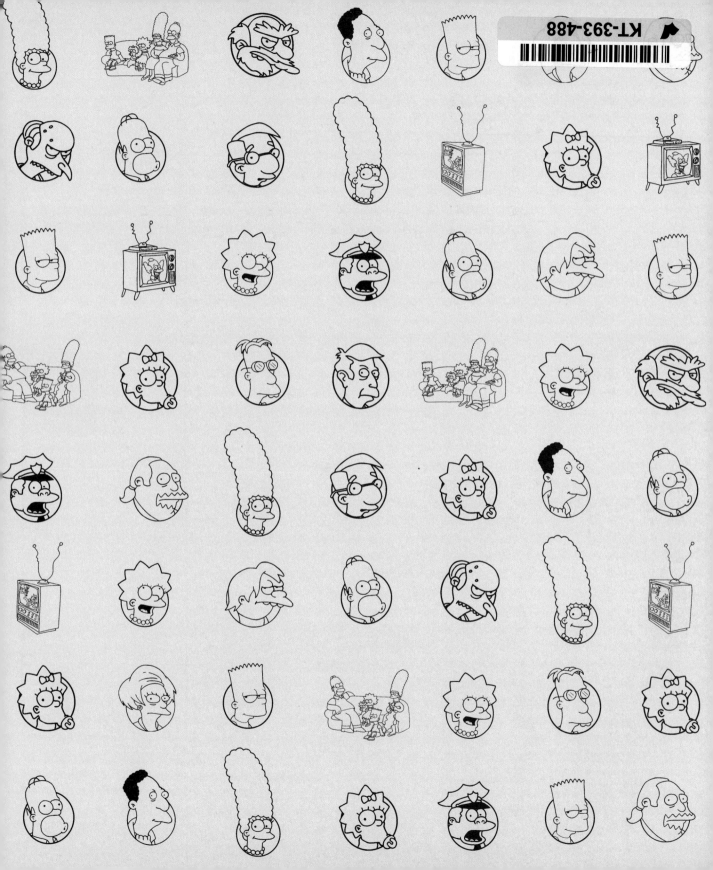

KT-393-488

THE SIMPSONS™
FOREVER!

**A COMPLETE GUIDE TO
OUR FAVORITE FAMILY
...CONTINUED**

Created by Matt Groening
Edited by Scott M. Gimple

HarperCollins*Entertainment*
An Imprint of HarperCollins*Publishers*

TO THE LOVING MEMORY OF
SNOWBALL I:
YOU MAY BE GONE, BUT WE
ARE STILL FINDING YOUR HAIRBALLS
IN THE CLOSET

The Simpsons™, created by Matt Groening, is the
copyrighted and trademarked property of Twentieth Century Fox Film Corporation.
Used with permission. All rights reserved.

THE SIMPSONS FOREVER! A COMPLETE GUIDE TO OUR FAVORITE FAMILY … CONTINUED.
Copyright © 1999 by Matt Groening Productions, Inc.
All rights reserved.
No part of this book may be used or reproduced in any manner whatsoever without written
permission except in the case of brief quotations embodied in critical articles and reviews.

Published by HarperCollins*Entertainment* 1999

HarperCollins*Entertainment*
An Imprint of HarperCollins*Publishers*
77–85 Fulham Palace Road
London W6 8JB

www.**fire**and**water**.com

First Edition

ISBN 0 00 653168 7

Printed in Great Britain by Scotprint Ltd, Musselburgh

1 3 5 7 9 8 6 4 2

A catalogue record for this book is available from the British Library

Concept and Design
Mili Smythe, Serban Cristescu, Bill Morrison

Art Direction
Bill Morrison

Computer Design & Layout
Christopher Ungar and Karen Bates

Contributing Artists
Shaun Cashman, Bill Morrison, Phil Ortiz, Julius Preite, Mike Rote

Production Team
Karen Bates, Terry Delegeane, Chia-Hsien Jason Ho, Bill Morrison, Mike Rote,
Jessica Seymour, Christopher Ungar, Robert Zaugh

HarperCollins Editors
Susan Weinberg, Trena Keating, Susan Hoffner

Legal Guardian
Susan A. Grode

Special thanks to
Annette Andersen, Jeannine Black, Claudia de la Roca, N. Vyolet Diaz,
Deanna MacLellan, Antonia Coffman, Bonita Pietila, Laurie Biernacki, and
everyone who has contributed to The Simpsons over the last 12 years.

TABLE OF CONTENTS

Introduction 6
Season 9/Do The Bartman 8
The City of New York vs. Homer Simpson
The Principal and the Pauper
Lisa's Sax
Treehouse of Horror VIII
The Cartridge Family
Bart Star
The Two Mrs. Nahasapeemapetilons
Lisa the Skeptic
Realty Bites
Miracle on Evergreen Terrace
All Singing, All Dancing
Bart Carny
The Joy of Sect
Das Bus
The Last Temptation of Krust
Dumbbell Indemnity
Lisa the Simpson
This Little Wiggy
Simpson Tide
The Trouble with Trillions
Girly Edition
Trash of the Titans
King of the Hill
Lost Our Lisa
Natural Born Kissers
Season 10/Deep, Deep Trouble . . 44
Lard of the Dance
The Wizard of Evergreen Terrace
Bart the Mother

Treehouse of Horror IX
When You Dish Upon a Star
D'oh-in' in the Wind
Lisa Gets an "A"
Homer Simpson in: "Kidney Trouble"
Mayored to the Mob
Viva Ned Flanders
Wild Barts Can't be Broken
Sunday, Cruddy Sunday
Homer to the Max
I'm with Cupid
Marge Simpson in: "Screaming Yellow Honkers"
Make Room for Lisa
Maximum Homerdrive
Simpsons Bible Stories
Mom and Pop Art
The Old Man and the "C" Student
Monty Can't Buy Me Love
They Saved Lisa's Brain
30 Minutes over Tokyo

A Tribute to Troy McClure . . 80
Homer Says 82
Couch Gags 84
Who Does What Voice 86
Songs Sung Simpson 88
Index 90

DON'T TOUCH THAT DIAL: AN INTRODUCTION

Ladies and Gentlemen, Boys and Girls, Geezers and Toddlers:

OK, here's the deal. A few decades back, we cobbled together this other book, *The Simpsons: A Complete Guide to Our Favorite Family*. It was filled with huge amounts of technical data, memorable lines, succinct plot summaries, pesky details, vital measurements, and national secrets. In the generally dismal genre of TV-show companions, the book was a profusely illustrated masterpiece, if I do say so myself. And for a short amount of time, our work was done.

But time has a peculiar way of slogging on. And slogging on with time were the writers, actors, and animators of "The Simpsons," who kept churning out new episodes of the show—a whole mess of new episodes, in fact. Now, we could have just added a few juicy chapters to the old book, slapped a snazzy embossed cover on it, called it the *Special Deluxe Revised Edition*, and charged all you loyal Simpsons nuts one more time for the same material—but we said no! You maniacs deserve better.

Hence this thing: a companion to the first companion. Here are all the nitty-gritty details about the rib-ticklin', knee-slappin' episodes from seasons nine and ten, along with bonus peeks into the nooks and crannies of "The Simpsons," including all the various d'ohs, mmms, and couch gags. We think it deserves a proud place of honor in your book nook—it's that nifty. And we call it *The Simpsons Forever!* for the same reason we called the first book *Complete*—because we're big fat liars.

Enjoy!

Your pal,

MATT GROENING

Writer:
Bryan Loren
Director:
Brad Bird

Do The Bartman

Original Airdate:
12/6/90

A music video in which the Simpson family goes to see Bart perform at the Fourth Grade Dance Recital at Springfield Elementary. Goofing around with the curtain before the show, Bart gets in trouble and is told by Mrs. Krabappel to stand offstage during the recital. Bart plugs his tape player into the sound system and takes over the recital, rapping his own song, "Do the Bartman."

(Bart starts his own music, and the kids onstage look at each other. Mrs. Krabappel gestures for them to dance to the music. Bart makes his way through the crowd of students dancing onstage. He puts his fist in the air.)
Bart: *Yo!*
(He then suddenly pops out of the group.)
Bart:
Hey, what's happenin', dude?
I'm a guy with a rep for bein' rude.
Terrorizin' people wherever I go
It's not intentional, just keepin' the flow.
Fixin' test scores to get the best scores...
(Bart tosses his jacket away; it hits Principal Skinner, standing offstage, in the face.)
Droppin' banana peels all over the floor,
I'm the kid that made delinquency an art.
Last name, Simpson; first name, Bart.
(Skinner turns to a nearby file cabinet and pulls out Bart's file.)
I'm here today to introduce the next phase,
The next step in the big Bart craze.
I got a dance, real easy to do.
I learned it with no rhythm and so can you!
(Skinner tries to snare Bart with a hook to pull him offstage, but misses. Mrs. Krabappel snaps her fingers in disappointment.)

So move your body, if you got the notion,
Front to back in a rock-like motion.
Now that you got it, if you think you can
Do it to the music, that's the Bartman.
(An unnamed student, Martin, and Milhouse step out of the crowd, singing and dancing the "Bartman.")
Student, Martin, and Milhouse: *Everybody if you can, do the Bartman!*
Bart: *Whoa!*
Student, Martin, and Milhouse: *Shake your body, turn it out, if you can, man!*
Bart: *Check it out, man!*
(The audience grooves to the music as the Simpsons look around in awe.)
Student, Martin, and Milhouse: *Move your butt to the side, as you can, can!*
Bart: *Bartman!*
Student, Martin, and Milhouse: *Everybody in the house, do the Bartman...do the Bartman.*
Bart: *Uh-huh!*
(Mrs. Krabappel hands Skinner a flask. He takes a draught, hands it back, and shudders.)
Student, Martin, and Milhouse: *Everybody if you can, do the Bartman! Shake your body, turn it out, if you can, man!*
Bart: *Whooooa, mama!*
Student, Martin, and Milhouse: *Move your butt to the side, as you can, can! Everybody in the house...*
(Bart appears in a line drawing, standing in the corner of a plain room.)
Bart: *It wasn't long ago, just a couple of weeks, I got in trouble, yeah, pretty deep. Homer was yellin'...*
(Homer and Marge's silhouettes surround Bart, à la Bongo in Matt Groening's "Life in Hell" cartoons.)
Homer: *Bart!*

Bart: *Mom was, too. Because I put mothballs in the beef stew.*
(Homer tries some stew as Marge looks on. Homer immediately spits it out, disgusted, and we cut to Bart, posed in a mugshot.)
Punishment time, in the air lurks gloom,
Sittin' by myself, confined to my room.
(Bart walks down the hall into his room. A barred door clanks shut behind him. He lays on his bed, looking dejected.)
When all else fails, nothin' else left to do,
I turn on the music, so I can feel the groove!
(Bart turns on his radio and the room lights up. He starts dancing to the music.)
Back-up Singer: *Move your body, if you got the notion...*
Bart: *I'm feelin' the groove now, baby!*
Back-up Singer: *Front to back in a rock-like motion...*
Bart: *Bring it back! Whoa!*
Back-up Singer: *Move your hips from side to side now...*
Bart: *Do the Bartman! Whoa!*
(Lisa looks into Bart's room.)
Back-up Singer: *Don't ya slip...*
Bart: *Lisa!*
Back-up Singer: *Let's reply now...*
(Bart leaps on the bed, striking a dance pose. Lisa joins him and swings him around.)
Back-up Singer: *If you've got the groove...*
Bart: *Yeah!*
(Bart flies off the bed.)
Back-up Singer: *You gotta use it. Rock rhythm in time with the music...*
(Bart laughs, flying out the window, to the tree branch outside his room.)
Bart: *Check it out!*

(Bart falls off the branch.)
Back-up Singer: *You just might start a chain reaction...*
(Bart hits another branch, breaking it. He looks to the camera, and he gets a curl on top of his forehead like Michael Jackson.)
Bart: *If you can do the Bart, you're bad, like Michael Jackson!*
(Bart lands on a city street, in an alley.)
Back-up Singers and Bart: *Everybody if you can, do the Bartman!*
Back-up Singers: *Shake your body, turn it out...*
(People on a tour ship near the Statue of Liberty groove to the music.)
Bart: *Check it out!*
Back-up Singers: *If you can, man!*
Bart: *Whoooa, mama!*
Back-up Singers: *Move your butt to the side as you can, can!*
Bart: *I'm bad! I'm bad!*
(People at a cafe in Paris groove to the music.)
Back-up Singers: *Everybody in the house...Do the Bartman!*
Bart: *Do the Bartman! Everybody back and forth, from side to side.*
(Germans by the ruins of the Berlin Wall dance to the music.)
Back-up Singer: *Do the Bartman!*
Bart: *Do the Bartman! Now here's a dance beat that you can't deny!*
(On the city street, Bart goes through a complex dance routine with a group of dancers. Homer pops out of a manhole cover.)
Homer: *Turn it down! Will you stop that infernal racket?*
(Lights go on in buildings all around Homer, and suddenly,

THE STUFF YOU MAY HAVE MISSED

According to the background in Bart's mugshot, he stands at three and a half feet tall. His number in the mugshot is A-113.

Adil Hoxha, introduced in 7G13, "The Crepes of Wrath," can be seen dancing by the fallen Berlin Wall.

A sign in the alley advertises, "Ben & His Rat Army — Oct. 25."

Springfielders seen in the conga line include: Mrs. Krabappel, Principal Skinner, Patty Bouvier, and Herman.

Jacques's dancing partners include: Helen Lovejoy; Princess Kashmir (introduced in 7G10, "Homer's Night Out"); Ms. Mellon, Bart's teacher from the Enriched Learning Center for Gifted Children (introduced in 7G02, "Bart the Genius"); and Karl (from 7F02, "Simpson and Delilah").

Seen among the people dancing in the town square is the Capital City Goofball.

he's surrounded by people from the neighborhood, shouting at him.)

Neighborhood People: *Do the Bartman!*

(Lisa stands on a bridge, playing a sax solo. Bart holds his ears.)

Bart: *Oh my ears! Lisa! Put that saxophone away!*

(Lisa keeps playing. Bart stands at the back door of the Springfield Dog Pound truck.)

Bart: *Ya can't touch this!*

(He opens the door and dogs race off, knocking him down. He pops back up.)

Bart: *I didn't do it. Nobody saw me do it. You can't prove anything.*

(A little dog bumps into him and keeps running. Bart starts walking along with the boys he was dancing with.)

Bart: *Now, I'm in the house feelin' good to be home. 'Til Lisa starts blowin' that damn saxophone...*

(Bart passes Lisa and Bleeding Gums Murphy, playing saxophone on the stoop of a brownstone.)

Bart: *And if it was mine, you know they'd take it away. But still I'm feelin' good, so that's okay. I'm up in my room, just a-singin' a song, Listen to the kickdrum kickin' along. Yeah, Lisa likes jazz, she's her number one fan. But I know I'm bad, 'cause I do the Bartman!*

Back-up Singers: *Everybody, if you can do the Bartman...*

(People standing by the pyramids dance like an Egyptian to the music.)

Bart: *Hey, everybody, need I remind you?*

Back-up Singers: *Shake your body, turn it out if you can, man! Move your butt to the side, as you can, can!*

Bart: *I! Am! Bart! Man!*

Back-up Singers: *Everybody in the house...*

(People on the Great Wall of China dance to the music.)

Back-up Singers: *Do the Bartman! Do the Bartman!*

(Bart is on a pay phone, rapping.)

Bart: *Do the Bartman!*

(Moe is listening at his bar as Larry, Barney, and an unnamed woman sit at the bar.)

Bart: *Everybody back and forth from side to side.*

(Larry, Barney, and the woman move their butts on their stools to the music. They dance out of the bar as a conga line of Springfielders walks down the street. Bart runs by them.)

Back-up Singers: *Do the Bartman!*

Bart: *Do the Bartman! She can do it, he can do it, so can I!*

(Bart dances and scats to the music on a cart being driven through the Springfield Nuclear Power Plant.)

Back-up Singer: *If you've got the groove, you gotta use it.*

Rock rhythm in time with the music. You just might start a chain reaction...

(Nuclear technicians dance in front of a chamber with plutonium rods in it. One of the mechanical arms inside the chamber drops its rod, causing the screen to white out. Bart appears, first as a skeleton, then coming into focus as himself.)

Bart: *I'm a Bartman.*

(He flicks a remote control, changing the "channel" to Krusty, advertising his pork products before a grill covered with dancing ham and bacon.)

Back-up Singers: *Everybody, if you can, do the Bartman!*

Bart: *Bring it, baby!*

(We pull away from the TV screen to reveal that Sideshow Bob is watching the Krusty commercial in jail. Prisoners dance in the background to the music. Itchy & Scratchy appear on TV, hitting each other with a club and a mallet.)

Back-up Singers: *Shake your body, turn it out, if you can, man! Move your butt to the side, as you can, can! Everybody in the house do the Bartman!*

(Itchy & Scratchy blow each other up with bombs and the scene switches to Kent Brockman reading the news. Bart slides through frame.)

Bart: *Oh, yeah! You call that dancing?*

(A graphic of the town square appears by Brockman. We then cut to the town square, where all of Springfield dances around to the music.)

Back-up Singers: *Move your body, if you got the notion. Shake your body to the rock-like motion!*

(Four men manipulate Mr. Burns's body so it appears that he's dancing.)

Bart: *Watch his rhythm!*

(Jacques dances into frame with a partner who phases into several Springfield women and then, finally, a man. His eyes open wide in shock.)

Back-up Singers: *Move your hips from side to side now...*

Bart: *Yeah!*

Back-up Singers: *Don't ya slip, let's reply now...*

(Reverend Lovejoy dances with the Devil. The Simpsons dance by the Jebediah Springfield statue, which waves.)

Back-up Singers: *If you've got your groove, you gotta use it!*

Bart: *Wing it!*

Back-up Singers: *Shake your rhythm in time with the music...*

Bart: *Eat your heart out, Michael!*

Back-up Singers: *You just might start a chain reaction...*

(The crowd starts tossing Bart around, and he lands in front of the Jebediah Springfield statue.)

Back-up Singers: *Everybody in the house...Do the Bartman!*

(Bart dances around and then suddenly is pulled offscreen. He's back at the recital. Mrs. Krabappel walks him to the side of the stage and makes him stand there.)

Bart: *Oh wow, man.*

(The kids onstage start dancing blandly to quiet music.)

DUFFMAN

Appearance fee:
10,000 Duff labels sent to Duff Brewery.

What he presents to the honored Duff drinker:
A giant, bottomless mug of new Duff Extra Cold.

His theme song:
"Oh Yeah," by Yello.

His assistants:
Two Duff cheerleaders.

His most handy accessory:
A belt that holds eight cans of beer.

> ARE YOU READY TO GET *DUFFED*?

After Moe tells the guys at the bar that they need to have a designated driver, Barney loses the draw and has to spend the night sober. Although he makes it through the night without a drink, he takes off with Homer's car and disappears for two months.

After Barney returns without the vehicle, Homer gives up on ever finding it. He receives a letter from the City of New York, informing him that his car is illegally parked. Marge, Lisa, and Bart are excited to go, but Homer, who had a bad experience in New York as a young man, would rather stay home.

Upon arriving in New York, Homer and the rest of the family split up, agreeing to meet in Central Park at the end of the day. Homer discovers his car is parked between the two towers of the World Trade Center. While he waits for a parking officer to remove the boot on his car, Marge and the kids see the sights of Manhattan. Homer misses the parking officer when he runs to the bathroom and drives away with the boot still on his car. Homer reunites with the family in Central Park, ushers them into the car, and speeds away from New York City.

SHOW HIGHLIGHTS

Moe: *The Springfield Police have told me that 91% of all traffic accidents are caused by you six guys.* (The guys high-five and cheer.)
Moe: *Yeah, I know, I know. But the bad news is, we gotta start havin' designated drivers.* (The guys all grumble.)
Moe: *We'll choose the same way they pick the pope.* (Moe reaches under the counter, grabs a large jar, and places it on the table.)
Moe: *Everybody reach in and draw a pickled egg. Whoever gets the black egg stays sober tonight.*

"Hey, it's Duffman, the guy in a costume that creates awareness of Duff!"

(The very drunk Lenny, Carl, and Homer drink beer in Homer's car as Barney drives them home.)
Lenny: *Hey, let's go to the girls' college!*
Carl: *No, the Playboy mansion! Playboy mansion!*
Homer: *Shut up! It's my car, and I say we're going the Lost City of Gold!*
Barney: (incensed) *Well, that's just drunk talk, beautiful drunk talk...*

"All I remember about the last two months is giving a guest lecture at Villanova. Or maybe it was a street corner."

(Homer attaches a wheel to a car he's built out of mattresses.)
Marge: *Homer, I don't want you driving around in a car you built yourself.*
Homer: *Marge, you can stand there finding fault, or you can knit me some seatbelts!*

The City of New York's letter:
"Dear motorist,
Your vehicle is illegally parked in the borough of Manhattan. If you do not remedy this malparkage within 72 hours, your car will be thrown into the East River at your expense."

"Oh, Homer, of course you'll have a bad impression of New York if you only focus on the pimps and the C.H.U.D.s."

What Happens to Homer on His First Trip to New York:
A con man runs off with his camera. A cop steals his suitcase. A pickpocket takes his wallet. A bird snatches his hot dog. Woody Allen empties a garbage can on him. An angry pimp chases him into an alley where he falls into a manhole.

"Awright, New York, I'm comin' back! But you're not gettin' this!" Homer, shortly before he tosses his wallet into the fireplace.

"You guys rock!" Bart, calling out to three Hasidic Jews he mistakes for ZZ Top.

"No, it's *Mademoiselle*. We're buyin' our sign on the installment plan." The receptionist, to Bart when he asks if he is in the offices of *Mad* magazine.

Kickin' It: A Musical Journey through the Betty Ford Center: The Broadway show Marge and the kids go to see.

"We're gettin' out of here, now! Jump in, Marge, trust me! Throw the kids—no time for the baby!" Homer, picking up his family from Central Park.

Homer Calls to Get His Boot Removed:
Pleasant Female Voice: *Thank you for calling the Parking Violations Bureau. To plead "Not Guilty" press one now.*
(Homer presses one.)
Pleasant Female Voice: *Thank you. Your plea has been—*
Gruff Male Voice: *Rejected.*
Pleasant Female Voice: *You will be assessed the full fine, plus a small—*
Gruff Male Voice: *Large lateness penalty.*
Pleasant Female Voice: *Please wait by your vehicle between nine A.M. and five P.M. for Parking Officer Steve—*
Gruff Male Voice: *Grabowski.*

VS. HOMER SIMPSON

Episode 4F22
Original Airdate: 9/21/97
Writer: Ian Maxtone-Graham

Director: Jim Reardon
Executive Producers:
Bill Oakley and Josh Weinstein

Movie Moment:
Homer races alongside the horse drawn carriage in Central Park à la the chariot race in *Ben Hur*. This same scene was also parodied in 8F07, "Saturdays of Thunder."

THE STUFF YOU MAY HAVE MISSED

Duffman arrives in the Duff Partymobile. The Partymobile has a scrolling digital sign above the windshield that says "Drink Duff," a satellite dish, and a large rearview mirror shaped like a bottle of beer.

During Homer's flashback to his trip to New York, he passes by the Merry Pervert and the Fascination theaters. They're respectively playing *The Godfather's Parts, II* and *Jeremiah's Johnson. Five Sleazy Pieces* plays at another theater.

Woody Allen was last seen in a spinning newspaper in the "King Homer" story in 9F04, "Treehouse of Horror III."

The Simpsons ride Sit-N-Stare Bus Lines.

The Very Tall Man who sits behind Homer on the bus was last seen in 3F18, "22 Short Films about Springfield."

The "Welcome to Manhattan" sign also reads, "Home of the World-Weary Poseur."

One of the immigrants seen on the ship passing by the Statue of Liberty looks like Adil Hoxha from 7G13, "The Crepes of Wrath."

Ads in the subway car Marge and the kids take include, "Have You Been Injured in a Subway Accident? Call NY Metro 555-5680," "Trade Food Stamps for Lottery Tickets," "Beware of Subway," and "Can You Throw a Football? Become a New York Jet Today! Call 1-800-4NYJETS."

The sign on the pizza place Homer wants to go to reads, "Original Famous Ray's" with, "Not Affiliated with Famous Original Ray's."

Signs in Chinatown read, "The Emperor's Used Clothes," "99¢ Furniture Store," and "Yee's Olde Tavern."

Signs on Broadway read, "Tommy Tune in Gotta Mince!", "David Copperfield's Astonishing Girlfriend!", "Ernest Goes to Broadway!", "Hoofin'-n-Mouthin'," and "Midtown Urine Disposal."

THE PRINCIPAL AND THE PAUPER

Episode 4F23 Original Airdate: 9/28/97 Writer: Ken Keeler Director: Steve Moore Executive Producers: Bill Oakley and Josh Weinstein

SERGEANT SEYMOUR SKINNER

Where he's been:
Spent five years as a prisoner in a secret POW camp and was then sold to China for slave labor. Until recently, he had been making sneakers at gunpoint in a sweatshop in Wuhan.

Lifelong ambition:
To become principal of Springfield Elementary.

Annoys Agnes:
By not cowering before her and by borrowing the car without permission.

Dislikes:
Tamzarian's aqua suit and lavender shirt.

Wears:
A maroon V-necked sweater. When going out on the town, he changes into a turtleneck.

I MUST SAY, IN MANY WAYS SPRINGFIELD REALLY BEATS THE OL' SLAVE LABOR CAMP.

Guest Voice:
Martin Sheen as
Sergeant Seymour Skinner

A salute to Seymour Skinner honoring his twentieth year as principal is interrupted by a stranger claiming to be the real Sergeant Seymour Skinner. Skinner admits to being an impostor, revealing that his real name is Armin Tamzarian, and that he is actually an orphan from Capital City that spent his youth as a "no-good street punk." After getting in trouble with the law, Tamzarian was sent to the army and shipped to Vietnam, where Sgt. Skinner took him under his wing.

When Sgt. Skinner was presumed dead after a mortar explosion, Tamzarian returned to Springfield, where he assumed the identity of Skinner and became the principal of Springfield Elementary. Exposed as a fraud, Tamzarian resigns his position, turning it over to Sgt. Skinner. As Sgt. Skinner assumes the role of son and principal, Tamzarian returns to being a lowlife in Capital City.

Soon, it becomes apparent that Springfield prefers the old Skinner to the new one. Agnes, Mrs. Krabappel, and the Simpsons travel to Capital City to bring Tamzarian back. Sgt. Skinner is sent out of town on a rail and Tamzarian is officially declared to be the one, true Principal Seymour Skinner.

SHOW HIGHLIGHTS

"Good lord! The rod up that man's butt must have a rod up its butt!"
Superintendent Chalmers, on Principal Skinner.

Break Time in the Teachers' Lounge:
Mrs. Krabappel: *Oh, Superintendent Chalmers! Can I offer you a cup of coffee-flavored Bevering?*
Chalmers: *Yeah, I take it gray with Cremium. But first, before Skinner shows up, I have a secret announcement. In honor of Seymour's twentieth year as principal, we've decided to hold a surprise tribute Friday night.*
Willie: *It's my twentieth year, too.*
Chalmers: *(rolling his eyes) The teachers' lounge is for teachers, Willie.*

Lisa and Ralph's Salute to Skinner:
Lisa: *...so, in 1966, a brave young man named Seymour Skinner enlisted and shipped out to Vietnam where he rose to become platoon sergeant. Ralph?*
Ralph: *Principal Skinner is an old man who lives at the school. Lisa?*
Lisa: *Sergeant Skinner was a hero. He risked capture many times behind enemy lines.*
Ralph: *Teacher made me go to Principal Skinner's office when I was dirty.*
Lisa: *And he survived to make it back to Springfield, where he became the fine educator we salute tonight.*
Ralph: *When I grow up, I want to be a principal or a caterpillar. I love you, Principal Skinner.*

"Keep looking shocked and move slowly towards the cake."
Homer's brain, just after Skinner admits to being an impostor.

 "My real name is Armin Tamzarian. I'm an orphan from Capital City and those who recall my fight to outlaw teenage rudeness may be shocked to learn that I myself was once a street punk."

"They gave me a choice: jail, the army, or apologizing to the judge and the old lady. Of course, if I had known there was a war going on, I probably would have apologized."

"My dreams all involve combing my hair."
The young Tamzarian, talking about his future to Sgt. Skinner.

"There's nothin' corny about fresh-faced youngsters skippin' to school, scrapin' knees and spellin' bees and pies cooling softly on the windowsill. Well sir, if that's corny, then corn me up."
Sgt. Skinner, telling Tamzarian about his dream to become principal of Springfield Elementary.

Skinner, Speaking before Springfield:
Skinner: *I've called this assembly to announce my retirement, effective as of the end of this sentence...*
(The crowd stares blankly at him.)
Skinner: *...this sentence I'm speaking...right now...*
(The crowd continues to stare, unmoved.)
Skinner: *...period.*
(The crowd bursts into gasps and shocked murmurs.)

"Armin Tamzarian's reign of terror is over. Now, let us welcome our new Principal Skinner...Principal Seymour Skinner."

"Up yours, children."
Skinner, to Bart, Milhouse, and Martin, after returning to the life of a "no-good street punk."

The Simpsons, on Names:
Lisa: *A rose by any other name would smell as sweet.*
Bart: *Not if you called 'em stenchblossoms.*
Homer: *Or crapweeds.*
Marge: *I'd sure hate to get a dozen crapweeds for Valentine's Day. I'd rather have candy.*
Homer: *Not if they were called scumdrops.*

It's Made Official:
Judge Snyder: *By authority of the City of Springfield, I hereby confer upon you the name of Seymour Skinner, as well as his past, present, future, and mother.*
Skinner: *Okay.*
Judge Snyder: *And I further decree that everything will be just like it was before all this happened. And no one will ever mention it again, under penalty of torture.*

THE STUFF YOU MAY HAVE MISSED

The SuperFriends, last seen in 2F11, "Bart's Comet," are all in the choir at the salute to Skinner. Report Card, who originally was of Indian descent, now looks Caucasian.

Agnes's line, "I have no son," was last said by Rabbi Krustofsky in episode 8F05, "Like Father, Like Clown." Also spoken by Lunchlady Doris to Squeaky-Voiced Teenager in episode 3F10, "Team Homer," and by Abe to Homer in episode 7F17, "Old Money."

In Capital City, Armin Tamzarian stays at "The Ritz-Carlton Hotel for Transients."

As Homer drives Tamzarian back into Springfield, they pass Luann Van Houten standing with Chase, a.k.a. Pyro, the American Gladiator she started dating in 4F04, "A Milhouse Divided."

LISA'S SAX

Episode 3G02 Original Airdate: 10/19/97 Writer: Al Jean Director: Dominic Polcino
Executive Producers: Al Jean and Mike Reiss Guest Voice: Fyvush Finkel as "Krusty the Klown"

When Bart tries to get Lisa to stop practicing her saxophone, he gets in a struggle with her that results in the instrument flying out her bedroom window and onto the street. The sax is instantly flattened by oncoming traffic. Crushed by the loss, Lisa is consoled by Homer, who tells her the story of how she got her saxophone.

The story revolves around Bart's adjustment to school. He has difficulty fitting in and becomes depressed. Homer and Marge bring little Lisa with them when they meet with the school psychologist, Dr. J. Loren Pryor, to discuss Bart's problem. Though he offers little advice for Bart's situation, he discovers Lisa is gifted and encourages the Simpsons to nurture her talents.

The Simpsons can't afford to send her to private school, so they look for another outlet to foster Lisa's gift. Meanwhile, Springfield is suffering through the hottest summer on record. Bart discovers he's good at making people laugh at school and decides to become a class clown. Homer decides to forgo the air conditioner he planned to buy and instead purchases a sax for Lisa.

After finishing his story, Homer is told by Marge to use the money in the current air-conditioner fund to buy Lisa another sax. He does.

I NO LONGER
WANT MY MTV
I NO LONGER
WANT MY MTV
I NO LONGER
WANT MY MTV

SHOW HIGHLIGHTS

Those Were the Days
(the Homer and Marge Version):

Boy, the way the Bee Gees played/ Movies John Travolta made/ Guessing how much Elvis weighed/ Those were the days/
And you knew where you were then/ Watching shows like "Gentle Ben"/ Mister, we could use a man like Sheriff Lobo again/ "Disco Duck" and Fleetwood Mac/ Coming out of my eight-track/ Michael Jackson still was black/ Those were the days.
(Added lyric:)
Bart was feeling mighty blue!/ It's a shame what school can do/ For no reason here's Apu/ Those were the days.

"The Krusty the Klown Story: Booze, Drugs, Guns, Lies, Blackmail, and Laughter." The WB-produced TV movie starring Fyvush Finkel.

"Back then, The Artist Formerly Known As Prince was currently known as Prince. Tracey Ullman was entertaining America with songs, sketches, and crudely drawn filler material." Homer, on 1990.

"That's it, I've lost them forever." Principal Skinner, after accidentally introducing himself as Principal Sinner before Bart's kindergarten class.

Curious George and the Ebola Virus: What Marge offers to read Bart when he's feeling down.

"Mr. and Mrs. Simpson, there's nothing to be alarmed about. Public school can be intimidating to a young child, particularly one with as many flamboyantly homosexual tendencies as your son." Dr. J. Loren Pryor, accidentally mistaking Milhouse's file for Bart's.

"Well, sir, I hate to be a suspicious Aloysius on you, but did you steal my air conditioner?"

"So, what do you like, Lisa? Vio-ma-lin? Tuba-ma-ba? Obo-mo-boe?"

Young Bart at Storytime:
Teacher: (reading) "...and the ugly duckling was amazed to realize it had grown into a beautiful swan." So you see children, there is hope for anyone.
Bart: Even me?
Teacher: No.

Bart's First Performance:
(Bart sings and dances on a picnic table in front of the other kindergartners.)
Bart: (singing) *Skinner is a nut/He has a rubber butt!*
(Principal Skinner appears from behind a tree.)
Skinner: Young man, I can assure you my posterior is nothing more than flesh, bone, and that metal plate I got in 'Nam. Now I want you to knock off that potty talk right now.
Bart: The principal said potty!
Skinner: You listen to me, son. You've just started school, and the path you choose now may be the one you follow for the rest of your life. Now, what do you say?
Bart: Eat my shorts.

THE STUFF YOU MAY HAVE MISSED

This episode marks the third mention of Sheriff Lobo on "The Simpsons." The first occurred in 9F20, "Marge in Chains." He was last mentioned in 1F01, "Rosebud."

Hans Moleman drives the truck that flattens Lisa's sax.

The man on the tricycle who falls down before running over Lisa's sax appears to be Arte Johnson. Just after he falls over, the musical joke sting from "Rowan & Martin's Laugh-In" plays.

This episode marks the first appearance of Dr. J. Loren Pryor since 9F10, "Marge vs. the Monorail."

Michelangelo's *David* appears with a fig leaf over his crotch—he was last seen without the fig leaf in 7F09, "Itchy & Scratchy & Marge."

Homer last rubbed himself with frozen foods to keep cool in 1F22, "Bart of Darkness."

The white cat in the Simpsons' living room is the original Snowball.

Homer almost buys an air conditioner at It Blows.

At King Toot's Music Store, a 1984-era, Eddie Van Halen–style, red and white-striped guitar hangs on the wall.

YOUNG MILHOUSE

Most striking feature:
His disproportionately large head.

Vulnerability:
Drinking regular milk can kill him.

Notable accomplishment:
Encouraged Bart's first attempts at bad behavior.

Talent:
Laughing while drinking soy milk causes it to come out his nose.

THE WORLD NEEDS A CLOWN.

Opening Sequence:

(A man sits at a desk, reading a copy of the script to "The Simpsons," episode 5F02. The nameplate on the desk reads, "Fox Censor." He takes a black magic marker to the pages.)
Censor: No.
(He crosses something out.)
Censor: No.
(He crosses something else out.)
Censor: No.
(He crosses something else out. He reads part of the script and starts laughing. Then he crosses something else out.)
Censor: No.
(He turns the page, sees something, and crosses it out.)
Censor: I think we can do without the crack pipe. Oh, hi. As the Fox censor, it's my job to protect you from reality. And thanks to my prudent editing, tonight's special Halloween show has been rated TV-G.

(A TV-G logo appears in the upper left-hand corner of the screen.)
Censor: This means there will be no raunchy NBC-style sex, or senseless CBS-style violence. So sit back and enjoy a night of worry-free—
(An arm with a sword appears out of the TV-G logo. It stabs the censor in the back. The TV-G turns to TV-PG.)
Censor: What the fudge?
(It stabs the censor again and turns to TV-14.)
Censor: Oh, for Pete's sake!
(It stabs the censor in the back again and turns to TV-MA.)
Censor: Jiminy Christmas!
(It stabs him again and turns to TV-21. It stabs him again and turns to TV-666. The censor collapses on his desk, awash in blood.)
Censor: Darn it.

THE HΩMEGA MAN

France threatens massive retaliation against Springfield unless Mayor Quimby takes back an ethnic slur against its people. When Quimby refuses, the Simpson family urges Homer to purchase a bomb shelter. While Homer looks over a shelter for sale, a French neutron bomb hits Springfield. When Homer exits the shelter, he discovers Springfield has been decimated. Homer quickly gets over his grief and, as the last person alive in Springfield, decides to do as he pleases. Accosted by horribly mutated Springfieldians trying to kill him, Homer escapes, arriving back at the Simpson house. There, he finds his family alive and well, having been protected by the house's many layers of lead paint. Witnessing the Simpsons' tender reunion, the mutants decide to pursue peace with the Simpsons. In turn, the Simpsons blast them with shotguns.

SHOW HIGHLIGHTS

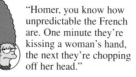

"Homer, you know how unpredictable the French are. One minute they're kissing a woman's hand, the next they're chopping off her head."

The Withstandinator: The bomb shelter Homer considers buying from Herman.

"But Aquaman, you cannot marry a woman without gills! You're from two different worlds! Oh, I've wasted my life." The Comic Book Guy, speaking to the comic book he reads and then realizing he's about to be struck by a neutron bomb.

"Geez, what's with all the death?" Homer, noticing that everyone in Springfield has become an ashy skeleton.

Things Homer does as the last man in Springfield: He watches a movie at the Aztec and while there, kicks off someone's skull and eats everyone else's snacks; he changes the Springfield Community Church's "Today's Sermon" marquee to read, "Homer Rocks." He also dances naked in the church to Edwin Starr's "War."

"Die, you chalk-faced goons!" Homer, to the nonmutated Johnny and Edgar Winter, shortly before running them over with a hearse.

"In the midst of all the killing and skin-eating, somehow we forgot the love." The mutated Dr. Hibbert, upon seeing the tender reunion of the Simpsons.

Homer's Loss

(Homer collapses in the middle of the street, realizing everyone has been killed by France's neutron bomb.)
Homer: *Everyone's gone! Little Bart!*
(A ghostlike image of Bart holding a bat floats by Homer's head; the ghost Bart swings and hits an unseen ball.)
Homer: *Little Lisa!*
(A ghostlike image of Lisa floats by; she, too, has a bat and hits an unseen ball.)
Homer: *Little Marge!*
(A ghostlike image of Marge floats by. She has a bat and swings, but she misses the ball with a whiff.)
Homer: *And the rest!*
(Ghostlike images of Santa's Little Helper, Maggie, Snowball II, and the TV float by.)

THE STUFF YOU MAY HAVE MISSED

In the model Withstandinator, cans labeled "STEAK" and "BEANS" can be seen on the shelves.

The neutron bomb is labeled with an "Intel Inside" logo.

The *Springfield Shopper* features the headlines, "Neutron Bomb Headed for Springfield!" and "Hippo Promoted to Detective."

Magazines for sale at the newsstand include, *Up & Away, Skywriter, Lifer, Wildlife,* and *News.*

After Springfield is hit by the neutron bomb, the long-burning fire in the tire yard apparently goes out.

Episode 5F02
Original Airdate: 10/26/97
Writers: Mike Scully, David S. Cohen, and Ned Goldreyer
Director: Mark Kirkland
Executive Producer: Mike Scully

FLY VS. FLY

Homer buys a matter transporter at Professor Frink's yard sale. Bart uses it to combine his DNA with a fly's, hoping to become a superhero. Instead, he and the fly merely switch heads. Afraid of being punished, Bart flies away, leaving his fly-headed body with his family. The family accepts Fly-Headed Bart. When Lisa finds out that Bart's head (and mind) is on the fly's body, she's about to try to set things right when Fly-Headed Bart attacks her. When Fly-Headed Bart tries to eat Bart-Headed Fly, Lisa pushes him into the transporter, changing Bart back to normal. Homer in turn chases him through the house with an ax for using his machine without permission.

SHOW HIGHLIGHTS

"Sorry, but this is a highly sophisti-ma-cated doowhacky."

"Look! In the sky! It's Superfly!" Bart, imagining his life as a half-boy, half-fly humanoid.

"Oh, well. He may be a horrible freak, but he's still my son." Marge, upon discovering Fly-Headed Bart.

"Get my filthy hands off my sister!" Bart-Headed Fly, to the Fly-Headed Bart attacking Lisa.

The Purchase:
(Homer walks around Frink's yard sale, whistling. He strolls right into a technological-looking booth. There's a flash of light and Homer appears in another booth a few yards away. Homer makes a little impressed noise, realizing what's happened.)
Frink: I take it from that little impressed noise that you are interested in purchasing that matter transporter, sir.
Homer: (looking at the price tag) Hmmm. Two bucks...and it only transports matter? Well, ah, I'll give ya thirty-five cents.
Frink: Sold, but I must warn you, this device carries a frighteningly high risk of catastrophic—
Homer: I said I'll take it.

THE STUFF YOU MAY HAVE MISSED

Among the items Professor Frink has at his yard sale is an Evel Knievel–style rocket cycle.

As Homer, Marge, and Fly-Headed Bart watch TV, the dog-rear/cat-rear thing lounges on the floor, slowly wagging its tails.

EASY BAKE COVEN

he year is 1649. Springfield is a puritanical society, bent on purging the specter of witchcraft from its homes. There are weekly burnings of those suspected of being witches, and at a town meeting, Marge is accused. When the town shoves her off a cliff, Marge reveals herself to truly be a witch. Marge and her witch sisters, Selma and Patty, go into the village to eat the townspeople's children. Goody Flanders, desperate to save her kids, offers them gingerbread children instead, and the witches take them. The rest of the town also offers treats in place of their kids to the witches—starting the Halloween custom.

THE STUFF YOU MAY HAVE MISSED

Sprynge-Fielde: Springfield's early name. Its motto: "First Toil, Then the Grave."

During the first scene, Snake can be seen in the town's stocks, and Moe's Inn can be seen in the background.

Goody Krabappel wears a scarlet A on her chest.

Lisa Simpson last said the line, "Doesn't the Bible say, 'Judge not lest ye be judged'?" in 2F04, "Bart's Girlfriend."

During the final scene, Nelson can be seen dressed as the Devil, and Jimbo is dressed like a skeleton. Flanders has a shepherd costume on, and Rod and Todd portray sheep.

During the first scene, it appears that Luann Van Houten is burnt at the stake along with Agnes Skinner and Miss Hoover. Yet she is seen later during Marge's transformation and again dressed like an angel among the trick or treaters.

SHOW HIGHLIGHTS

"See you in hell, Seymour!" Agnes Skinner, to Principal Skinner, as she's burned at the stake.

"Let's come to our senses everyone! This witch-hunt is turning into a circus!"

"Well, I'll be a son of a witch." Bart, upon discovering his mother flying on a broom.

"That's right. I'm a witch! And I'm the one who withered your livestock, soured your sheep's milk, and made your shirts itchy."

"If I knew you were coming, I would've baked a cat." The Witch Selma, greeting the Witch Marge.

The Due Witch Hunt Process:
(An angry mob has Goody Simpson [Marge] standing on the edge of a cliff.)
Wiggum: Okay, here's how the process works. You sit on the broom, and we shove you off the cliff.
Goody Simpson: What?
Wiggum: Well, hear me out. If you're innocent, you will fall to an honorable Christian death. If, however, you are the bride of Satan, you will surely fly your broom to safety. At that point you will report back here for torture and beheading.
Skinner: Tough, but fair.

GUN SALESMAN

Place of business:
Bloodbath & Beyond Gun Shop.

Gun accessories he sells:
Holster, bandoleer, silencer, loudener, speed cocker, and a special attachment that enables the owner to shoot down police helicopters.

Examples of calmness:
Doesn't react strongly to Homer repeatedly firing an unloaded gun in his face; shrugs off Homer's threat on his life.

Claim to fame:
Caused Homer to continually grumble and murmur for dozens of hours straight.

Example of integrity:
Allows "potentially dangerous" gun applicants to buy only three handguns.

The citizens of Springfield riot after a boring Continental Soccer Association match between Mexico and Portugal. Afterward, the Simpsons decide to make their home more secure. Without the money for an electronic security system, Homer decides to buy a gun.

Homer, though excited about his purchase, manages to make it through the five-day waiting period. Marge is shocked that Homer has bought a gun and demands that he get rid of it. Homer asks her to attend an NRA meeting, with the intention of showing her that the Simpson household needs a gun.

After a dinner-table gun accident, Marge pleads with Homer to get rid of the gun. He agrees, but Marge soon discovers that he lied. She leaves the house and takes the kids with her. Homer goes on to host an NRA meeting that night, but the members kick him out when they see how recklessly he

uses his pistol. He goes to the sleazy hotel where Marge and the kids are staying and tells her that he's gotten rid of the gun. As they check out of the hotel, Snake runs into the lobby, brandishing a knife and demanding the contents of the register. Homer pulls his gun on Snake, breaking up the robbery. Homer apologizes to Marge for lying again, saying that the gun had an almost hypnotic hold on him—she forgives him and is about to throw away the pistol when she decides to keep it for herself.

SHOW HIGHLIGHTS

"Tonight: Soccer, Tomorrow: Monsters of Poetry":
Sign outside Springfield Stadium.

"It's hard to believe this used to be an internment camp." Marge, sitting in Springfield Stadium.

The Start of the Springfield Soccer Riot

Sideshow Mel: *I can't bear this any longer. I'm leaving.*
Moe: *Yeah, not before me you ain't.*
Ned: *Now, now. There's plenty of exits for everyone.*
(Moe puts Ned in a headlock.)
Moe: *Oh, that's it! You're dead, pal!*
Skinner: *Hey now, that's uncalled for!*
Lenny: *Shut your hole, Skinner!*
(Lenny punches him in the stomach, causing him to knock into Barney and send Barney's tray of beer flying. Barney screams and dives into the fray.)

"What began as a traditional soccer riot has escalated into a citywide orgy of destruction. Reacting swiftly, Mayor Quimby has declared mob rule. So, for the next several years, it's every family for itself."

Homer Shows the Salesman the Door:

Security Salesman: *But surely you can't put a price on your family's lives.*
Homer: *I wouldn't have thought so either, but here we are.*

EVERYONE IS TIRED OF THAT
RICHARD GERE STORY
EVERYONE IS TIRED OF THAT
RICHARD GERE STORY
EVERYONE IS TIRED OF THAT
RICHARD GERE STORY

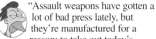

"I don't have to be careful, I got a gun."

Target store truck, flock of ducks, group of rabbits, Patty and Selma, and Flanders:
Things that pass Homer as he sits in his front yard, waiting for the waiting period to end, allowing him to finally shoot something.

The Waiting:

(Homer grabs for his gun, but the cashier holds onto it.)
Cashier: *Sorry, the law requires a five-day waiting period. We've got to run a background check.*
Homer: *Five days? But I'm mad now!*
(The cashier pulls the gun away from Homer.)
Homer: *I'd kill you if I had my gun.*
Cashier: *Yeah, well, you don't.*

Who Shot Mr. Burns?

Homer: *It's a handgun! Isn't it great? This is the trigger, and this is the thing you point at whatever you want to die.*
Marge: *Homer, I don't want guns in my house! Don't you remember when Maggie shot Mr. Burns?*
Homer: *I thought Smithers did it.*
Lisa: *That would have made a lot more sense.*

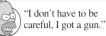

"Assault weapons have gotten a lot of bad press lately, but they're manufactured for a reason: to take out today's modern superanimals, such as the flying squirrel and the electric eel."

Marge Finds Out That Homer Kept the Gun:

Marge: *Of all the terrible things you've ever done in your life, this is the worst—the most despicable!*
Homer: *But Marge, I swear to you—I never thought you'd find out!*

Spinster City Apartments:
The name of Patty and Selma's building.

Gun Warming Tonight
***Nachos* Rifles *Alcohol*:**
Homer's sign for the meeting.

"Hey, yutz! Guns aren't toys! They're for family protection, hunting dangerous or delicious animals, and keeping the King of England out of your face."

"...this gun had a hold on me. I felt this incredible surge of power, like God must feel when he's holding a gun."
Homer, explaining to Marge why he lied about getting rid of the gun.

THE STUFF YOU MAY HAVE MISSED

At the soccer riot, Dr. Hibbert chokes Dr. Riviera.

The slogan for Ex-Con Security is, "From the Big House...to Your House."

This episode featured the second instance this season of Homer desperately needing a bathroom.

Among the members of the Springfield NRA are Agnes Skinner, Moe, Krusty, Lenny, Dr. Hibbert, Ruth Powers, and Cletus.

BART STAR

Episode 5F03 Original Airdate: 11/9/97 Writer: David M. Stern Director: Mark Kirkland
Executive Producer: Mike Scully Guest Voices: Joe Namath and Roy Firestone as Themselves, Mike Judge as Hank Hill

SHERRI & TERRI

Specialties:
Taunting and tattling,
with some conniving, on occasion.

**Notable
accomplishments:**
Convincing Bart the pilgrims landed
in "sunny Acapulco"; being among
the guests at Milhouse's exclusive
birthday party; telling Lisa that she
had a head made out of lettuce
because she is a vegetarian;
respectively representing Trinidad
and Tobago for the Springfield
Elementary Model UN club.

**What they hate
being asked:**
Which one of them
is the evil twin.

> YOU RUINED OUR UNDEFEATED SEASON! YOU RUINED EVERYTHING, RUINER...MY SISTER LIKES YOU.

SHOW HIGHLIGHTS

"Your cholesterol level is lethally high, Homer, but I'm more concerned about your gravy level." Dr. Hibbert, examining Homer.

"I've got to quit smoking." Nelson, panting heavily after running to catch his own long-bomb for a touchdown.

"We drove 2,000 miles for this?" Hank Hill, lamenting Springfield's 28–3 defeat of Arlen.

Luann: *You know, Milhouse, you are getting a little doughy.*
Milhouse: *Aw, can't I just have the surgery?*

Marge: *You know, Homer, it's very easy to criticize.*
Homer: *Fun, too.*

---

omer volunteers Bart for the Springfield Wildcats, the town's peewee football team. Ned Flanders decides to coach, and soon Nelson is named as quarterback. Despite a string of wins, Homer constantly heckles Flanders's coaching style from the bleachers. Not being able to take any more of Homer's abuse, Flanders quits, telling Homer that he can take over.

As the new coach, Homer pressures Bart to work harder, treating him badly. Marge reminds Homer of how Abe had made Homer feel he was never good enough at sports. Homer vows not to make the same mistake and overcompensates, making Bart the quarterback of the Wildcats. Bart is awful and causes the team's first loss. To gracefully bow out, Bart fakes several injuries on the day of the next game. When Homer decides to forfeit rather than start another quarterback, Bart reveals that he'd been faking his injuries and tells him he quits.

Homer's anger at Bart fades when he's left alone after the Wildcats' next victory. He apologizes to Bart for pressuring him and asks him to come back as an offensive tackle. The two make up. At the championship game, Chief Wiggum shows up with an arrest warrant for Nelson Muntz. Bart tells Homer that he'll fill in and goes off with Wiggum, claiming to be Nelson. Nelson goes on to lead the team to victory.

(Bart walks out of the dressing room in Sportacus, wearing a football uniform. Milhouse stands nearby.)
Bart: *Okay, Milhouse, let's try out the new cup.*
(Milhouse kicks Bart in the groin. Bart laughs.)
Bart: *Again.*
(Milhouse kicks Bart in the groin again, and Bart yawns.)
Bart: *Ho-hum.*
(Milhouse tries again and again, getting no reaction from Bart.)
Marge: *(off camera)* Milhouse! Stop that!

Homer: *I'm feelin' kinda low, Apu. Got any of that beer that has candy floatin' in it? You, know, Skittlebrau?*
Apu: *Such a product does not exist, sir. I think you must have dreamed it.*
Homer: *Oh. Well, then just give me a six-pack and a couple of bags of Skittles.*

THE STUFF YOU MAY HAVE MISSED

Text under the "Free Health Fair" sign reads, "Welcome Cheapskates."

At the Free Health Fair, Selma smokes while she runs the Lung Capacity booth, Mayor Quimby ogles a nurse at the Blood Pressure booth, and Groundskeeper Willie and Troy McClure wait in line outside the Are You Crazy? booth, while Sideshow Mel is on the couch and Kirk Van Houten is being questioned. Dr. Nick Riviera runs the What's Your Sex? booth.

The Simpsons shop for athletic equipment at Sportacus. (Depicted above the sign are two gladiators using tennis racquets and bats to battle each other.)

Springfield beats Victory City 34–0.

Rod Flanders's number on the team is 66. His brother Todd's is 6. When Homer announces that Bart will be the Wildcats' new starting quarterback, the Flanders boys stand next to each other, making the Sign of the Beast.

Bart plays an arcade game called "Cat Fight" in the Kwik-E-Mart.

Springfield plays "Capitol" City in the championship. The largest city nearest to Springfield is usually spelled "Capital" City.

Homer: *Let's hear it for Bart!*
(Homer walks off. The other players surround Bart.)
Bart: *(weakly)* Give me a B?
Nelson: *I won't give you a B, but I'll tear you a new A.*
Milhouse: *If I wasn't your friend, I'd tell you you sucked.*

(Marge gives a presentation in front of the First Aid booth.)
Marge: *Now make no mistake; when I say, "First Aid," I'm not talking about some sort of charity rock concert.*
(As Marge laughs at her own joke, the audience stares blankly.)
Marge: *I'm talking about treating serious injuries.*
(The crowd erupts with laughter. Krusty laughs along with them and then pulls out a notepad, jotting something down.)
Krusty: *Serious injuries...oh, that's gold!*

> I DID NOT INVENT IRISH DANCING
> I DID NOT INVENT IRISH DANCING
> I DID NOT INVENT IRISH DANCING

APU'S MOTHER

Demeanor:
Skeptical.

Qualities:
Persistence, resilience, and refusal to suffer fools gladly.

Knows:
How to take a fall; how to negotiate for better dowries.

Has no problem with:
Running up other people's long-distance bills and then insulting them in her native tongue.

> I HAVE COME TO SEE THE WOMAN FOR WHOM APU WAS WILLING TO DISGRACE HIS FAMILY AND SPIT ON HIS CULTURE.

Guest Voice:
Andrea Martin as Apu's Mother

THE TWO MRS.

When Marge volunteers him at the Charity Bachelor Auction, Apu becomes one of the most sought-after dates in Springfield. Shortly afterwards, Apu receives a letter from his mother: It is time for his long-arranged marriage to commence. Homer advises Apu to tell his mother that he is already married. This causes Mrs. Nahasapeemapetilon to come to Springfield to meet Apu's new wife. Seeing Apu in trouble, Homer offers Marge to play the role of Apu's betrothed. Apu brings Mrs. Nahasapeemapetilon to the Simpson home, pretending that Marge is his wife and Bart, Lisa, and Maggie are his children.

Meanwhile, Homer hides out at the Springfield Retirement Castle. Mistaken for one of the retirees named Cornelius Talmadge, Homer soon gets accustomed to life as an elderly person, eating supper at four o'clock and using a wheelchair instead of walking. When the real Talmadge shows up, Homer leaves the home and rejoins Marge and the family. When Mrs. Nahasapeemapetilon walks into the bedroom and finds Homer and Marge sleeping in the bed together and Apu sleeping on the floor, she realizes Apu's marriage is a ruse.

Apu admits his lie to his mother and the plans for the wedding continue. She tells his prospective bride to come out from India. Apu sinks into depression. At his wedding, he learns that Manjula is a beautiful, witty woman. Homer tries to disrupt the ceremony by pretending to be the Hindu god Ganesh, but is quickly subdued. Apu and Manjula are wed, hopeful and happy about their union.

SHOW HIGHLIGHTS

"I do like to cook, I'm not much of a talker but I love to listen, and in my leisure time I like to build furniture and then to have a discussion about where it could be placed in a room." Apu, describing himself at the Charity Bachelor Auction.

"All Kwik-E-Mart managers must be skilled in the deadly arts." Apu, explaining why he's a good shot.

Manjula's Dowry: Ten goats, an electric fan, and a textile factory.

Apu: *Is it me or do your plans always involve some horrible web of lies?*
Homer: *It's you.*

(Moe hangs up a sign on his bar reading, "On Vacation—Back Monday." Homer walks up.)
Homer: *But you can't leave! We're scammin' an old lady at my house, and I need a place to hide out.*
Moe: *Sorry, Homer, I've been planning this vacation for years—I'm finally gonna see Easter Island.*
Homer: *Oh right, with the giant heads.*
Moe: *With the what now?*

"The pink ones keep ya from screamin'." Grampa Simpson, on medication at the Springfield Retirement Castle.

What Homer likes about the Springfield Retirement Castle: Free medicine, electric wheelchairs, their kidney mush, and the liquid potato chips.

"It's like being a baby, only you're old enough to appreciate it." Homer, on living in a retirement home.

Bart: *What's a castrati?*
Marge: *I don't know, but I'm sure it's spicy.*

(At Apu's wedding, Lisa is about to put a necklace of flowers on Moe.)
Moe: *No, no, no, no, no, no. No pansies for me.*
Lisa: *It's the tradition in India.*
Moe: *Yeah, all right, it'll cover the gravy stains.*
(Moe bends down so Lisa can hang the necklace on him, and Bart kicks him in the pants.)
Moe: *Hey!*
Bart: *Tradition.*

"Nothin' like a depressant to chase the blues away." Lenny, on beer.

THE STUFF YOU MAY HAVE MISSED

The sign for the Springfield Civic Center reads, "Tonight: Charity Bachelor Auction, Tomorrow: I Retire, Ya Bastards!"

At the auction, Stacy Lovell from episode 1F12, "Lisa vs. Malibu Stacy," and Waylon Smithers sit behind the Simpson family.

The bachelor rejects: Otto, Captain McCallister, Professor Frink, Disco Stu, Kirk Van Houten, Hans Moleman, Barney, the Comic Book Guy, and Moe.

According to the Nahasapeemapetilon family chart, Apu has two brothers. He is also the oldest.

Apu gets his hair cut at Hairy Shearers.

The Foreigner song "Hot Blooded" plays over Apu's bachelor binge.

Apu Riverdances with four women in the disco.

When Apu drives through town with three screaming women hanging out of his car, sparks shoot out of the car's back. The license plate reads, "HI LIFE." He also drives by Lotsa Books and Dress Up Plus.

Moe wears an "Easter Island Is for Lovers" T-shirt upon his return from his vacation.

Air India's logo features a stewardess serving a drink to a steer. Their slogan is, "We Treat You Like Cattle."

Ernst and Gunter are seen at the airport. The tiger tamers from Mr. Burns's casino first appeared in 1F08, "Springfield (or, How I Learned to Stop Worrying and Love Legalized Gambling)."

NAHASAPEEMAPETILONS

Episode 5F04
Original Airdate: 11/16/97
Writer: Richard Appel
Director: Steven Dean Moore
Executive Producer: Mike Scully
Guest Voice: Jan Hooks as Manjula

(Bart sees the elephant Apu rides.)
Bart: *Wow. I wish I had an elephant.*
Lisa: *You did. His name was Stampy. You loved him.*
Bart: *Oh yeah.*
(Bart won Stampy in a radio contest in 1F15 "Bart Gets an Elephant.")

LISA THE SKEPTIC

Original Airdate: 11/23/97 **Writer:** David S. Cohen **Director:** Neil Affleck **Executive Producer:** Mike Scully
Guest Voice: Stephen Jay Gould as Himself

Discovered in:
Sabertooth Meadow.

What it is:
A shameless publicity stunt that exploits people's most deeply held beliefs.

What Homer uses it for:
An exhibit in his garage, which he charges people fifty cents to view.

Ultimate resting place:
Atop the main entrance to the Heavenly Hills Mall.

L isa discovers that a new mall is being constructed on Sabertooth Meadow, where several fossils were found. Worried that there still might be prehistoric remains in the meadow, Lisa complains to the developers and wins the right to hold an archeological survey on the site. During the dig, Lisa unearths what appears to be the skeleton of an angel. While the town determines who should keep the skeleton, Homer loads it onto his car and drives it home. Displaying it in the Simpson garage, Homer charges admission to anyone who wants to view the supposed angel. Insistent that the fossil can't really be an angel, Lisa takes a sample from the skeleton to Dr. Stephen Jay Gould for testing.

Though the test proves to be inconclusive, Lisa is still skeptical. When she goes on "Smartline" to refute the angel, the town lashes out against the Springfield scientific community. During the chaos, the angel is stolen from the Simpson garage. It's found on a hillside, with a message carved into it: "The End Will Come at Sundown." The whole town gathers around the angel as the sun sets. The skeleton floats up and a voice is heard announcing the end...of high prices. The voice goes on to trumpet the grand opening of the Heavenly Hills Mall. Soon, it's revealed that the "angel" was planted by the mall developers as a publicity stunt.

SHOW HIGHLIGHTS

"Sheesh! You're the most paranoid family I've ever been affiliated with!"

Homer Gets Grilled:
Bart: *Dad, why aren't you saying anything? Where's our motorboat?*
Homer: *I didn't like it. The mast had termites.*
Lisa: *Why would a motorboat have a mast?*
Homer: *Because! The thingy was...shut up!*

"Principal Skinner, remember how I didn't sue when I found that scorpion in my applesauce? Well, I'm calling in a favor."

Rounding Up the Diggers:
Principal Skinner: (via the intercom) *Attention! All honor students will be rewarded with a trip to an archeological dig!*
(Martin, Sherri, and Terri cheer.)
Principal Skinner: (via the intercom) *Conversely, all detention students will be punished with a trip to an archeological dig.*
(Bart, Milhouse, and Nelson mutter.)

"Ah. We elected the wrong Carter." Homer, after taking a nostalgic swig of Billy Beer.

"Miss Simpson, how can you maintain your skepticism in spite of the fact that this thing really, really looks like an angel?"

Movie Moment:
The shot silhouetting the students on the dig under the rippling sunset is a visual tip of the hat to *Raiders of the Lost Ark.*

(The townspeople find the angel on a hillside by the courthouse.)
Lenny: *Wow, do you think it flew up here?*
Moe: *Well, it didn't ride up on no zebra.*

THE STUFF YOU MAY HAVE MISSED

Among the suspects rounded up by the Springfield Police Department is Jimmy the Scumbag, last seen in 4F01, "Lisa's Date with Density."

Items in Homer's "Safe Deposit Closet" include: the Flanderses' antique three-cornered hat and the town crier bell (from 3F13, "Lisa the Iconoclast"), a six-pack of Billy Beer (from 8F21, "The Otto Show"), Homer's boxing gloves (from 4F03, "The Homer They Fall"), Homer's Grammy (from 9F21, "Homer's Barbershop Quartet"), a bag of Farmer Homer's XX Sugar (from 1F17, "Lisa's Rival"), Homer's white cowboy hat (from 8F19, "Colonel Homer"), a box of Mr. Sparkle (from 4F18, "In Marge We Trust"), the animatronic heads of Itchy & Scratchy (from 2F01, "Itchy & Scratchy Land"), the helmet to Homer's spacesuit (from 1F13, "Deep Space Homer"), his "Mr. Plow" jacket (from 9F07, "Mr. Plow"), the shirt from his Dancin' Homer days (from 7F05, "Dancin' Homer"), and a bowling trophy (from 3F10, "Team Homer").

A sign outside the Museum of Natural History reads, "Now Hiring Stuffers."

Seen with the people waiting around the angel for sundown to come is a yellow version of Dr. Hibbert's wife.

I WILL NOT TEASE FATTY
I WILL NOT TEASE FATTY
I WILL NOT TEASE FATTY
I WILL NOT TEASE FATTY
I WILL NOT TEASE FATTY

Can't, Ain't, Am:
Lisa: *But it can't be an angel!*
Moe: *Oh no? Well, if you're so sure what it ain't, how about tellin' us what it am!*
Lisa: *Well, maybe it's a...a Neanderthal who got bitten by some angry fish.*
Ned: *Well, I gotta say, Lisa, it sounds like you're strainin' to do some explainin'!*
Wiggum: *Yeah, everyone's heard of angels. But who's ever heard of a "Neanderthal"?*

Hibbert: *Now, regardless of what this thing is, it's a priceless scientific find. So our most pressing concern now is determining who owns such a valuable skeleton and I'd like to suggest that I do.*
(The crowd clamors in discontent.)
Sideshow Mel: *I'd like to hear from Lionel Hutz!*
Lionel Hutz: *It's a thorny legal issue, all right. I'll need to refer to the case of Finders versus Keepers.*
Ned: *Oh, we can work this out, friends. In the spirit of sharing, let's say we simply place the sacred bones in—*
(A car horn blares. Everyone turns to discover Homer has tied the angel bones to the roof of his car.)
Homer: *So long, suckers!*

(Homer and the family discover the angel is gone.)
Homer: *Oh no! This can't be happening! What the hell are we gonna do with ten thousand angel ashtrays?*
Bart: *I could take up smoking.*
Homer: *You damn well better.*

PREPARE FOR THE END...THE END OF HIGH PRICES!

REALTY BITES

Episode 5F06   Original Airdate: 12/7/97   Writer: Dan Greaney   Director: Swinton Scott   Executive Producer: Mike Scully

omer takes Marge out to the Police Seized-Property Auction for a fun-filled Saturday. There, Homer buys a souped-up sports car. When he takes Marge out for a dangerous ride, she has Homer pull over and drop her off. Walking around the neighborhood, Marge runs into Lionel Hutz, who now works as a Realtor for Red Blazer Realty. Interested in getting involved in real estate, Marge studies for the Real Estate Law test. With a little help from Bart and Lisa, she passes the exam.

Marge is made an employee of Red Blazer Realty. She soon learns that her honest, earnest approach doesn't work for selling homes. She also learns that if she doesn't sell a house her first week, she'll be fired. Marge shows Ned and Maude Flanders a house in which some grisly murders occurred several years ago. When they offer to buy it, she fails to tell them of the house's history.

After the Flanderses spend a night in the house, Marge comes clean. Amazingly, the Flanderses are thrilled with their new home's rich history. Their excitement is short-lived, however. Homer crashes his car through the house while fighting with Snake, the original owner of the vehicle. The house collapses and Marge is fired. But all is not lost: The family is thrilled that Marge now qualifies for unemployment benefits.

> THERE WAS NO ROMAN GOD
> NAMED "FARTACUS"
> THERE WAS NO ROMAN GOD
> NAMED "FARTACUS"
> THERE WAS NO ROMAN GOD
> NAMED "FARTACUS"

SHOW HIGHLIGHTS

"I don't know, Marge. Trying is the first step towards failure."

"What in the heck is a dwelling?" Marge, reading her Real Estate Law book.

Marge: You bought a car? Without consulting me?
Homer: I don't recall being consulted when you bought that hat!
Marge: I found this hat!

"Time's up. You may now undermine each other's confidence."
The real estate test proctor, at the end of the exam.

"Yaaar! I nailed that one about houseboats, did you?"
Captain McCallister, to Marge, after the real estate test.

Selling Houses the Hutz Way:
(Hutz opens a listing book, showing Marge a picture of a small house.)
Marge: It's awfully small.
Hutz: I'd say it's awfully...cozy.
(He shows her a beat-up shack.)
Marge: That's dilapidated.
Hutz: Rustic.
(He shows her a house we can't see.)
Marge: That house is on fire.
Hutz: Motivated seller.

"Screw the honor system—my car needs me!"
Snake, walking out a prison gate labeled, "No Escaping Please."

"Please don't tell anyone how I live."
Lenny, after his dining room wall falls, revealing that he sits in his underwear, eating from a can.

"What'd you use Marge, huh? The old buff and bluff? The Hail Murray? The Susquehanna Shuffle, huh, huh, huh?"
Gil to Marge, after she unloads the murder house.

"And right here's where they found the torso heap! In front of our very own fireplace!"
Ned, excited by his new home's history.

"You're one of a kind, Marge. And nobody deserves this more than you."
Hutz, putting the "FIRED" blazer on Marge.

Marge: Ooh! There's an azalea festival at the public garden!
Homer: Aw, I went yesterday.
(Marge makes a disappointed sound.)
Homer: Lenny really wanted to go.
Marge: I'm tired of being cooped up in this house all the time.
Homer: Open a window.

At the Police Seized-Property Auction:
(Chief Wiggum stands at a podium, gesturing to some metal gates with the name "Johnny D." inscribed in them.)
Chief Wiggum: These prestigious wrought-iron security gates are bulletproof, bombproof, and battering-ram resistant. Now—
Skinner: Then what happened to Johnny D.?
Chief Wiggum: He forgot to lock 'em. Now what am I bid?
Patron: One kilo!
Chief Wiggum: Sold!

The Flanderses Look at the Murder House:
Ned: Oh my, diddily-I! Will you look at this place! And the price has been slashed repeatedly!
Maude: It's sure built solid. The kids could scream bloody murder, and no one would hear!
Ned: Well, I'm just gonna spill my guts. I love it to death!

THE STUFF YOU MAY HAVE MISSED

The slogan on Lionel Hutz's Red Blazer Realty card is, "You'll go nuts for Lionel's Huts!"

A sign at the real estate test reads, "$75.00 or Best Offer."

Red Blazer Realty has a sign in their window, proudly proclaiming themselves "The 6% Commission People."

Gil has a bottle of Bromo Seltzer on his desk.

Maggie nods (along with the rest of the family) when Marge asks if they see her as a "spineless, potato-cooking housewife."

Snake uses Acme Piano Wire in his attempt to decapitate Homer.

The Flanderses rent their truck from U-Break-It Van Rental.

Snake's license plate is "GR8 68."

Kirk Van Houten's arm is cut off by Snake's piano wire. Later, at the unemployment office, he's seen wearing a cast on one arm. Also in line at the unemployment office are a woman who looks to be a disheveled Lurleen Lumpkin, Larry Burns (first seen in 4F05, "Burns, Baby Burns"), Jimbo Jones, Simpson scribe George Meyer, and George Bush.

GIL

Appearance:
Tired, beaten-down, desperate.

Past jobs:
Realtor, shoe salesman, used car salesman, Canyonero salesman, doorbell salesman, Coleco computer salesman.

What haunts him:
His chronic inability to close the deal.

How he communicates on the road:
A rotary cell phone that's bigger than his head.

Former bosses:
Lionel Hutz, Señor Ding-Dong, and several other disappointed people.

His biggest mistakes:
Losing the company payroll in Vegas; believing his wife when she said things were over with Fred; embezzling money from his employers.

How he refers to himself:
In the third person.

AH, SHE'S A BEAUT! YOU CAN'T BEAT A COLECO! HOW MANY CAN I PUT YOU DOWN FOR? A LOT? PLEASE SAY A LOT. I NEED THIS.

PATCHES AND POOR VIOLET

Familial status:
Orphans.

Signs of classic orphanhood:
The patches on their clothing; the rings under their eyes; their beige pallor; their larger-than-normal eyes; the fact that they're wearing shorts in the dead of winter.

Their vitamin money:
One tattered dollar.

I'D KISS YOU, BUT DOCTOR SAYS I'M SICK.

Bart wakes up before the rest of the family on Christmas morning to open his presents. Playing with a new remote control fire truck, Bart accidentally sets fire to the family's plastic Christmas tree, causing it to melt and envelop all of the family's presents. Bart drags the melted plastic-present conglomeration outside and buries it in the snow. Finding the family inside, Bart tells them that he came down early and saw a burglar stealing their presents and the tree.

After Kent Brockman reports on the Simpsons' supposed plight, the community rallies to their aid, gathering fifteen thousand dollars for them. The family buys a new car, which Homer drives into a frozen lake shortly after leaving the lot. Consumed by guilt, Bart admits that there was no burglar—that he burned down the tree and the presents.

When the town finds out the truth, they're outraged. The Simpsons are shunned by the community, have their house pelted by rotten fruit, and are sent bags of hate mail. Homer decides the only solution is to pay the town back. Marge goes on "Jeopardy!" to win the fifteen thousand dollars they need to set things right, but loses miserably. When the Simpsons return home, they find their house being looted by the townspeople. Having stripped the Simpsons of all their possessions save a lone washcloth, the town forgives them.

SHOW HIGHLIGHTS

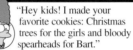 "Hey kids! I made your favorite cookies: Christmas trees for the girls and bloody spearheads for Bart."

"It's crap-tacular." Bart, commenting on Homer's disastrous Christmas light arrangement.

Bart, the Christmas Clairvoyant:

(Bart takes a present from under the tree, holds it up to his head, and shuts his eyes as Lisa watches.)
Bart: *Hocus pocus, mucus pukus. My powers of deduction tell me you're getting a handmade sweater, possibly...yellow.*
Lisa: *Mom! Make him stop!*
Marge: *Bart, put down that yellow sweater!*

Bart's Christmas Bargain:

(Bart kneels at his bed in his pajamas, hands pressed together, seemingly in prayer.)
Bart: *Dear Santa, if you bring me lots of good stuff, I promise not to do anything bad between now and when I wake up.*
(When Bart opens his arms, he hits his elbow on his nightstand.)
Bart: *Ow! I'll kill you!*
(Bart lunges for his nightstand to smash it.)

"Go! Go! Go! We're number one! Gimme a P! P! Go! Go! Go!" Cheers Bart hears in his dreams after drinking twelve glasses of water before bed.

Chief Wiggum: *Now, um, what did this, uh, Christmas thief look like?*
Bart: *Well, he had a glass eye, a wooden leg, um, big scar on his cheek...*
Chief Wiggum: *Anything unusual?*
Bart: *Hooks for hands. Um, oh, oh, he was wearing a striped convict's shirt, and he was carrying a big sack with a dollar sign on it.*
Lou: *Classic burglar.*

"Aren't we forgetting the true meaning of this day—the birth of Santa?"

"So while you're home today, eating your sweet, sweet holiday turkey, I hope you'll all choke just a little bit." Kent Brockman, trying to impart his disgust to his viewing audience.

"Does anyone have change for a button?" Montgomery Burns, about to make a donation to the impromptu charity fund.

"Fifteen thousand mazzulians! Holy shlamola! Whaddya gonna do with all that kablingy?"

At Kliff's Kar Chalet:

(Homer sits in a new car with "12,000" on the windshield. He holds up a wad of cash to the salesman.)
Homer: *Is this car fifteen thousand dollars?*
(The salesman discreetly rubs the "12,000" off the windshield.)
Salesman: *It is now. And because of your loss, folks, I'll throw in the undercoating for two hundre—no, four hundred and ninety bucks.*
Homer: *What a deal! I'd be a sucker not to get it.*
Bart: *I don't know about this, Dad. Shouldn't we give the money to charity or som—ow!*
Salesman: *Oh, I'm sorry, I jabbed you with my pen.*
Bart: *Ow! You're still doing it!*
Salesman: *Yeah, I know.*

"H-hello, jerk. We may never find you and we should probably all stop looking. But one thing's for sure, you do exist." Homer's response to Brockman asking him if he has any words for the Christmas thief, shortly after learning it was Bart who burned down the tree and presents.

"Oh, it's true! We weren't robbed—that part we made up! But the rest is true!"

Moe: *So this was all a scam! And on Christmas!*
Barney: *Yeah! Jesus must be spinning in his grave.*

"There's no shame in being a pariah."

THE STUFF YOU MAY HAVE MISSED

This is the third Christmas episode of "The Simpsons." The others are 7G08, "Simpsons Roasting on an Open Fire," and 3F07, "Marge Be Not Proud."

Homer parks across three disabled parking spaces at the Try-N-Save.

While investigating the "crime" at the Simpsons', Lou wears a Christmas tree tie and Eddie wears a Santa hat. Also, although we see Wiggum and Lou walk out of the house, we never see Eddie leave.

The eldest Hibbert child (last seen in 3F02, "Bart Sells His Soul") isn't with the Hibbert family on Christmas.

Many of the dancing residents of the Springfield Retirement Castle are mimicking moves seen in "A Charlie Brown Christmas."

The last time "sweet, sweet" was used as an adjective was in 2F06, "Homer Badman," when Homer referred to the Gummi Venus de Milo as "sweet, sweet candy."

Barney is seen driving his Plow King truck, last seen in 9F07, "Mr. Plow."

After the new car explodes underwater, Homer is hit in the face by a fish among the flying debris.

Under the *Springfield Shopper* headline, "Simpsons Scam Springfield," is the subheadline, "Angry Mob Mulls Options."

A Santa hat has been placed on Krusty's head on the Krustyburger sign.

Graffiti on the Simpson car includes, "I Keell You," and "Die."

Among the stuffed animals Wiggum is stealing from the Simpson home are a "Life in Hell"–style rabbit and a monkey in a fez.

EVERGREEN TERRACE

Episode 5F07
Original Airdate: 12/21/97
Writer: Ron Hauge
Director: Bob Anderson
Executive Producer: Mike Scully
Guest Voice: Alex Trebek as Himself

RUDOLPH'S RED NOSE IS NOT ALCOHOL-RELATED. RUDOLPH'S RED NOSE IS NOT ALCOHOL-RELATED. RUDOLPH'S RED NOSE IS ALCOHOL-RELATED.

Movie Moment:

Marge's line, "...you won't believe what's happened! It's a miracle!", was also used by Maude Flanders, speaking to Ned in 7F23, "When Flanders Failed." The line and the subsequent scene of the town coming together to help the Simpsons is reminiscent of *It's A Wonderful Life*.

(As the Simpsons leave the "Jeopardy!" set, Alex Trebek calls after them.)
Alex Trebek: *Aren't we forgetting something, Marge? You were down fifty-two hundred dollars.*
Marge: *But Mr. Trebek—*
Alex Trebek: *I asked you before the game if you knew the rules and you said you did. Judges?*
(Two thugs carrying clubs step out from the shadows.)
Lisa: *Run, Mom!*

ALL SINGING, ALL DANCING

Episode 5F24 Original Airdate: 1/4/98 Writer: Steve O'Donnell Director: Mark Ervin Executive Producer: David Mirkin

Role:
Springfield's chief convenience store armed robber, rioter, and unrepentant smoker.

Has a tattoo of:
A snake.

Prison ID#:
7F20 (also the production number of the episode in which he was introduced).

His car:
Li'l Bandit.

Dubious acts:
Trying to run over Bart; stealing the entire Kwik-E-Mart; using "Nacho Cheez" as hair gel; stealing a Beta VCR when he was hoping for VHS.

One of the reasons he steals:
To pay off his student loans, presumably to Middlebury College.

Former cellmate of:
Sideshow Bob.

IF ONLY THEY HAD PEEWEE HOCKEY WHEN I WAS A LAD.

SHOW HIGHLIGHTS

(Homer, carrying a plastic bag, walks into the house with Bart. Marge meets them at the door, standing with Lisa. Marge holds Maggie with one hand and a bowl of popcorn in the other.)
Marge: We got the popcorn! Did you get Waiting to Exhale?
Homer: Well, they put us on the Waiting to Exhale waiting list, but they said don't hold yer breath.
(Homer walks into the living room.)
Lisa: Did you get Emma? Did you get Emma? Didja, didja, didja, huh?
Homer: Whoa, whoa. Calm down, little lady. Take it easy, take it easy, heh, heh. No.
Marge: What did you get?
Homer: Something very close, exactly along those lines. A Clint Eastwood–Lee Marvin shoot 'em up Western!
(Lisa and Marge share an annoyed murmur. Bart puts a tape in the VCR.)
Bart: So prepare yourself for the bloody mayhem and unholy carnage of Joshua Logan's Paint Your Wagon.
Homer: With blood, I bet!
(Homer and Bart laugh sinisterly and high-five.)

Homer: They're singing! They're singing, Marge! Why aren't they killing each other?
Bart: Yeah, their guns are right there!
(Homer sees something onscreen.)
Homer: Wait, wait, wait! Here comes Lee Marvin! Thank god! He's always drunk and violent!

"**Gonna paint your wagon, gonna paint it fine, gonna use oil-based paint, 'cause the wood is pine!**"
Lee Marvin's *Paint Your Wagon* solo.

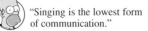 "Oh, why did they have to screw up a perfectly serviceable wagon story with all that fruity singing?"

"**I thought it was toe-tapping fun.**"
Marge's review of *Paint Your Wagon*.

"Singing is the lowest form of communication."

Marge: Who knew that Lee Marvin could do such marvelous splits?
Lisa: He's dreamy.

The Opening to *Paint Your Wagon*:
(A serape-wearing, spaghetti Western–style outlaw played by Clint Eastwood rides into a desolate Western town, lighting a cigarette. He is immediately accosted by one of the townsfolk, a tough-looking man who resembles Lee Van Cleef.)
Man: Hey, that's a pretty sorry lookin' wagon you've got there, mister.
Outlaw: I reckon it could use a...coat of paint.
Man: (calling out happily) Well, what are we waitin' for?
(Music suddenly starts and the man and the outlaw begin dancing.)
Outlaw and Man: (singing) Gonna paint our wagon, gonna paint it good, we ain't braggin', we're gonna coat that wood!

THE STUFF YOU MAY HAVE MISSED

The musical numbers in this episode were drawn from the following episodes: 9F21, "Homer's Barbershop Quartet"; 4F06, "Bart After Dark"; 1F06, "Boy Scoutz-N the Hood"; 1F10, "Homer and Apu"; 9F19, "Krusty Gets Kancelled"; 2F18, "Two Dozen and One Greyhounds"; 9F10, "Marge vs. the Monorail"; 3F02, "Bart Sells His Soul"; and 1F09, "Homer the Great."

The other "Simpsons" clip shows the banner refers to are: 9F17, "So It's Come to This: A Simpsons Clip Show"; 2F33, "Another Simpsons Clip Show"; and 3F31, "The Simpsons 138th Episode Spectacular."

Homer: All right, Marge! You've convinced me there are more terrible things than musical comedies where everyone sings!
(Lisa, Maggie, and Bart start a kick line.)
Lisa: There is something worse!
Bart: And it really does blow!
Simpsons: When a long-running series does a cheesy clip show!
(Confetti and streamers fall from above, and a banner is lowered, reading, "The Simpsons Clip Show #4 '5F24.'" Just then, Snake leaps in through the open window and points his shotgun at the family.)

Homer rents a shoot 'em up Western for the family to watch on their VCR. When the film turns out to be a musical, Homer is disgusted. Marge reminds Homer of all the times he's sung and danced, and soon, the entire family is singing and reminiscing about the past musical numbers in their lives. After they sing and watch an old video of Bart's musical prowess, Snake leaps in through the window, wielding a shotgun. When he hears the Simpsons singing everything they say, he leaves, believing they wouldn't make good hostages. Lisa croons about how Krusty, Mr. Burns, and Apu have done their share of singing in the past.

Snake soon returns, ready to kill the family for putting an annoying tune in his head. When he tries to shoot the Simpsons, he realizes he's out of ammunition and leaves. Marge sings about how the churches, clubs, and government institutions often burst into song. Homer admits that there are worse things than musical comedies.

Snake comes back to threaten the Simpson family again, but they tell him they are done singing, and he leaves. Marge absently hums by the living room window, and Snake fires a blast through it. Then throughout the final credits, Snake fires and threatens his way through the end music.

THE SIMPSONS CLIP SHOW #4 "5F24"

BART CARNY

Episode 5F08 Original Airdate: 1/11/98 Writer: John Swartzwelder Director: Mark Kirkland Executive Producer: Mike Scully

O n a Simpson family outing to a traveling carnival, Bart accidentally crashes Hitler's car, the fair's main attraction. To pay off the debt, Bart and Homer get jobs helping with the booths and exhibits. They befriend Cooder and Spud, a father-and-son carny team.

While manning Cooder and Spud's Ring Toss booth, Homer fails to recognize that he's being asked for a bribe by Chief Wiggum. Wiggum shuts down the booth, and Cooder and Spud are left homeless. Feeling guilty, Homer lets them stay at the Simpson home. During dinner that evening, a grateful Spud offers the family tickets to a glass-bottom boat ride.

When the Simpsons return, they find the house's windows boarded up and the locks changed; Cooder and Spud have taken over their home. Chief Wiggum, still bitter over not receiving a bribe from Homer, refuses to help. Ultimately, Homer makes a bet with the carnies: If he can throw a hula hoop over the home's chimney, he can keep the house—if he misses, he'll sign the deed over to them. When Cooder and Spud step outside the house to watch Homer's attempt, the family rushes inside and shuts the door, locking the carnies out.

SHOW HIGHLIGHTS

(Marge tries to push Santa's Little Helper out the back door as Homer eats in the kitchen.)
Marge: *Come on! You have to go outside to do your...business.*
Homer: *The experts say that if you want an animal to do something, you should do it yourself first, to show 'em how.*
Marge: *I'm not going to the bathroom in the backyard.*
Homer: *Pfft. Sor-ree, Your Majesty.*

Marge: *...no chores, no allowance.*
Lisa: *Okay, we get our room and board free anyway.*
Bart: *And Santy Claus provides the rest.*

(Marge has dressed Bart and Lisa in overalls, gloves, and straw hats. She brings them to the back door to go out and clean the backyard.)
Bart: *I can't go out dressed like this! What if someone sees me?*
Marge: *You're just going into our backyard. No one will see you.*
(Bart opens the door and looks out.)
Nelson: (in the distance, off camera) *Ha...*
(Bart slams the door. Marge frowns and points him outside. Bart opens the door again.)
Nelson: (in the distance, off camera) *Ha!*

 "Carnies built this country, the carnival part of it, anyway. And though they may be ratlike in appearance, they are truly kings among men."

The Tooth Chipper; the Scream-atorium of Dr. Frightmarestein: Rides at the carnival.

Homer Learns the Tricks of the Trade:
Cooder: *You see, the trick here is the rings won't fit over the good prizes.*
(Homer takes out a wad of money.)
Homer: *We'll see about that. Gimme ten rings.*

"Wow, it's Fuhreriffic!" Bart, seeing Hitler's car.

"Yeah, we could start our own game where people throw ducks at balloons and nothing's the way it seems." Homer, responding to Bart's dream of leaving town to become full-time carnies.

Homer, Just Not Getting It:
Wiggum: *Let me put it this way. I'm looking for my friend Bill. Have you seen any bills around here?*
(Wiggum looks at the cash box.)
Homer: *No. He's Bart.*
(Wiggum, frustrated, runs a hand over his face and groans. He winks while he talks.)
Wiggum: *Listen carefully and watch me wink as I speak, okay?*
Homer: *Okay.*
Wiggum: *The guy I'm really looking for, wink, is Mr. Bribe, wink, wink.*
(Wiggum holds out his palm.)
Homer: *It's a ring toss game.*
Wiggum: *That's it, I'm shutting this game down.*

"It must've taken you years to win all this stuff." Spud, looking over the Simpson home.

Revealed:
Spud refers to Lisa's blue eyes in this episode.

(Marge talks to Homer in the kitchen.)
Marge: *How long are those roustabouts going to be staying here?*
Homer: *Oh, it won't be long. Once their résumé gets out, they'll have all kinds of offers. The older one can pull out his left eye.*
(A glass eye rolls into the kitchen from the living room.)
Cooder: (from the living room) *Little help?*

"I was wrong about the Cooders, Dad. They're the nicest of all the transients you've ever brought home."

"Listen to 'em. Watchin' my television, sittin' on my couch... You better not be in my ass-groove!" Homer, shouting to the Cooders occupying the Simpson home.

THE STUFF YOU MAY HAVE MISSED

This episode marks the third time someone has been squirted in the face with a water gun intended for a "squirt the clown-head, blow up the balloon" carnival booth. Krusty is squirted in the face by Bart in 3F22, "Summer of 4 Ft. 2," and Martin is in 9F02, "Lisa the Beauty Queen."

One of the games at the carnival is called, "Knock Over the Fuzzy Guy."

Prizes at the Ring Toss include: a Def Leppard mirror, a camera, a matador lamp, a Rubik's cube, a Magic Eight Ball, a hunter's knife, an antique TV (it has a sign on it reading, "The appliance everyone's talking about"), a stuffed monkey, a Happy Little Elf, and a white stuffed seal.

Karl, introduced in 7F02, "Simpson and Delilah," is seen on the glass-bottom boat ride, standing next to Lisa. He appears later in the season standing in line at the post office in 5F14, "The Trouble with Trillions."

Items seen on the glass-bottom boat ride include shopping carts, a muffler, a vat of Li'l Lisa Slurry (from 4F17, "The Old Man and the Lisa"), a radio, tires, and a vat of radioactive waste.

Though the Cooders presumably boarded up all of the Simpsons' windows, just before Homer falls out of the treehouse, the home's rear windows can be seen without boards.

COODER AND SPUD

Live:
In the Ring Toss game.

Work:
In the Ring Toss game.

Their usual breakfast:
Cotton candy, Sno-Kones, and caramel apples.

Unique physical abilities:
Cooder can pull out his left eye; Spud can unhinge all his joints at once.

OH HELL, THE COODERS HAVE BEEN CARNIES EVER SINCE WE CAME HERE IN 1620, CLINGIN' TO THE SIDE OF THE MAYFLOWER.

Guest Voice: Jim Varney as Cooder

GLEN AND JANE

Their beat:
The Springfield International Airport, just to the right of the Hare Krishnas and Christians.

What they believe in:
An unwavering devotion to the Leader.

What they believe Homer to be:
The Most Powerful Mind They've Ever Dealt With.

What they use to break his will:
The "Batman" Theme Song.

Their deadliest weapon:
Their lawyers.

> WOULD YOU RATHER HAVE BEER OR COMPLETE AND UTTER CONTENTMENT?

THE JOY

SHOOTING PAINTBALLS IS NOT
AN ART FORM
SHOOTING PAINTBALLS IS NOT
AN ART FORM
SHOOTING PAINTBALLS IS NOT
AN ART FORM

After encountering two recruiters from "the Movementarians," a sect dedicated to serving an omniscient leader who promises to take them away in a spaceship bound for a cosmic paradise known as Blisstonia, Homer attends their "get acquainted session" and finds himself wanting to join the group.

Homer moves the family to the sect's compound. The Movementarians quickly convert all of the Simpsons, save Marge, to their way of life. Marge escapes the compound and hires Willie to kidnap her family and deprogram them in the Flanderses' rumpus room. They succeed in bringing the kids back to reality, but lawyers burst in before they're seemingly done with Homer, and he opts to return to the compound.

There, Homer reveals that he no longer believes in the group, and exposes the spaceship to be a fake. The group disbands and the Simpsons return home.

SHOW HIGHLIGHTS

"Look at the outrageous markup! You magnificent bastard, I salute you." Apu, commenting to the clerk on the prices at the Springfield International Airport newsstand.

(Bart and Homer pass a Hare Krishna in the airport. He offers them some literature.)
Hare Krishna: *Have you heard of Krishna consciousness?*
Homer: *This, Bart, is a crazy man.*
(They pass a man holding up a Bible.)
Man: *Do unto others as you would have them do unto you.*
Homer: (sarcastic) *Right, that'll work.*
(A man and woman, Glen and Jane, stand nearby. Jane hands Homer a pamphlet.)
Jane: *A new and better life awaits you on our distant home planet, Blisstonia.*
(Homer looks at their pamphlet. It's titled "The Movementarians." It has a picture of a man on it with words underneath, reading "The Leader.")
Homer: *Hmm. Makes sense.*

Li'l Bastard General Mischief Kit: Bart's general mischief kit of choice.

Li'l Bastard Brainwashing Kit: The Movementarians' brainwashing kit of choice.

"Marge, when I join an underground cult I expect a little support from my family."

THE STUFF YOU MAY HAVE MISSED

The Springfield International Airport sign reads, "No Crashes Since" with a hanging sign that says, "Tuesday."

The Springfield Airport houses the Just Crichton and King Bookstore.

Homer also asked the question, "Will there be beer?" in 5F13, "This Little Wiggy."

Homer says, "Outta my way, jerkass!" twice in the episode.

In this episode, Homer runs off in the middle of a conversation to go chase a bird; in 1F02, "Homer Goes to College," Homer runs off before a review session to chase a squirrel; and in 2F08, "Fear of Flying," he runs off to chase a dog with a puffy tail.

Books in the Movementarians' classroom include *Arithmetic the Leader's Way* and *Science for Leader Lovers*. On the board is written, "Leadership starts with 'Leader'."

When Marge escapes from the compound, she's chased by a giant bubble that pops out of the river—it winds up encapsulating Hans Moleman—a reference to the cult TV series "The Prisoner."

The lawyers from the Springfield Lawyer House ride around in fire trucks with the letters SPLT on them. They stand for Springfield Lawyer Truck.

"This so-called new religion is nothing but a pack of weird rituals and chants designed to take away the money of fools. Let us say the Lord's Prayer forty times, but first, let's pass the collection plate."

"When we got married, you promised me my harvesting days were over." Marge, to Homer, as they participate in the lima bean harvest at the Movementarians' compound.

OF SECT

Episode 5F23
Original Airdate: 2/8/98
Writer: Steve O'Donnell
Director: Steven Dean Moore
Executive Producer: David Mirkin

Lisa: *Dad, do you think you might have been brainwashed?*
Homer: *I have not been brainwashed.* (Then, as if in a trance) *Kill the girl. Kill the girl.*
(Homer slowly reaches for Lisa. Marge hits him.)
Marge: *Homer!*
Homer: *What, what'd I say?*

Marge: *I've never heard of these Movementarians. Are they some kind of church?*
Homer: *Who cares what it is? The point is these are some decent, generous people that I can take advantage of!*

Lisa: *Watch yourself, Dad. You're the highly suggestible type.*
Homer: *Yes, I am the highly suggestible type.*

Glen: *Why don't you come chat with us about the Leader at the welcome center?*
Homer: *Will there be beer?*
Glen: *Beer is not allowed.*
Homer: *Homer no function beer well without.*

Movie Moment:

Willie captures Marge's and Reverend Lovejoy's attention by scratching his nails along a stained glass window. Bart captured Homer's, Benjamin's, Doug's, and Gary's attention by doing the same thing with a chalkboard in 1F02, "Homer Goes To College." In both instances, this is a direct reference to Robert Shaw's attention-getting technique as Quint in *Jaws*.

"Ahoy hoy, lowly mortals." Burns's new greeting, after proclaiming himself a god.

"Oh, I never thought I'd have to do this again." Reverend Lovejoy, as he douses the church with gasoline.

"Gimme that, ya noodle-armed choirboy." Willie, requesting the bat from Reverend Lovejoy, after Lovejoy fails to knock Homer out with a baseball bat.

"Damn it! It fell apart like everything else I've ever believed in. Oh, I guess it's back to good old-fashioned voodoo."

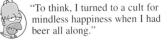

"To think, I turned to a cult for mindless happiness when I had beer all along."

DAS BUS

Episode 5F11   Original Airdate: 2/15/98   Writer: David S. Cohen   Director: Pete Michels
Executive Producer: Mike Scully   Guest Voice: James Earl Jones as Narrator

WENDELL

Typical state of being:
Nauseous. (Sometimes dizzy.)

Most dangerous:
On field trip bus rides.

Pet peeves:
Gear shifting, backslapping.

Sad fact:
Once sent to his death when a pencil rolled off his desk.

Often seen with:
Richard and Lewis.

> PLEASE TRY NOT TO SHAKE THE SEAT LIKE THAT.

E n route to a Model UN conference, the Springfield Elementary school bus crashes off of a bridge into a river, and then is swept into the ocean. Otto is carried away by the current, and the children wash ashore on a deserted island.

Meanwhile, Homer decides to start a business on the Internet, but his operation is ultimately bought out by Bill Gates in a very hostile takeover.

After the children fail to find anything edible on the island, Bart swims back to the sunken school bus and retrieves their cooler full of food. The kids agree to ration out the cooler's contents, but the next morning they find it empty. Milhouse, surrounded by discarded candy wrappers, is accused of eating everything. He claims a monster did it.

With Bart presiding as judge, Lisa as the defense, and Nelson as the prosecutor, Milhouse is put on trial. When he's found innocent due to lack of evidence, the other kids, displeased with the verdict, turn on Bart, Lisa, and Milhouse, chasing them down, presumably, to kill them. When the kids corner the trio in a cave, they all discover that there is a "monster" on the island—a wild boar. They see a potato chip bag from the cooler stuck on one of its tusks and realize that Milhouse wasn't lying. The kids cook the boar for food, and, at the end of the story, a narrator assures us that the children are rescued by Moe.

SHOW HIGHLIGHTS

(Troy McClure, as Noah, stands on a cliff before a darkened sky. God's voice calls out to him.)
God: *Noah, thou shalt build thyself an ark measuring three hundred cubits in length.*
(Noah writes the figure down on a tablet as he responds.)
Noah: *Three hundred cubits, give or take...*
(The sky thunders.)
God: *Exactly three hundred! And thou shalt takest two of every creature...*
Noah: *Two creatures...*
(The sky thunders again.)
God: *Two of every creature!*
Noah: *Even stinkbeetles?*
God: *Especially stinkbeetles!*

The Simpsons, Watching the Noah's Ark Movie:
Bart: *Whoa, cool! God is so in-your-face!*
Homer: *Yeah. He's my favorite fictional character.*

"You let us stay up to watch Troy McClure in such other Bible epics as *David vs. Super-Goliath* and *Suddenly Last Supper!*" Lisa, citing precedent to stay up late.

"I'd like to, but I'm afraid he has diplomatic immunity." Principal Skinner, explaining why he won't stop Nelson from pinching Wendell's nose shut with chopsticks during a meeting of the Model UN Club.

 "Order! Order! Do you kids want to be like the real UN? Or do you just want to squabble and waste time?"

Historical Moment:
Principal Skinner calls for order by banging his shoe on the table, à la Nikita Khrushchev during his infamous "We Will Bury You" speech at the UN.

"Zeppelin rules!" Otto's last words before being carried off by the current.

 "I'm glad we're stranded. It'll be just like the Swiss Family Robinson—only with more cursing! We're gonna live like kings. Damn hell ass kings!"

Compu-Global Hyper-Mega Net:
The name Marge suggests for Homer's new company.

Movie Moment:
After Milhouse uses the vine to swing across the chasm, Bart asks him to throw it back and is refused, much like Indiana Jones in *Raiders of the Lost Ark*. The entire episode is derived from *Lord of the Flies*.

"They taste like burning." Ralph's review of the berries the food patrol gathered for dinner.

"Kill the dorks! Bash their butts! Kick their shins!" The children's chant at the start of the hunt for Milhouse, Bart, and Lisa.

"Oh, they have the Internet on computers now." Homer, reading *Internet for Dummies*.

"Sorry about that whole tryin' to kill ya thing." Nelson, apologizing to Milhouse after discovering the boar ate the kids' food.

THE STUFF YOU MAY HAVE MISSED

The banner on the bus reads, "Model UN 'Order At Any Cost.'" It features a dove holding a machine gun.

Otto listens to "Songs to Enrage Bus Drivers."

On his desk, Homer has the drinking bird first seen in 8F23, "Brother, Can You Spare Two Dimes?", and a pin sculpture with the impression of his face on it.

An "Ah Fudge!" bar and a bag of "Chippos" are seen among the other food in the cooler.

Ralph paints his face like Kiss member Peter Criss.

THE LAST TEMPTATION OF KRUST

Episode 5F10 Original Airdate: 2/22/98 Writer: Donick Cary Director: Mike B. Anderson Executive Producer: Mike Scully
Guest Voices: Steven Wright, Janeane Garofalo, Bobcat Goldthwait, Bruce Baum, Jay Leno, and Hank Williams Jr. as Themselves

PAIN IS NOT THE CLEANSER
PAIN IS NOT THE CLEANSER
PAIN IS NOT THE CLEANSER
PAIN IS NOT THE CLEANSER
PAIN IS NOT THE CLEANSER
PAIN IS NOT THE CLEANSER

Bart learns that a big comedy benefit show in Springfield isn't including Krusty the Clown on the bill. He rectifies the situation by speaking with Jay Leno, organizer of the event. Krusty's appearance at the show goes badly as he tells dated, offensive jokes.

Discouraged by his failure at the show, Krusty goes on an all-night bender, winding up passed out on the Flanderses' lawn. Bart rescues Krusty and brings him to his room. There, Krusty sees all of Bart's Krusty merchandise and realizes that he should have spent his time over the years honing his act instead of selling out. Bart has Jay Leno over to help Krusty update his comedy, but Krusty's attempts to modernize don't work out. Yet, when he announces his retirement, his tirade against modern comedy has all the reporters in attendance laughing. He decides to give show business another go.

Krusty's new "tell it like it is" image is a hit, and he becomes a popular comedian in Springfield once more. Krusty's new-found credibility is noticed by a couple of ad executives who approach him about endorsing a new sport-utility vehicle. Krusty initially rebuffs the execs, but in the end, he relents. Seeing Krusty as a sellout once more, Krusty's audience turns on him, ending his stand-up comedy comeback.

SHOW HIGHLIGHTS

"They need a good, stiff, all-purpose dress shoe. Something for church, but also for doctor's appointments, dental checkups, piano recitals, building dedications, visiting elderly relatives, haircuts, and shoe shopping."

"That's where you're wrong, pal. It's not enough to want a cracker, you have to earn it." Homer, arguing with the bird.

Prince of Pies; Sultan of Seltzer: Two oft-used nicknames for Krusty the Clown.

Bart: Hey, Krusty, great set.
Krusty: Are you kidding? I stunk up the joint.
Bart: No, no. I was talkin' to Lisa back there—we both agreed; you killed!
Krusty: Really? Lisa, huh?

Corpsy the Clown: Janeane Garofalo's nickname for Krusty.

"Hey, hey. I'm Kent Brockman the Clown, filling in for Krusty the Clown, who didn't come in today. He is presumed dead or on vacation. Today's top joke: It seems a local moron threw his clock out the window. We'll tell you why, right after this."

Bart: Anyway, don't you have some advice for Krusty?
Jay Leno: Well, these days people like observational humor, you know, about things they deal with in everyday life.
Krusty: Oh yeah! You mean, like when your lazy butler washes your sock garters and they're still covered with schmutz?
Jay Leno: Well, kinda, but more universal. And maybe lose the "Me so solly" bit.
Bart: Hey, whoa, whoa, let's not tamper with the classics.
Krusty: Shut up, kid. C'mon, Leno! Tamper, teach, impart!

"Then, you got these lady comics talkin' about stuff that would embarrass Redd Foxx, God rest his smutty soul. Who they slept with, what time they sit on the can. This is supposed to get you a husband?"

Krusty: I guess you Wall Street weasels didn't get the word: Krusty's not for sale.
Ad Exec #1: But you endorse everything! In fact, this endorsement contract comes from your line of legal forms!
Krusty: It's a quality form. But those days are behind me—I don't shill for nobody no more!

Bart: What do we need church shoes for? Jesus wore sandals.
Homer: Well, maybe if he had better arch support they wouldn't have caught him.
(Marge makes a disapproving sound and notices something.)
Marge: Look, Homer—here's that bird you like to argue with!
(Homer looks over and sees a parrot sitting atop a perch in front of All Pets Great and Cheap.)
Homer: Well, well, well, if it isn't Professor Know-It-All. Excuse me, Marge.
(Homer walks off.)

Bart: Well, if you're running the show, how could you leave out Krusty the Clown?
Jay Leno: Ah, Krusty the Clown. That takes me back. Didn't he die in a grease fire?
Bart: No, he's alive and he is so funny you could plotz. At least according to his press release.
Jay Leno: Well, if he's half as alive as you say he is, he's in!

THE STUFF YOU MAY HAVE MISSED

Gil is the salesman at Goody New Shoes. He was first seen in episode 5F06, "Realty Bites."

On his "bender to end all benders," Krusty visits The Gutter Room, Blottos, and The Bloated Liver.

Among the Krusty items in Bart's room are: a talking Krusty doll; a Krusty toy chest; a Krusty mug; a "Krusty the Clown Show" poster; a Krusty lamp; a Krusty phone; a "Krusty #1" pennant; a Krusty tongue pendulum clock (first seen in 8F24, "Kamp Krusty"); two Krusty photographs; a Krusty poster; a Krusty model plane; stacks of Krusty magazines; a Krusty bedspread; a Krusty "Hey, Hey!" rug; a Krusty snowglobe; a regular Krusty doll; a Krusty in the box; a Krusty radon detector; a Krusty calendar; a Kamp Krusty banner; Krusty's personal swabs; a Krusty T-shirt; a Krusty wastebasket; a Krusty-firing-Mel-out-of-a-cannon toy; a Krusty-throwing-bomb toy; a Krusty alarm clock; a Krusty globe; a Krusty brand seal of approval; a Krusty toolbox; a Krusty ball; a Krusty walkie-talkie (Milhouse owns the other one, last seen in 8F04, "Homer Defined"); a Krusty book, a bottle of Krusty eyewash; and a Krusty flashlight.

This episode marks the first time a "Simpsons" character's eyes have appeared bloodshot.

While Krusty is taking a bath, his pacemaker scar and his superfluous third nipple can be seen. Both were last seen in 3F13, "Bart the Fink."

Krusty drinks coffee with Jay Leno at Java the Hutt.

The contract from Krusty's line of legal forms has a picture of Krusty dressed as a judge, saying, "Hey, hey! They're binding!"

AD EXECS

Chutzpah level:
High.

Marketing strategy:
To exploit people by exploiting other people with high credibility.

Working dynamic:
Rife with unrequited attraction.

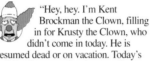

YOUR CREDIBILITY IS JUST...WOW!

RENEE

Job:
Professional flower vendor.

Most puzzling behavior:
Finds Moe charming.

Chief charitable act:
Pity dates.

Enjoys:
Bow ties, balloons, in-line skating, whales, fine dining, movies, Hawaii.

Admires:
Men who are willing to face the music for their mistakes.

Dislikes:
Men who are willing to dig up corpses to use in faking their deaths to avoid facing the music for their mistakes.

WELL, HELLO, MARY SUNSHINE.

Guest Voice:
Helen Hunt as Renee

 omer tries to help Moe meet a woman. After having no luck at Stu's Disco, Moe finally meets a woman named Renee selling flowers. They strike up a conversation, and Moe asks her out. She accepts.

Romance blossoms between Moe and Renee. Moe begins to spend a great deal of money on her, and soon his Players Club card is maxed out. Desperate to get more money, Moe decides to commit insurance fraud by asking Homer to steal his car and park it in front of the 10:15 train while he and Renee are on the Police Midnight Charity Cruise.

Homer steals the car but fails to stick to the plan. Missing the train because he goes to a drive-in movie, Homer decides to dump the car into the ocean, but winds up getting caught in the act by the police on the charity cruise. Moe lets Homer take the rap.

Moe takes the money from the insurance company, but instead of bailing Homer out of jail, he plans a trip to Hawaii with Renee. Before they can leave, Moe is seized with guilt and confesses the whole thing to Renee. Renee is initially forgiving, but when Moe tries to put together another scheme to avoid telling the truth, she leaves. Moe accidentally sets the bar on fire, just as an escaped Homer arrives to exact his revenge on Moe. Homer and Moe succumb to smoke inhalation and are saved by Barney after he first saves some kegs of beer. When the duo come to, they wake up and apologize to each other. To help him get back on his feet again, Homer allows Moe to convert the Simpson home into the new site of Moe's Tavern.

SHOW HIGHLIGHTS

Homer: *Hey, I thought your mother told you to take a bath.*
Bart: *Yeah, Mom says a lot of things.*
Homer: *Oh, I understand, kids. I'm not a bath man myself, more of a cologne man.*

How Homer Chooses to Fix the Water Heater: He hits it repeatedly with a wrench.

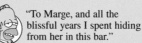 "To Marge, and all the blissful years I spent hiding from her in this bar."

"It's been four years since my last date with a whatchoo-call-it, uh, woman."

Moe: *No girl wants to end up with a Joe Pukepail like me.*
Homer: *Now, now, I won't hear of it, Moe—you're a fabulous catch!*
Moe: *Oh yeah? Well, uh, how come I ain't fending off movie starlets with a pointy stick?*
Homer: *Oh, it's probably due to your ugliness, but that doesn't mean we can't find you a woman. C'mon! We're going to the darkest bar in town!*

In Stu's Disco:
Moe: *Uh, I don't know, Homer. Women can smell panic, and, uh, right now I gotta be reekin' of it.*
Homer: *Relax, all I smell is garlic and fish.*

Moe's Opening Lines to Women in Stu's Disco:
"You look pretty clean" and "So, hi there. Uh, don't scream."

Renee: *Really? You think I'm gorgeous?*
Moe: *Yeah, well, the part that's showin'. Guess you could have a lotta weird scars or a fake ass or somethin'.*
Renee: *You don't talk to a lot of women, do you?*

"Aw, there's nobody for Moe. I'm just gonna die lonely and ugly and dead."

"Hot damn! All right, don't eat nothin' for the next three days 'cause I'm takin' you out for a steak the size of a toilet seat!" Moe, asking Renee out on a date.

Moe: *Hey, hey, Sabu! I need another magnum of your best champagne here, ah, and bring us the finest food you got, stuffed with the second finest.*
Maitre d': *Excellent, sir. Lobster stuffed with tacos.*

"He's got this insecure, sweaty charm." Renee's explanation as to why Moe has grown on her.

Moe: *(into phone) Yeah, I want to send her two dozen roses and I want to put somethin' nice on the card like, um, ah, "Renee, my treasure—"* (Suddenly, Barney starts laughing at Moe. Moe turns to him.)
Moe: *Hey, shut up or I'll ram a stool down your throat! (getting back on the phone) I, ah, no, no, no—I don't want that on the card. Well, let me hear how it sounds. (pause) Nah, nah, take it out, take it out.*

(Homer sits at the dinner table, dressed in black with a black wool cap on. He keeps stealing glances at the clock. The family notices.)
Marge: *Why all the black?*
Homer: *Why all the pearls, why all the hair, why anything?*
Lisa: *You look a little nervous, Dad.*
Homer: *No, you look a little nervous, Lisa.*
Bart: *You're up to somethin', aren't you?*
(Homer pushes his chair away from the table and gets up.)
Homer: *No, I'm just going out to commit certain deeds.*

"Stealing, stealing, stealing a car for Moe! Da-da-da-da da-da-da-duh, insurance fraud today!" Homer's car-stealing song, sung to the tune of "Sailing, Sailing."

 "You know, fingerprints are just like snowflakes. They're both very pretty."

"Ukulele, pineapples, beach pistol, scandalously revealing thong..." Moe, packing for Hawaii.

"I could never stay mad at you, Moe. After all, you get me drunk."

THE STUFF YOU MAY HAVE MISSED

The sign outside Stu's Disco depicts Apu's cousin Sanjay and reads, "You must be at least this swarthy to enter."

While dancing in Stu's Disco, Luann Van Houten appears to have brown hair.

Other patrons of Stu's Disco include: Otto, Princess Kashmir, Pyro (a.k.a Chase), and Willie.

A sign introducing the whale at Marine World reads, "'Willie' (formerly 'Shamu')."

Moe, Renee, Homer, and Marge double-date at The Gilded Truffle, first seen in 8F02, "Treehouse of Horror II."

It appears that the lobsters Moe and Renee dine on at The Gilded Truffle wear sombreros.

In *Hail to the Chimp*, the Oval Office is full of paintings and pictures depicting chimps in historical poses.

Principal Skinner and Mrs. Krabappel are among the guests on the Police Moonlight Charity Cruise.

Songs in this episode include: "One Bourbon, One Scotch, One Beer" by George Thorogood & the Destroyers, "Brick House" by The Commodores and "I'm a Believer" by The Monkees.

INDEMNITY

Episode 5F12
Original Airdate: 3/1/98
Writer: Ron Hauge
Director: Dominic Polcino
Executive Producer: Mike Scully

Hail to the Chimp:
(Homer watches the film at the Springfield Drive-in. On the screen, several politicians confront the chimp president in the Oval Office.)
Politician: *Mr. President, your welfare proposal is nothing but a lot of technical jargon and partisan rhetoric and—*
(The chimp president leaps at the politician, scratching at his face. Sitting in Moe's car, Homer leans back and laughs, eating popcorn.)
Homer: *That's what you get for not hailing to the chimp.*

THE SIMPSON MEN

Their occupations:
Unsuccessful shrimp company manager; airport bird shooter; aspiring millionaire impersonator; insurance fraud perpetrator; celebrity harasser; prison snitch; and jug band manager.

Traits in common:
Baldness; dimwittedness; obesity; perpetual five o'clock shadow; willingness to show up somewhere for five bucks.

Favorite sport:
Wearing pots on their heads and ramming into each other.

LISA THE SIMPSON

Episode 4F24 Original Airdate: 3/8/98 Writer: Ned Goldreyer Director: Susie Dietter
Executive Producers: Bill Oakley and Josh Weinstein

SHOW HIGHLIGHTS

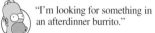

"I'm looking for something in an afterdinner burrito."

Someone's in the Kitchen with DNA! The film Hibbert shows to Lisa to answer her questions on genetics.

"Hi, I'm Troy McClure! (*A siren sounds and everyone but Troy leaves the room.*) You may remember me from such medical films as *Alice Doesn't Live Anymore* and *Mommy, What's Wrong with That Man's Face?*"

"DNA is God's recipe for making you. You take a dash of Dad, a pinch of Mom, then we bake for nine months and...Mmm! That's good Billy!" Troy McClure, explaining genetics.

"Isn't there any way I can change my DNA, like sitting on the microwave?"

"Well, we better leave him in there. Moving him now could kill him and tire us out." Dr. Nick Riviera, on Jasper frozen in Apu's freezer.

"Come one, come all! See the amazing frozen man! Also gaze at the Frito found in a bag of Doritos. Marvel at the floor that just won't come clean!"

"The best part was when the buildings fell down." Bart's review of the Fox special, "When Buildings Collapse."

Frostillicus: What Apu names the frozen Jasper.

"Marge, get me your address book, four beers, and my conversation hat."

"I got it! Woo-hoo! I mean, 'splendid.'" Lisa, finally getting the brain teaser.

Apu, Making a Deal:

Big Texan: *Son, I represent a group of oil tycoons who make foolish purchases. We already bought us a stained glass bathroom and the world's fattest racehorse. And now we need your iceman.*
Apu: *Oh no, I could never sell him. He's like a frozen father to me.*
Big Texan: *How much for just the head?*
(As Apu mulls it over, Jasper walks out of the freezer.)
Jasper: *By gum, it worked. I've awakened in the future.*
(He takes a snack cake from a display and reads the wrapper.)
Jasper: *(in awe) Moon Pie. What a time to be alive.*

Jasper's Letter to Apu:

"I have frozen myself so I may live to see the wonders of the future. Thaw me out when robot wives are cheap and effective. P.S. Please alter my pants as fashion dictates."

The Sad Truth, According to Grampa:

(Up in the attic, Grampa shows Lisa a picture of Homer after he won his first-grade spelling bee.)
Lisa: *Wow. Dad was a good speller?*
Grampa: *Oh, your dad used to be smart as a monkey, then his mind started gettin' lazy and now he's as dumb as a chimp.*
Lisa: *Grampa!*
Grampa: *Hey, I am, too. And your brother's coming along nicely. Look at Bart's homework. Back when he was your age, he was smart as a chimp.*
(Grampa opens up a box labeled "Bart." On top of a stack of homework is a paper of Bart's from the second grade. It has a smiley face on it with the comment, "Great Work!")
Lisa: *This is just two years ago!*
Grampa: *That's right. Then the Simpson genes kick in!*
(Grampa leafs through the papers like an animator's flip book and the smiley faces on the corners of the papers gradually turn to frowns and eventually to a skull and crossbones.)

THE STUFF YOU MAY HAVE MISSED

Lisa eats a Portion Time brand, vacuum-packed, vegetarian meal with applesauce.

Milhouse's case of head lice is not the first in his class. Bart had it in episode 3F01, "Home Sweet Homediddly-Dum-Doodily."

At the beginning of the episode, when the kids run out of the school happily screaming after the bell rings, Mrs. Krabappel, Miss Hoover, and the rest of the teachers join them.

After Apu changes his store's name to the Freak-E-Mart, he hangs signs in the window that read, "See the incredible siamese hot dog" and "Astonishing rubber check from mysterious unknown bank."

Buildings that collapse in "When Buildings Collapse" include the Old Printers' Home; Leaning Tower of Pizza; the headquarters of the Society of Structural Engineers; and The House of Usher.

A sign above the Haunted Cash Machine in the Freak-E-Mart reads, "Dispenses Images of Dead Presidents."

In Lisa's vision of the future, an Elvis painting hangs on the wall of her and Ralph's trailer.

After Apu changes his store's name to the Nude-E-Mart, he hangs a sign that reads, "Topless Dancers! Bottomless Coffee!"

L isa fails to solve a brain teaser that Martin, Milhouse, and Nelson easily figure out. When she then forgets her locker combination, her science homework, and her saxophone technique, she suspects that something may be wrong. Meanwhile, Jasper freezes himself in the Kwik-E-Mart ice cream freezer, in the hopes of seeing the far future. Overhearing Lisa worrying, Grampa tells her that all Simpsons start to lose their intelligence in their late childhood.

After authorities do not allow Apu to move Jasper, kids start offering to pay admission to see the frozen senior. Apu then converts the Kwik-E-Mart into a freakshow. Convinced that she can't escape genetics, Lisa surrenders to a life of stupidity.

After trying to live like Homer and Bart, Lisa becomes disgusted and storms out of the house, saying that she doesn't want to turn out like them. Inspired by a performer at The Jazz Hole, Lisa schemes her way onto the Channel 6 newscast and pleads with Springfield to treasure their brains. Homer sees Lisa's speech and decides to show her that all Simpsons are not stupid. He gathers all of the Simpson relatives in the tri-city area, and it's discovered that the defective gene is only passed on to males. At the Freak-E-Mart (formerly the Kwik-E-Mart), Jasper wakes from his hibernation, believing himself to be in the future, and leaves. Losing his cash cow, Apu changes the Freak-E-Mart into the Nude-E-Mart, a strip club/convenience store.

THIS LITTLE WIGGY

Episode 5F13 Original Airdate: 3/22/98 Writer: Dan Greaney Director: Neil Affleck Executive Producer: Mike Scully

O n a family trip to the Springfield Knowledgeum, Marge sees that Chief Wiggum's son, Ralph, has no friends. Feeling sorry for him, Marge volunteers an embarrassed Bart to be his new pal, setting a play date for them.

At Ralph's house, Bart discovers that Chief Wiggum has a master key to all the locks in the city. The next night, he and Ralph sneak out and run rampant through Springfield, using the key. They run into Jimbo, Dolph, Kearney, and Nelson. In the hopes of looking cool, Bart tells them about the key and takes them to an abandoned penitentiary to sneak around. Before they go in, a scared Ralph says he wants to go home. Bart decides he can't leave his friend behind, but the bullies throw the master key into the prison.

When Bart and Ralph go in to retrieve the key, they discover and activate the jail's electric chair to see how it works. The next afternoon, the mayor holds a press conference from the jail to announce its reopening. He straps himself into the electric chair to demonstrate what Springfield criminals could face. Bart tries to call the jail to warn them that the chair is activated, but the line is busy. Ralph suggests they ask Lisa what to do. Lisa has them write out a note that says, "The electric chair is on," and tie it to a model rocket, which they fire at the prison. The rocket lands in Montgomery Burns's office. Burns reads the note and is outraged that the prison has been receiving free electricity. He turns off the power, saving the mayor.

SHOW HIGHLIGHTS

"Welcome to the Knowledgeum, I'm Troy McClure. You may remember me from such automated information kiosks as 'Welcome to Springfield Airport' and 'Where's Nordstrom?' While you're enjoying our Hall of Wonders, your car will unfortunately be subject to repeated break-ins..."

"Ovulate, damn you! Ovulate!" Homer, on the "Let's Make a Baby" interactive exhibit.

(Marge and Chief Wiggum watch Ralph run around, barking.)
Marge: Is that normal?
Chief Wiggum: Yeah, he's just playing "Wiggle Puppy." That's a dog he made up who flies by wagging his tail. I tell ya, that dog has had some amazing adventures.

Marge: Bart, it's too nice a day to leave Ralph in a closet. You boys should go play outside.
Bart: But people will see me paired up with a doofus. You have no idea what that's like.
(Just then, a saw pops out of the floor between Marge and Bart. It saws a circle, and Homer's head pops out of the floor.)
Homer: Uh-oh.
(He pops back down.)

(Ralph shows Bart a large rock in his backyard.)
Ralph: That's where I saw the leprechaun.
Bart: Riiiight, a leprechaun.
Ralph: He told me to burn things.

"C'mon Ralph, your dad's a cop! There must be some cool stuff around here—bullets, dead body photos, what have you..." Bart, hanging out with Ralph at his house.

"Wow! Dad's been in jail six times! Aw, Mom's only been in twice." Bart, looking through Homer's police file.

"You know you're not supposed to go in there. What is your fascination with my 'Forbidden Closet of Mystery'?"

(Homer and Marge stand at their answering machine, looking at a book titled, 99 Hilarious Phone Messages. Reading from the book, Homer hits a button on the machine.)
Homer: Hi, this is Jerry Maguire. Show me the message! Show me the message!
Marge: No, that stinks. Let me try one.
(Marge takes the book and hits a button on the machine.)
Marge: This is Geraldine, and the devil made me miss your call, so here comes the beep, here comes the beep!
(As Marge laughs, Homer swipes the book and hits the button on the answering machine.)
Homer: (to the tune of "The Hustle") Do the message! Do, duh, do, da-dit, da-dit, da-dit...

"Wow! Look at all these toilets! And just inches from your bed—talk about luxury!" Bart, looking at the cells in the abandoned Morningwood Penitentiary.

(Bart and Ralph open a door marked, "Danger—No Entry." They gasp, discovering an electric chair.)
Bart: Whoa, mama! The electric chair! Smell that, Ralph? That's the smell of justice.
Ralph: Smells like hot dogs.

"I will now strap myself into this electric chair which was deactivated over thirty years ago, and, I can only assume, still is." Mayor Quimby, holding a penitentiary news conference to demonstrate what violent criminals in Springfield have to fear.

"Aw, you've done grand, laddie! Now you know what you have to do: Burn the house down. Burn 'em all!" Ralph's evil leprechaun, congratulating him on saving the mayor.

I WAS NOT TOLD TO DO THIS
I WAS NOT TOLD TO DO THIS
I WAS NOT TOLD TO DO THIS
I WAS NOT TOLD TO DO THIS
I WAS NOT TOLD TO DO THIS
I WAS NOT TOLD TO DO THIS

THE STUFF YOU MAY HAVE MISSED

The Springfield Knowledgeum sign reads, "Where Science Is Explained with Brightly Colored Balls."

In the Knowledgeum, we see Database, Ham, and Report Card, all members of SuperFriends. They (and their organization) were introduced in 2F11, "Bart's Comet," and last seen in 4F23, "The Principal and the Pauper."

The "Let's Make a Baby" exhibit sign features a cartoon sperm offering flowers to a cartoon egg.

Among Ralph's toys is a "Life in Hell"-style rabbit and a monkey in a fez. Both of these toys were last seen in 5F07, "Miracle on Evergreen Terrace," as Chief Wiggum was stealing them from the Simpson home.

All of the files in Chief Wiggum's "Forbidden Closet of Mystery" have labels on them reading, "Confidential—Do Not Remove from Police Station." Bart leafs through files belonging to "Riviera, Dr. N.," "Krustofsky, H." (a.k.a. Krusty the Clown), "Terwilliger, R." (a.k.a. Sideshow Bob), and "Simpson, Homer."

The toy store Bart and Ralph visit is called J. R. R. Toykin's. Among the toys there is a Big Ben slide, a giant piano, a train, a pirate's mast, a giant stuffed giraffe, giant tinkertoys, and a giant erector set–style ferris wheel.

Robbie the Automaton is apparently the same model as the robot named Floyd in 5F02, "Treehouse of Horror VIII: Fly Vs. Fly."

ROBBIE THE AUTOMATON

Usual salutation:
"Greetings, Earth children!"

Where he's from:
Earth.

Secret shame:
He's actually controlled by a guy in a tree.

Default setting (after command link is severed):
Crush, kill, destroy.

SIMPSON

CAPTAIN TENILLE

Describes himself as:
A man of few words.

Likes:
The cut of Homer's jib.

Unusual beliefs:
Homer is competent; "In the Navy" by the Village People is an ancient sea chantey.

Worst decision:
Tie: leaving Homer in charge; climbing into a torpedo tube while Homer is in charge.

> MAYBE IT'S THE SALT WATER IN MY VEINS OR THE NITROGEN BUBBLES IN MY BRAIN, BUT I'VE TAKEN A REAL SHINE TO YOU.

Guest Voice:
Rod Steiger as Captain Tenille

After being fired for causing a near meltdown, Homer joins the Naval Reserve. Meanwhile, Bart gets an earring after seeing how it transforms Milhouse from being a nerd to being cool. Homer disapproves. After graduating from basic training, Homer goes off on a mission of war games; before he leaves, he chides Bart about the earring, and Bart gives it to him.

Assigned to a navy sub, Homer makes fast friends with the captain, who leaves him in charge when he goes to check on a blocked torpedo tube. When Homer believes the ship is being attacked, he orders the torpedoes fired, accidentally ejecting the captain.

Homer gets the sub lost, so that it is directly en route to Russia. The media labels Homer a traitor. When the sub is bombarded by depth charges from the United States

Navy, it springs a pinhole leak. Things look dire until Homer realizes he can use Bart's earring to fix it. He has the sub surface and is taken into custody by the navy. Court-martialed, Homer beats the rap when the navy judges all must resign from the case due to various scandals in which they're involved.

> MY BUTT DOES NOT DESERVE
> ITS OWN WEBSITE
> MY BUTT DOES NOT DESER*
> ITS OWN WEBSITE
> MY BUTT DOES NOT DES*
> ITS OWN WEBSITE

SHOW HIGHLIGHTS

"Mmm...Homer." The Big Donut, eating Homer in his dream about the Planet of the Donuts.

"Next on *Exploitation Theater: Blackula*, followed by *Blackenstein*, and the *Blunchblack of Blotre Blame!*" Overheard on the Simpson television.

"After basic training, you only have to work one weekend a month, and most of that time you're drunk off your ass." Part of the Naval Reserve ad campaign.

> Homer: *Well, guys, I won't be seeing you for a while.*
> Barney: *Where are you going?*
> Homer: *I've joined the Naval Reserve.*
> Barney: *Well, I'm not going to let anything happen to my best friend. I'm joining, too.*
> Moe: *Well, I'm not going to let anything happen to my two best customers. I'm joining, too.*
> Apu: *And although my religion strictly forbids military service, what the hey? I'm in, too.*
> Homer: *Gee thanks, guys. This is just like The Deer Hunter.*

> Lisa: *Good luck, Dad. Although I am morally opposed to the military-industrial complex of which you are now a part.*
> Homer: *Aw, that's sweet, honey. I'll bring you back a hat.*
> Bart: *Hey, Homer! Bring me back a torpedo.*
> Homer: *No.*
> Bart: *But Flanders got his kids torpedoes.*
> Homer: *Oh, he did, did he? I'll show him! I'll bring you a weapon of unimaginable destructive power!*

"Oh, I'm a freak!" Homer, after having his head shaved in Naval Reserve boot camp.

"That is so 1991." Ralph, commenting on Bart's rendition of "Do the Bartman."

Bob Hope and Cindy Crawford: The star attractions on the USO Tour.

Bob Denver and Cindy Williams: The star attractions on the Naval Reserve Tour.

> "You know, Marge, joining the reserves was the best thing I ever did. I feel good about myself, I'm helping my country, and later I'm gonna get Gilligan's autograph."

> "An earring! How rebellious, in a conformist sort of way."

> Captain Tenille: *Oh, Simpson, you're like the son I never had.*
> Homer: *And you're like the father I never visit.*

"We're losing power. We're losing backup power! We're down to mood lighting here!" Moe, informing Captain Homer of the torpedo damage.

> Homer: *Damage report, Mr. Moe.*
> Moe: *Sonar out, navigation out, radio out.*
> Homer: *Enough of what's out. What's in?*
> Moe: *Ice-blended mocha drinks and David Schwimmer.*
> Homer: *Yes, he is handsome in an ugly sort of way.*

> "Well, sir, treason season started early this year as a nuclear sub was hijacked by local man, Homer Simpson."

> "My Homer is not a communist. He may be a liar, a pig, an idiot, a communist, but he is not a porn star!"

> "Children, I'll be frank. In the event of nuclear war we can only save our best and brightest. Therefore, space in the fallout shelter will be reserved for Lisa Simpson, Martin Prince, our championship kickball team, and Sherri, but not Terri."

"The engine room has sprung a leak! It's filling up with a clear, nonalcoholic liquid." Barney, reporting the damage from the depth charges.

I'm with Admiral Stupid: Homer's novelty navy shirt.

> Marge: *A dishonorable discharge! It's the best we coulda hoped for!*
> Homer: *You can't spell "dishonorable" without "honorable"!*

Movie Moment:

Homer's dream of the Planet of the Donuts is a direct reference to *Planet of the Apes*. Other episodes that reference the film are 1F13, "Deep Space Homer" and 3F13, "A Fish Called Selma."

TIDE

Episode 3G04
Original Airdate: 3/29/98
Writer: Joshua Sternin & Jeffrey Ventimilia
Director: Milton Gray
Executive Producer: Al Jean & Mike Reiss
Guest Voice: Bob Denver as Himself

THE STUFF YOU MAY HAVE MISSED

Homer's big-handed co-worker was first seen in 1F07, "The Last Temptation of Homer."

When Homer sees the Naval Reserve TV ad, Lisa is reading *Junior Skeptic* magazine.

Text on the Naval Reserve sign reads, "It's not just a job...it's a really easy job."

When Homer does his Columbo impression, one of his pupils goes off in an odd direction.

Barney's mother is seen standing outside of the Officer's Club.

The Veterans of Unpopular Wars Hall has text on its sign, reading, "(Two War-Story Minimum)."

In 'n' Out Ear Piercing's motto is, "If It Dangles, We'll Punch a Hole in It."

A sign along the former site of the Berlin Wall reads, "Berlin reunited and it feels so good."

This episode marks the first appearance of Moe's cat, Mr. Snookums.

THE TROUBLE WITH TRILLIONS

Episode 5F14 Original Airdate: 4/5/98 Writer: Ian Maxtone-Graham Director: Swinton Scott Executive Producer: Mike Scully
Guest Voice: Paul Winfield as Lucius Sweet

CHARLIE

Trained as:
A dangerous emissions supervisor.

Replaced by:
Mindy Simmons.

Example of bad luck 1:
Mr. Burns once sent him through a tube to a foreign land where he was forced to dance for cackling men in fezzes and turbans.

Example of bad luck 2:
He was arrested for threatening to beat up local officials over the slow progress of HDTV.

Example of bad judgment:
Once used his sister's wooden leg as a softball bat.

> I WON'T BORE YOU WITH THE DETAILS OF OUR MIRACULOUS ESCAPE, BUT WE DESPERATELY NEED A REAL EMERGENCY EXIT.

S hortly before midnight on April 15th, Homer discovers he didn't do his annual taxes. In a rush, he fakes deductions and provides false information on his form. Soon, Homer is arrested for tax fraud. Homer strikes a deal: He'll work for the FBI for immunity from IRS prosecution.

Homer successfully assists the FBI in foiling his co-worker Charlie's scheme against government officials. Pleased with his work, the bureau enlists Homer for a more important project. In 1945, on behalf of the U.S. government, Mr. Burns was supposed to deliver a trillion-dollar bill to postwar Europe for reconstruction. It never arrived. The FBI suspects Burns still has the bill and asks Homer to infiltrate his mansion to find it.

Homer makes it into Mr. Burns's home, and, after he mistakes Homer for a reporter from *Collier's*, Burns shows Homer the bill. The FBI immediately rushes in and arrests Burns, who loudly criticizes the government's taxation and spending policies. Burns's words reach Homer, and at the last moment, he snatches Burns from the FBI.

Burns enlists the help of Smithers, and, together with Homer, they flee the country in Burns's plane. Burns decides to land in Cuba and offer Castro the trillion-dollar bill in exchange for the country. When they meet with Castro, he tells them Cuba is not for sale, but asks if he can see the bill. Burns lets him have the bill for a moment, and when Burns asks for it back, it's gone.

Floating on a makeshift raft with Homer, Burns decides that they should return to the United States, saying that he'll merely bribe the jury when the government brings him to trial for handing over a trillion dollars to Cuba.

SHOW HIGHLIGHTS

"January 1st! Better get goin' on those taxes, Neddy!"

"Let's see, cash-register ink. Well, that's a business expense, isn't it? Oh, but then I do enjoy the smell of the stuff, don't I? Better not risk it." Ned Flanders, preparing his tax return.

"Why, everything! Policemen, trees, sunshine, and let's not forget the folks who just don't feel like workin', God bless 'em!" Ned Flanders, explaining what taxes pay for.

"Will you look at those morons! I paid my taxes over a year ago!"

Dr. Hibbert, Physician:
(Ned, walking out of the post office, runs into Dr. Hibbert.)
Ned: *Get your taxes out of the way?*
Hibbert: *No, just mailing out death certificates for holiday-related fatalities, ah-heh, heh, heh!*

I WILL NOT DEMAND
WHAT I'M WORTH.
I WILL NOT DEMAND
WHAT I'M WORTH.
I WILL NOT DEMAND
WHAT I'M WORTH.

"Quiet, honey, you don't know how big this government is! It goes all the way to the president!"

Homer Does His Taxes:
Homer: *Marge, how many kids do we have? Oh, no time to count—I'll just estimate! Uh, nine!*
Marge: *Homer, you know we don't have—*
Homer: *Shut up, shut up! If I don't hear you, it's not illegal! Okay, I need some deductions, deductions... Oh, business gifts!*
(Homer takes the sailboat painting from above the couch and hands it to Marge.)
Homer: *Here you go, keep using nuclear power!*
Marge: *Homer, I painted that for you.*
Homer: *Okay, Marge, if anyone asks, you require twenty-four-hour nursing care, Lisa's a clergyman, Maggie is seven people, and Bart was wounded in Vietnam.*
Bart: *Cool!*

"We believe Burns still has that bill hidden somewhere in his house, but all we've ascertained from satellite photos is that it's not on the roof." Agent Johnson, explaining why Homer is needed.

"Wow! That must be worth a fortune!" Homer, admiring Burns's trillion-dollar bill.

Business/Pleasure, Smuggle Cigars, Assassinate Castro:
The three choices listed on the official "Purpose of Visit" form at Cuban customs.

"Well, if it's a crime to love one's country, then I'm guilty. And if it's a crime to steal a trillion dollars from our government and hand it over to communist Cuba, then I'm guilty of that, too. And if it's a crime to bribe a jury, then so help me, I'll soon be guilty of that!"

The Interrogation:
Agent Johnson: *Okay, kids, I want some answers. Where do you think your father would go with a trillion dollars?*
Bart: *My dad has a trillion dollars? Wow! I can buy and sell your sorry ass! I'll give you a billion dollars to empty the cat box for me.*
Marge: *No, no. Bart, that money is going towards your college education.*
Lisa: *Who needs college, Mom? We're trillionaires—let's buy dune buggies!*

THE STUFF YOU MAY HAVE MISSED

Lucius Sweet, last seen in 4F03, "The Homer They Fall," wipes his brow with a hundred-dollar bill in the IRS office waiting room.

Several Malibu Stacy dolls are on a shelf during the scene in Smithers's apartment. His love of the dolls was revealed in 1F12, "Lisa vs. Malibu Stacy."

The Springfield Airport sign reads, "Birthplace of Wind Shear."

The "El Duffo O Muerte" (The Duff or Die) sign in Cuba features a picture of communist revolutionary Che Guevara. He was last referenced in 2F20, "Who Shot Mr. Burns? (Part Two)"—Tito Puente played in a club called Chez Guevara.

GIRLY EDITION

Episode 5F15 Original Airdate: 4/19/98 Writer: Larry Doyle Director: Mark Kirkland
Executive Producer: Mike Scully

SHOW HIGHLIGHTS

Krusty: *(laughing) Man, you think the quality would dip after fifty-five hundred shows, but...* *(laughter)*
Channel 6 Executive: *Well, the FCC isn't laughing. They don't believe kids are learning anything from "Itchy & Scratchy."*
Krusty: *Oh, please. What don't they learn? Don't trust mice, cats are made of glass...*

"The Mattel and Mars Bar Quick Energy Chocobot Hour": The closest thing to educational programming on Channel 6.

Skinner: *Lisa, Channel 6 is launching a children's news program, and they've asked me to select an outstanding student to be anchorchild.*
Lisa: *Oh my gosh! Today's top story, little girl on cloud nine as dream comes true!*

"This isn't right. This isn't right at all!" Willie, upon waking up and discovering his shack is nearly filled with creamed corn.

"...and I'll be able to tackle all the hard-hitting children's news the grown-up-controlled media won't touch. Plus, I get to be on TV!"

A Question of Zazz

Lisa: *I don't need a co-anchor! I'm a straight-A student!*
Channel 6 Executive: *Lisa, Bart's got something you can't learn in school—zazz.*
Lisa: *What is zazz?*
Channel 6 Executive: *Zing, zork, kapowza. Call it what you want, in any language it spells mazuma in the bank!*
Lisa: *Zork? What is zork?*
Channel 6 Executive: *I didn't say zork.*

Marge Meets the Monkey

Marge: *There's a monkey in the house!*
Homer: *Relax, it's only Mojo. Mojo, Marge. Marge, Mojo.*

"They tug at the heart and fog the mind." Kent Brockman, revealing his secret to success: human interest stories.

"Bart, look up here. This is where the tears would be if I could cry. But I can't—botched facelift." The Channel 6 Exec, congratulating Bart on his "Bart's People" newscast.

"They want cheap sentiment? I'll pump 'em so full of sap they'll be blowin' their nose with a pancake!"

"I'm proud of you, honey. You're finally giving something back to the community after taking so, so much." Marge, talking to Bart about "Bart's People."

Marge: *Oh, for Pete's sakes! Why is that monkey wearing a diaper? I thought he was housebroken!*
Homer and Mojo: *Eh.*
Marge: *You said this monkey would be sweeping the floors and cleaning the gutters, and now he just lies there, struggling to breathe.*
Homer: *What do you want? His cholesterol's through the roof!*

(The Animal Assistants coordinator discovers a bloated, diapered Mojo on the step of their building.)
Coordinator: *Mojo, what have they done to you?*
(The coordinator offers Mojo a keyboard device, on which Mojo slowly types a message. The message appears on the device's screen as a computer voice says it aloud.)
Computer voice: *Pray for Mojo.*

THE STUFF YOU MAY HAVE MISSED

The Animal Assistants sign reads, "As Felt in Braille Weekly."

Bart does a report from the Veterans of Popular Wars Hall.

Major Nougat, Gooey, Coco, Colonel Kataffy: various characters on "The Mattel and Mars Bar Quick Energy Chocobot Hour."

To satisfy the FCC's educational programming requirement, Channel 6 enlists Lisa Simpson to anchor a kids' news segment on the "Krusty the Clown Show." At school, Bart rides through Willie's leaf pile, causing Willie to take his skateboard away. In revenge, Bart fills Willie's shack with creamed corn, destroying it.

Homer discovers that Apu has a helper monkey to assist him after being shot on the job. Homer then cons an Animal Assistants organization into giving him a helper monkey named Mojo. Meanwhile, Marge makes Lisa allow Bart to host the sports segment on her news program. Bart does so well that Channel 6 management promotes him to co-anchor. To prove to Lisa that he's good enough, he starts producing reports called "Bart's People"—fluff human interest pieces designed to tug at the heart. The reports become incredibly popular.

Seeing that Mojo has adopted his slovenly lifestyle, Homer returns him to the Animal Assistants organization. Meanwhile, Lisa, resentful of Bart's success, gives him a fake letter describing an immigrant who's lost his home. Bart rushes to do a live "Bart's People" with the person, only to discover it's Willie. Willie goes after Bart, but Lisa shows up. Using Bart's fluff-talk, she convinces Willie to let Bart go.

Trained for:
Assisting the differently abled, physically challenged, or enfeebled.

What Homer has him do:
Make orange juice; steal donuts; act as a drinkin' buddy; act as an eatin' buddy; act as a nappin' buddy.

Pre-Homer condition:
Happy, eager, healthy, toilet-trained.

Post-Homer condition:
Bloated, lazy, diapered, with breathing difficulties.

After a local department store invents a holiday called Love Day, Homer is left with the task of taking out all of the garbage generated by the festivities at the Simpson home. Not making it to the curb in time for the garbage truck, Homer shouts insults after the garbagemen. They get into an argument that results in the Simpsons having their garbage collection service cut off. Soon, their front lawn is full of trash. Marge writes a letter of apology to the sanitation commissioner and signs Homer's name to it. When Homer finds out, he goes to city hall to rescind it. After an angry meeting with Ray Patterson, the sanitation commissioner, Homer decides to run for the position.

Though he campaigns at the plant and a local U2 concert, Homer fails to win much support. He then comes up with the slogan, "Can't Somebody Else Do It?", and proceeds to promise such things as around-the-clock garbage pick up and free car washes. He wins in a landslide.

He goes on to spend his entire year's budget frivolously within a month. Fearing they won't be paid, the garbagemen threaten to strike. To come up with more revenue, Homer offers to let other cities dump their trash in one of Springfield's abandoned mines. Soon, trash is bursting out of the ground. When the town asks Ray Patterson to come back, he refuses. Left with a trash problem they can no longer manage, the people of Springfield decide to move their entire town five miles away.

SHOW HIGHLIGHTS

"Gentlemen, I am pleased to report strong holiday sales from the Christmas-Hanu-Kwanzaa spend phase, and things look good for the Mom-Dad-Grad gift corridor..." A Costington's sales analyst, addressing the board of directors.

Homer's Love Day Present: Sir Lovesalot, the bear who loves to love.

The Costington's Board Meeting:
Chairman: Okay, people, we need to cook up a new holiday for the summer. Something with gifts, cards, assorted gougeables.
Board Member #1: How about something religious? We had great penetration last spring with "Christmas II."
Board Member #2: Oh, I know, "Spendover." Like Passover, but less talk, more presents.
Board Member #3: "Product Day"?

"Stupid trash...rotten, stinking...hate world, revenge soon...take out on everyone..." Homer, taking out the trash.

Garbageman #1: You called us trash-eating stinkbags.
Garbageman #2: Didn't you learn anything from Love Day?
Homer: That was yesterday, moron.

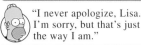 **"I never apologize, Lisa. I'm sorry, but that's just the way I am."**

Marge: Homer, that crazy lady who lives in our trash pile attacked me again.
Homer: That's not the way she tells it.

Marge: Homer, this has gone far enough. Will you please just apologize to the garbagemen?
Lisa: Yeah, Dad. You're always telling me and Bart to apologize.
Homer: Yeah, but I'm always secretly disappointed when you do.

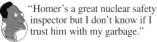 **"Homer's a great nuclear safety inspector but I don't know if I trust him with my garbage."**

The Awful Truth:
Marge: Oh, Homer, you didn't beat city hall! They picked up our trash because I wrote a letter of apology to the sanitation commissioner and signed your name, period.
Homer: You signed my name? I feel so violated!
Marge: You've signed my name lots of times.
Homer: But this isn't like a loan application or a will! You signed away my dignity!

Homer: I came to fight city hall! I want to shake things up, Patterson. Stir up some controversy! Rattle a few cages!
(Homer grabs a birdcage holding a parrot and starts shaking it.)
Patterson: Hey, stop that!
Homer: You'll never silence me! I'm the last angry man, Patterson! A crusader for the little guy!
(Homer shakes the birdcage some more.)
Patterson: Leave the bird alone!
Homer: Never!

Bono: Why should they vote for you?
Homer: That's a good question, Bono. 'Cause I'd be the most wack, tripped-out sanitation commissioner ever! Can you dig it?

Patterson: You told people I lured children into my gingerbread house.
Homer: Yeah, that was just a lie.

"Oh gosh. You know, I'm not much on speeches, but, it's so gratifying to leave you wallowing in the mess you've made. You're screwed, thank you, bye." Ray Patterson, speaking before the town.

TITANS

Episode 5F09
Original Airdate: 4/26/98
Writer: Ian Maxtone-Graham
Director: Jim Reardon
Executive Producer: Mike Scully

Guest Voices: U2 (Bono, The Edge, Adam Clayton, and Larry Mullen) as Themselves

THE STUFF YOU MAY HAVE MISSED

Costington's slogan reads, "Over a Century without a Slogan."

The sex offender registration line is made up of Jimmy the Scumbag, Patty and Selma, Freddy Quimby, and Moe.

In the *Springfield Shopper*, under the headline, "New Face in Trash Race" is a picture of Homer with another headline, reading, "Local Nut at It Again."

A later issue of the *Springfield Shopper* has the headlines, "Simpson Wins in Landslide," and "Says 'Crazy Promises' the Key."

As trash is bulldozed into the abandoned mine, Sir Lovesalot can be seen in the heap, with four hypodermic needles stuck in him.

Mayor Quimby says, "What the hell is that?" when a bubble of trash pops up on his golfing green. He last said the phrase in 4F13, "My Sister, My Sitter."

The band at the town meeting (possibly The Larry Davis Experience) plays the theme to "Sanford and Son" after reinstated Sanitation Commissioner Ray Patterson is introduced.

This episode was dedicated to the memory of Linda McCartney. She taught Lisa about living a meat-free lifestyle in 3F03, "Lisa the Vegetarian."

Marge: *How could you spend 4.6 million dollars in a month?*
Homer: *They let me sign checks with a stamp, Marge. A stamp!*

Marge: *Good God, Homer. You're turning our wonderful little town into America's trashhole!*
Homer: *Marge, ix-nay on the asshole-tray.*

Homer: *Okay, before I show ya, who wants to guess how I got the money?*
Bart: *Dealing drugs?*
Lisa: *Drugs?*
Marge: *I'd have to say drugs, too.*
Homer: *Close, but you're way off.*

RAY PATTERSON

Position:
Former sanitation commissioner.

Election record:
Sixteen wins, one loss.

Personality traits:
Solid work ethic, droll attitude, unabashed use of five-dollar words, willingness to carry a grudge, love of parrots.

Endorsed by:
Bono.

Believes Homer is:
A fatheaded, loudmouth malcontent (among other things).

ALL RIGHT, FINE. IF YOU WANT AN EXPERIENCED PUBLIC SERVANT, VOTE FOR ME. BUT IF YOU WANT TO BELIEVE A BUNCH OF CRAZY PROMISES ABOUT GARBAGEMEN CLEANING YOUR GUTTERS AND WAXING YOUR CAR, THEN BY ALL MEANS, VOTE FOR THIS SLEAZY LUNATIC.

Guest Voice:
Steve Martin as Ray Patterson

BRAD AND NEIL

Roles in life:
Powersauce hucksters supreme.

Neil's most annoying habit:
Using the word "Powersauce" as a verb.

Brad's most annoying habit:
A tie between catching people's attention by shouting, "Yo, yo!" and offering people free samples after telling them that a relative has died.

Co-hosts on:
The Powersauce Newsbreak.

What they believe in:
Sending a man to risk death in the hopes of promoting their product.

THIS JUST IN--POWERSAUCE IS AMAZING!

Guest Voices:
Brendan Fraser as Brad
Steven Weber as Neil

SHOW HIGHLIGHTS

Commie-nazis: McBain's latest foes.

"It appears I will have to find a new Fortress of Solitude." The Comic Book Guy, shortly after Homer knocks away the walls and ceiling of the portable toilet he's using.

"What will it be, Mr. Simpson? Your usual bucket of ice cream covered with miniature pies?"

"A bushel of apples packed in each bar, plus a secret ingredient that unleashes the awesome power of apples!" The wrapper copy for Powersauce bars.

(At the dinner table, Homer eats Powersauce bars as the rest of the family eats plates of gray stuff.)
Homer: How can you put that filth into your bodies?
Marge: My casserole is not filth. (to kids) Eat it!
Homer: Look at you people! Bart's a tub, Lisa's as weak as a little girl, and Maggie doesn't seem to be growing at all!
Marge: Now that's just not—
Homer: You too, Marge. If you toned up a little, you'd probably get a lot more action.

"Sorry, I only eat food in bar form. When you concentrate food, you unleash its awesome power, I'm told. That's why I'm compressing five pounds of spaghetti into one handy mouth-sized bar!"

The Murderhorn: The highest mountain in Springfield.

"Son, don't go up that mountain—you'll die up there, just like I did!"

Sherpa #1: I foresaw your death last night.
Sherpa #2: Stop saying that.

"Aw, good-bye, everyone. Don't touch my stuff." Homer's parting words to his family.

Homer: (into radio) Homer Simpson here. I've sent the Sherpas home, and I'm heading for the top—solo!
Brad: (radioing back) Are you crazy? You'll never make it!
Homer: (into radio) The hell I won't! You're forgetting I've got my Powersauce bars!
Neil: (radioing back) Wake up, Homer! Those bars are just junk! They're made of apple cores and Chinese newspapers.
(Homer looks at the bar he's eating.)
Homer: (into radio) Hey, Deng Xiaoping died.

Lisa: (into radio) Family to Dad, family to Dad, come in, Dad.
Brad: Uh, I'm pretty sure he's dead, little girl. Here, have a Powersauce bar. It's on the house.

Bart and Rod Choose Their Teams:
Rod: I pick my dad! Do you wanna play 'Capture the Flag,' Daddy?
Flanders: Sports on a Sunday. Hmmm. I better check with Reverend—
Reverend Lovejoy: (off camera) Oh, just play the damn game, Ned!

Homer: Oh, Marge! How could you let me let myself go like this?
Marge: Me? I'm not the one who puts butter in your coffee!

(About to go jogging, Homer stands with Santa's Little Helper.)
Homer: Okay, boy, I want you to keep this exercise thing under your hat. That way, I won't be embarrassed if I fail.
(Santa's Little Helper barks. Snowball II meows, springs from the bushes, and races inside.)
Homer: Oh, great, now the cat knows!

Homer Meets McBain:
Homer: Rainier Wolfcastle! Oh, I love your movies and your Powersauce bars and your taut, rippling—
Wolfcastle: Hey, hey, hey, that's enough.

Neil: New angle: Joe Schlub eats Powersauce bar—becomes world's mightiest man.
Brad: It's believable; that's what I like about it.

The Press Conference
Brad: ...and when he reaches the top, Mr. Simpson here will plant this Powersauce flag as an eternal symbol of man's contempt for nature. (aside, to Neil) Wait, is contempt the word I want here? (Neil nods.)
Brad: Homer, you're the world's greatest hero. Do you owe it all to Powersauce?
Homer: That's right, Brad and Neil. I only eat Powersauce: the bar with applesauce-icity.

Bart: Dad, wait. You're not risking your life just to impress me, are you?
Homer: Well, yeah.
Bart: Oh, cool! Now get going, chop, chop!

THE STUFF YOU MAY HAVE MISSED

The Comic Book Guy reads a "Zebra Girl" comic book.

At dinner, Maggie has knocked over her casserole bowl.

The Butterbaby Flapjack can reads, "Flapjacks in Oil."

A t a church picnic, Bart and the other kids play "Capture the Flag" together. When Rod Flanders picks Ned to be on his team, Bart picks Homer to be on his. In a mad dash to bring the flag back to their side, Homer collapses, too out of shape to run a short distance. Bart feels humiliated.

Homer starts an exercise regimen at night, keeping his efforts secret from the family. He starts eating Powersauce sports bars and joins a gym. There, he runs into Rainier Wolfcastle, who starts training him. After two months of working out, Homer is thinner and stronger. At the gym, two Powersauce execs try to draft Wolfcastle into climbing the tallest mountain in Springfield, the Murderhorn, as a Powersauce publicity stunt. Wolfcastle refuses. Bart, overhearing the conversation, has them approach Homer. Homer accepts, not wanting to disappoint Bart. Grampa tries to warn him off the expedition, recounting his own adventure on the Murderhorn and the betrayal of his climbing partner, McAllister.

The execs partner him with two Sherpas to make sure that Homer gets to the top. By day, Homer makes little progress up the mountain, but when Homer wakes up at night and discovers the Sherpas dragging him up the mountain, he fires them and goes for the top, solo. After a long climb, he reaches a plateau, thinking he has reached the peak, only to discover he still has a long climb ahead. Homer crawls into a cave for shelter and discovers the frozen body of C.W. McAllister along with evidence that it was Grampa who betrayed him. Giving up, Homer nails a flag on the ledge. The flagpole creates a crack that topples the rest of the mountain, making where Homer stands the top of the mountain. When Homer gets down, using the frozen body as a makeshift sled, Bart tells him that he's the coolest dad ever.

LOST OUR LISA

Episode 5F17 Original Airdate: 5/10/98 Writer: Brian Scully Director: Pete Michels
Executive Producer: Mike Scully

When Bart arrives home with comedy props glued to his face, Marge panics. To bring Bart to the emergency room, she has to back out of a promise to take Lisa to the Springsonian Museum to attend the last day of the "Treasures of Isis" exhibit. Lisa asks Marge if she can take the bus, and as she leaves with Bart, Marge tells Lisa no. Lisa decides to ask Homer and quickly manipulates him into saying yes. She takes the wrong bus and winds up in the middle of nowhere.

When Lenny and Carl discover that Homer let Lisa take a bus downtown, they're horrified. Realizing his mistake, Homer goes after Lisa. From the outskirts of town through Springfield's Russian district, Lisa finally makes it to the museum, just as Homer arrives. In order to spot Lisa easier, Homer commandeers an extended cherry picker. Just as Homer spots her, the cherry picker goes out of control, rolls off a pier, and floats quickly downstream toward a drawbridge. Thinking quickly, Lisa tells the bridge operator to lower the bridge, catching Homer by the head and saving him. By this time, the exhibit has closed for good.

On the ride home, Lisa tells Homer that she's never going to take a stupid risk like riding the bus alone again. Homer tells Lisa that taking stupid risks is what life's all about. To prove it to her, he breaks into the museum with her to see the "Secrets of Isis" exhibit. Looking at the mysterious Orb of Isis, Homer accidentally knocks it over, hitting a secret button that reveals it to be a music box. Lisa is amazed and decides that stupid risks can lead to wonderful discoveries.

SHOW HIGHLIGHTS

Etern-A-Bond: The adhesive Bart uses to glue stuff to his face. It bears a skull and crossbones with the blurb, "Now with Death Grip." It also bears the advisory, "Warning: In case of accidental ingestion consult a mortician."

"In a few years, when you're old enough to drive, then you can take a bus." Marge, telling Lisa she's too young to use public transportation alone.

"Why, if I had seventy-five dollars for every novelty I've removed... Oh, by the way, I'll need a check for seventy-five dollars." Dr. Hibbert, telling Marge he can help Bart.

Homer Simpson, Concerned Parent:
(Lisa calls Homer at the power plant.)
Lisa: *Dad?*
Homer: *Who is this?*
Lisa: *It's Lisa. I just called to tell you how much I love you, and can I take the bus to the museum?*
Homer: *Museum? Mmm, I don't like the sound of that. What'd your mother say?*
Lisa: *Um, I wasn't a hundred percent clear on that. She said something, but she was kind of in a rush to get Bart to the emergency room.*
Homer: *Hmm...So you wanna take the bus, huh?*

"I'm not normally a praying man, but if you're up there, please save me, Superman!"

(Lisa approaches Cletus, standing outside his pickup.)
Lisa: *Um, listen, I'm kind of lost. Do you think you could give me a lift downtown?*
(Brandine sticks her head out of the pickup.)
Brandine: *Cletus, what are you beating your gums about?*
Cletus: *Never you mind, Brandine; you just go back to birthin' that baby.*

"Stupid risks are what make life worth living. Now your mother, she's the steady type and that's fine in small doses, but me, I'm a risk-taker. That's why I have so many adventures!"

"What do you say, honey? Feelin' stupid? I know I am!" Homer, talking Lisa into breaking into the museum to see the Isis exhibit.

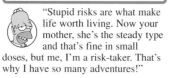
I AM NOT THE NEW
DALAI LAMA
I AM NOT THE NEW
DALAI LAMA
I AM NOT THE NEW
DALAI LAMA
I AM NOT THE NEW
DALAI LAMA

THE STUFF YOU MAY HAVE MISSED

The "ol' joke shop" is named Yuk-ingham Palace.

When Milhouse rings the doorbell at Yuk-ingham Palace, he's sprayed in the face by water. A doorbell/water-squirter was last featured in 1F05, "Bart's Inner Child."

Various gag powders available for purchase at Yuk-ingham Palace include: itching (featuring a picture of a man scratching all over); heart attack (featuring a man clutching his chest); and impotence (featuring a man clutching his groin area, turned away, ashamed). Other items for sale include: a Krusty mask (in which most of his face is flesh-colored); an alien mask, gag spiders; a giant eight ball; chattering teeth; gag anvils; seltzer bottles; lava lamps; and Groucho glasses.

Bart's gag toucan beak bears a striking resemblance to Froot Loop mascot Toucan Sam's.

Items in Homer's drawer: a gun, a bag of peanuts, a bag of Chippos, a half-eaten sandwich, a plutonium rod, a pencil, a playing card, a stick of gum, a wrapper for a peanut butter cup, a comb, a lotto ticket, a jar of nuts, various wrapped candies, and glue.

The Khlav Kalash salesman, last seen in 4F22, "The People of New York vs. Homer Simpson," appears in the Russian marketplace.

Communicates with passengers:
Usually by pointing to a "Do Not Talk to Driver" sign and tapping it.

His route:
The 22 on Mondays, Wednesdays, and Fridays; the 22A, Tuesdays and Thursdays.

Stops at:
Sycamore Avenue, Little Newark, Crackton, Industrial Access Road, Airport Refueling Way, Rural Route 9, Army Proving Ground, and the End of the Line.

His personal touches:
Occasionally saying the name of a stop twice; frowning and smiling menacingly while saying "End of the Line."

FARMER

Demeanor:
Grizzled, yet cosmopolitan.

Weapon of choice:
Shotgun with pitchfork tied to it.

Examples of sophistication:
Names his pigs Teresa and Steve; has a media room.

> IF SOMEBODY'S IN HERE, YOU'RE IN FOR SOME SERIOUS ASS-FORKIN'!

Homer and Marge are forced to take the kids along on their anniversary dinner. The dinner turns out to be completely unromantic. At the end of the night, the two are disinterested in "getting intimate." Later, when they go off to purchase a new refrigerator motor, their car gets stuck in the mud during a rainstorm, and they race into a barn for shelter. After the owner of the farm nearly discovers them, the two find themselves excited and amorous.

While they're away, Grampa gives Lisa and Bart his old metal detector, and they go in search of hidden treasure. Homer and Marge decide to spend a weekend at a bed and breakfast. Once there, they find themselves again romantically uninspired. When a

SHOW HIGHLIGHTS

"Okay, folks, this is your pilot speaking. If you'll look to the left side of the aircraft, you'll see Homer and Marge Sampson, who are celebrating with us today their eleventh 'air-niversary.' So hang on while we dip our wings to this happy couple." The pilot of Up, Up, and Buffet!, making an announcement just before the entire airplane-themed restaurant begins to shake.

(Marge opens the freezer and sees a piece of wedding cake with a plastic bride and groom on it.)
Marge: *Oh, look, Homie. Our wedding cake.*
Homer: *You mean there's been cake in our freezer for eleven years? Why was I not informed?*
Marge: *Look at this little plastic couple. Oh, so full of hopes, potential, dreams for the future...*
Homer: *Hey, Marge, wouldn't it be weird if they had little parties at night? Wee little parties?*

Marge: *When we got married, is this how you thought we'd be spending our Saturdays? Driving out to the boondocks to trade in a refrigerator motor?*
Homer: *Eh, I never thought I'd live this long.*

"When you think about it, mud is nothin' but wet dirt."

Homer Turns Down a Trip to Moe's:
Homer: *Sorry, guys. Marge and I are spending the weekend at a bed and breakfast.*
Carl: *Oh, tryin' to jumpstart the ol' marriage, huh?*
Lenny: *Can I come?*
Homer: *Now, it'd just be awkward. What with the sex and all.*

Marge: *You don't think there's anything wrong with what we're doing, do you?*
Homer: *I don't think anything I've ever done is wrong.*

Bart and Lisa, Treasure-Finders:
(Using the metal detector, Bart and Lisa dig up a chest containing a reel of film labeled, "Casablanca Alternate Ending.")
Lisa: *An alternate ending to Casablanca! Bart, this could be priceless!*
Bart: *Priceless like a mother's love, or the good kind of priceless?*

"It hasn't changed since that magical evening when I knocked you up." Homer, referring to his and Marge's old "love nest," the inside of the windmill on the Sir Putt's A Lot Merrie Olde Fun Centre miniature golf course.

Some of the Alternate Ending to Casablanca:
(As Ilsa's plane takes off and disappears into the fog, Rick and Louis walk off together.)
Rick: *Louis, I think this could be the start of a beautiful friendship.*
(Louis pulls a gun on Rick. Sam, who had been sitting at his piano on the tarmac, notices.)
Sam: *Look out, Rick! He's packing heat!*
(Sam shoves his piano at Louis, knocking him unconscious.)
Rick: *Good work, Sam. C'mon, I'll buy you a falafel.*
(Hitler pops out from inside the piano.)
Hitler: *Not so fast, schmartenheimer!*
(Hitler pulls out a grenade, but before he can throw it, Ilsa, in a parachute, lands on top of him, shutting him inside the piano. The grenade explodes inside.)
Ilsa: *Hope you don't mind my dropping in.*

***It's A Wonderful Life* (Killing Spree Ending):** The label on another reel given to Bart and Lisa by a former studio exec living at the Springfield Retirement Castle.

"Why are people always trying to kill me?" Homer, hiding in the mini-golf windmill with Marge, after Moe sticks a hose inside to fill it with carbon monoxide.

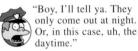

"Boy, I'll tell ya. They only come out at night. Or, in this case, uh, the daytime."

"Now listen very carefully. I want you to pull on the thing that's near the other thing." Homer, hanging off the hot air balloon, instructing Marge on how to operate it.

"Dear lord! Look at that blimp! He's hanging from a balloon!" Sideshow Mel, spotting Homer.

THE STUFF YOU MAY HAVE MISSED

Homer finds a program from Frank "Grimey" Grimes's funeral in his sports jacket. Grimes was introduced (and died in) 4F19, "Homer's Enemy."

The plane restaurant the Simpsons eat at is called Up, Up, and Buffet!

The restaurant Homer and Marge wanted to eat at, The Gilded Truffle, was first seen in 9F12, "Lisa the Greek."

The leftovers from Up, Up, and Buffet! are labeled, "Arf Bag."

Homer's car still features a Trackstar 8 Track stereo.

During the radio commercial for "The Divorce Specialists," the song "Spanish Flea" can be heard. Homer sung a version of the song in 8F21, "The Otto Show."

KISSERS

Episode 5F18
Original Airdate: 5/17/98
Writer: Matt Selman
Director: Klay Hall
Executive Producer: Mike Scully

maid discovers them lying on the bed, they realize that the fear of getting caught makes them frisky.

Using the metal detector near the Aztec Theater, Bart and Lisa find an old film can containing an alternate ending to *Casablanca*. They watch it with Grampa at the Retirement Castle. A resident who was one of the studio executives who ordered the ending gives Bart and Lisa twenty dollars to bury it again.

While Homer and Marge are getting intimate in the windmill at the local mini-golf course, the golfers start to realize that something is inside. A completely naked Homer and Marge narrowly escape a gathering crowd and make their way into town, looking for clothes. They steal a hot air balloon from a used car lot and wind up landing on a football field, only to be ogled by a stadium full of people.

THE STUFF YOU MAY HAVE MISSED

The miniature golf course in 7F08, "Dead Putting Society" was called "Sir-Putt-A-Lot's Merrie Olde Fun Centre"; in this episode, its sign reads, "Sir Putt's A Lot Merrie Olde Fun Centre." The sign also lists "Ye Go Karts," "Her Majesty's Batting Cage," "Merlin's Video Dungeon," and "Skee Ball."

Homer and Marge sneak into the windmill at the miniature golf course to "snuggle." Calling it "their old love nest," they imply that the windmill was the place in which they conceived Bart. Yet, in 8F10, "I Married Marge," Bart's conception occurred in the course's castle.

Moe's lament, "Won't somebody please think of the children?", was originally said by Helen Lovejoy in both 7F09, "Itchy & Scratchy & Marge," and 4F15, "Homer vs. the Eighteenth Amendment."

The balloon at the used car lot has a sign that reads, "Our Prices Are Sky High!"

Gil, now employed at the used car lot, was last seen working in a shoe store in 5F10, "The Last Temptation of Krust."

On the copy of the *Springfield Shopper* with the "Local Couple Bares All!" headline, another headline reads, "Police Dog Clings to Life." The dog had been seen earlier in the episode, running away and whimpering after sniffing Homer's underwear.

The Clash's "Rock the Casbah" is played over the end credits.

Writers: Matt Groening and D.J. Jazzy Jeff
Director: Greg Vanzo

Deep, Deep Trouble

Original Airdate: 3/7/91

> A music video in which Bart tells a tale of woe, recounting how exactly he wound up sent to his room.

(The silhouette of an open door is seen, and Bart's shadow flies through it. Strangely, the trademark spikes atop his head are gone. When the door shuts, it casts a shadow of prison bars across Bart's face. He looks at us, the top of his head obscured in shadow.)

Bart: *Let me start at the start. Let's move right along. You can all sing along at the sound of the gong.*
(We cut to Itchy slamming Scratchy with a mallet. The sound of a gong is heard.)
Once upon a time about a week ago, All of the sudden, trouble started to grow...
(The shadow of Homer is cast across Bart's face. The scene cuts to black. The face of a clock is seen.)
Alarm was buzzin', I was snoozin'...
(The room lights up, revealing the face of the clock is Bart's Krusty Alarm Clock. Bart rolls over in bed and pulls the covers over his head. Santa's Little Helper appears when Bart pulls his blankets.)

Supposed to get up now, But I was refusing. To let reality become an intrusion. 'Cause in dreamy-dreamland I was cruisin'...
(We see Bart's dream. A Homer-looking King Kong stands atop a building as Bart flies a biplane. Bart shoots Homer Kong off the building.)
But the buzz kept buzzin'. My head kept fuzzin'. Gave the radio a throw and heard an explosion...
(Bart, still in bed, tosses his Krusty Clock away. It connects with something offscreen.)

Homer: *D'oh!*

Bart: *I opened up my eyes to my surprise, There stood Homer and his temperature rised.*
(Homer stands with his hair mussed, holding his head. He begins to look angry, and his skin turns red. Bart sits on his bed, clutching Santa's Little Helper, smiling weakly, covered in Homer's shadow.)
I was chillin', he was yellin', Face all distorted, 'Cause he was propellin'...
(Homer leans into Bart, frowning and gritting his teeth.)
I said I'm real sorry...
(Cut back to Bart in the shadows of his room.)
That didn't cut it. I started to protest, but Dad said...
(We cut back to Bart and Homer.

Homer stands above him, pointing outside.)

Homer: *Shut it! Get up, mow the lawn! Move it on the double! 'Cause if you don't, you're in deep, deep, trouble!*
(Homer points and then makes a fist at Bart. Bart falls out of bed. Bart rolls down a long flight of stairs, landing in a courtroom, presided over by a Homer-looking Judge, a Homer-Lawyer, a Homer-Bailiff, and a jury of Homers.)

Back-up Singers: *Trouble!*
(The Homer-Judge, Homer-Lawyer, and Homer-Jury all point at Bart.)

Back-up Singers: *Deep, deep trouble!*
(Chief Wiggum appears on the witness stand, holding a skateboard labeled "A." Principal Skinner follows him, holding a spraypaint can labeled "B." The headless Jebediah Springfield statue follows Skinner, holding its own head, labeled "C.")

Back-up Singers: *One! Two! Trouble!*

Bart: *Where's your sense of humor, man?*
(Bart looks to his side and sees a statue of Marge as Lady Justice. Her scales tip to the right.)

Back-up Singers: *Deep, deep trouble!*
(The Homer-Jury huddle up and each turns around with his thumb down. The shadow of an ax falls on Bart, and we cut to the front yard of the Simpson home, where he mows the lawn with a push mower.)

Bart: *So I'm in the front yard Mowing like crazy,*
(Todd Flanders rolls by on a sit-down mower.
Sweating like a pig and the sun is blazy.
(Homer tries to pull the door open, hitting himself with it.)
Homer's in the driveway, gettin' in the car With Mom and Lis, I hope they're going real fa...
(The next exchange is cut between Bart in the shadows of his room, and Homer in the front yard.)

Bart: *Then Dad yells—*

THE STUFF YOU MAY HAVE MISSED

The episode in which Bart cuts off the statue of Jebediah Springfield's head is 7G07, "The Telltale Head."

Bart drinks a "Space Mutants" squishee.

Martin and Nelson play *Super Slugfest*, from 7G06 "Moaning Lisa."

Moe can be seen cleaning a glass full of beer.

Among the people laughing at Bart at the end of the song are Kearney, Dolph, Otto, and Krusty.

Homer: *Bart!*

Bart: *And I go, "Yo!" He goes—*

Homer: *You done yet?*

Bart: *And I go, "No." So he goes—*

Homer: *Oh, you're too slow!*

Homer hits his head on the horn. Bart leans on the mower, sending it forward. He falls down.)

Bart: *So I step on the gas, speed up the mow. Didn't see that sprinkler underneath that tree—*

(The mower connects with a sprinkler head.) *Wham!*

(Water shoots out the broken sprinkler head and soaks Bart.)

Rainin' on me! I go, "Whoa!" Homer goes—

Homer: *D'oh! Now you can't go, to the boat show!*

(Homer pulls the car away as Bart sinks in the mud.)

Bart: *Soaked to the bone, standin' in a puddle...*

(We cut back to Bart in the shadows as water rises from below screen.)

No one needs to tell me I'm in deep, deep trouble...

Back-up Singers: *Trouble!*

(Chains appear on Bart's wrists and he's yanked offscreen. He appears in a prison, with two Homer-Guards pulling him along. Prisoners point at Bart from inside their cells.)

Back-up Singers: *Deep, deep trouble!*

(Bart is brought to the electric chair, where Reverend Lovejoy stands with a bible. Bart pulls his chains together, causing the Homer-Guards to collide and the chains to pop off.)

Homer-Guards: *D'oh!*

Back-up Singers: *You're in trouble!*

(He runs off down the hall, into a room, slamming the door behind him. He dives into another room and another and another, slamming the doors behind him as well.)

Back-up Singers: *Deep, deep trouble!*

(Bart is in complete darkness when the lights are suddenly turned on. He faces Moe, Principal Skinner, Homer, Mrs. Krabappel, Chief Wiggum, and Sideshow Bob. They all pull a switch labeled "Extreme High Voltage." Bart, in the electric chair, gets violently shocked. We cut to Bart on the front lawn, drinking a squishee, wearing sunglasses, and listening to a personal stereo.)

Bart: *As soon as they're gone, I'm stretched on a lawn.*

(It's revealed that Bart is lying naked on the lawn, with his stereo acting as an impromptu fig leaf.)

Looking at the sky with my sunshades on. Now I never ever claimed that I was a smarty...

(Bart shakes his squishee cup to get the last bit, and the ice and syrup fall all over his face. He springs up.)

But inspiration hits me: "Let's have a party!"

(We wide out to see Flanders, an old couple, Martin, Sherri and Terri, and Reverend Lovejoy are standing in front of the Simpson lawn, gaping at the naked Bart. His personal stereo drops and he's completely naked. We cut to Bart at the telephone, making a call.)

I called up my posse. They were here in a flash...

(Bart opens his front door. Martin, Milhouse, and Richard stand at the front step.)

They brought all their pals...

(We wide out to reveal that a giant crowd of kids stands behind them. Bart closes the door and puts his back to it, but it's knocked down in a stampede of kids.)

We started to thrash!

(We see a shot of the house at night, each of the lit windows has silhouettes of dancing kids in it.)

There was rompin', and stompin', An occasional crash. A fist fight or two, and Nintendo for cash.

(A video game boxer smashes the other in the face. We wide out and see that Martin is playing Nelson in Nintendo. Martin holds out his hand, gesturing to be paid. Nelson smashes him in the face.)

We raided the fridge. Dogs raided the trash.

(The wiped-out refrigerator closes, revealing Wendell standing by Santa's Little Helper, eating out of the trashcan. Wendell throws up in the can. We cut to Bart in the shadows of his room.)

I got a little worried when the windows got smashed.

(Homer's car pulls up in front of the house.)

The next thing you know Mom and Dad are home. The kids disappear, and I'm all alone.

(Bart lies in front of the door as the house is in ruins.)

Everything is silent except for my moan And the low bluesy tone of a saxophone.

(The door opens. Homer, Marge, and Maggie stand in the doorway as Lisa plays her sax. Lisa, Homer, and Marge turn from Bart to talk to each other.)

They look at me, then they go into a huddle, Get the sinking sensation I'm in deep, deep trouble.

Back-up Singers: *Trouble!*

(The family's silhouettes close in on Bart. We cut to Bart crashing through the top of a vast red cavern with fire shooting out from underneath. He's in hell.)

Back-up Singers: *Deep, deep trouble!*

(He screams and then his shirt catches on a peg that's part of a Wheel of Misfortune. The Devil stands below. Each peg is labeled "Eternal Damnation.")

Back-up Singers: *You're in trouble!*

(Bart falls off the wheel, causing it to slowly spin. Both the Devil and Bart watch it spin.)

Back-up Singers: *Deep, deep trouble!*

(It lands on "Re-Incarnation.")

Bart: *Reincarnation?*

Devil: *D'oh!*

(Bart smiles and is beamed away. He reappears as a snail. We then cut back to Bart in the shadows of his room.)

Bart: *There's a little epilogue to my tale of sadness. I was dragged down the street by His Royal Dadness.*

(Homer drags Bart down a Springfield street, past Moe's, where Moe, Barney, Larry, and Sam wave to him.)

We rounded the corner and came to a stop. Threw me inside Jake's barber shop.

(The barber smiles, holding his scissors.)

I said, please sir just a little off the top...

(The barber starts on Bart's hair with clippers, as locks fall down. Bart screams.)

Dude shaved me bare, gave me a lollipop...

(We cut back to Bart in the shadows of his room.)

So on my head there's nothing but stubble...

(Bart leans his head down, revealing he's bald.)

Man, I hate bein' in deep, deep trouble!

Back-up Singers: *Trouble! Deep, deep trouble!*

(We pull out, revealing a crowd of people in the darkness, laughing and pointing at Bart.)

Bart: *Oh, come on, man.*

ALEX WHITNEY

Scent of choice:
Calvin Klein's Pretension.

Dislikes:
Dolls, the game of jacks, poor hygiene.

Likes:
Cellular phones, credit cards, dances.

How she pierces ears:
With thumbtacks and a "whole lot of paper towels."

> OH YEAH, LIKE I'D BE SEEN WITH A DISCOVER CARD.

Guest Voice:
Lisa Kudrow as Alex Whitney

When Homer learns that kitchen grease waste can be sold to rendering plants, he becomes obsessed with the idea and decides to make a grease fortune. At school, Lisa is asked to show a new student named Alex Whitney around. While Lisa is interested in dolls and jacks, Alex is like a mini-adult, wearing perfume and going on shopping excursions. Soon, Alex has become a hit with Lisa's friends, and Lisa feels left out.

Alex convinces Principal Skinner to change the school's annual "Apple Pick" to a dance. Lisa learns that everyone is bringing a date. Feeling as if she has to be like Alex, Lisa becomes desperate to get a boy to go with her. While bullying Milhouse into dropping his date and taking her instead, Lisa realizes she's becoming someone she doesn't want to be. She sadly decides to go without a date.

At the dance, all of the boys stay separate from the girls, and nobody has the nerve to ask anyone to dance. Alex doesn't understand, but Lisa explains that they're all acting like kids because they are still kids. Meanwhile, Homer and Bart sneak into the school to get the kitchen stove's grease. With a hose sucking the grease out of the stove, they're caught by Willie, who attacks Homer in order to protect his retirement grease. While pummeling Homer, Willie causes a massive grease explosion. Grease rains down upon the dance via the air ducts and the kids start to play with it like snow. Alex is initially disgusted, but soon she can't help but start playing in the grease like the rest of the kids.

SHOW HIGHLIGHTS

"Stay cool, Milly." Milhouse's advice to himself upon seeing Lisa.

"Without the grease, all you can taste is the hog anus." Homer, complaining that Apu cleaned the hot-dog machine.

"This is where all the hard work, sacrifice, and painful scaldings pay off."

"Ooh, twins! Which one is the evil one?" Alex, meeting Sherri and Terri.

Homer: *Lisa, I can't imagine anyone being more likable than you. But apparently, this new girl is. So my advice would be to start copying her in every way.*
Lisa: *But Dad—*
Homer: *Uh-uh! Think, "Is that what Alex would say?"*

"Am I the only one who just wants to play hopscotch and bake cookies and watch 'The McLaughlin Group?'"

"I've been muscled out of everything I've ever done, including my muscle-for-hire business."

Homer: *All right, son, we're about to embark on our most difficult mission. Let's bow our heads in prayer.* (Bart and Homer close their eyes, bow their heads, and clasp their hands.)
Homer: *Dear Lord, I know you're busy, seeing as how you can watch women changing clothes and all that, but if you help us steal this grease tonight, I promise we'll donate half the profits to charity.*
(Bart looks at Homer.)
Bart: *Dad, he's not stupid.*
Homer: *All right, screw it! Let's roll!*

"Lisa, I made you some homemade Pepsi for the dance; it's a little thick, but the price is right."

"My retirement grease! No!!!" Willie, catching Homer and Bart siphoning off the grease under the Springfield Elementary cafeteria stove.

(Willie grabs Homer, crawling in the air ducts.)
Willie: *Not so fast, boyo. Well, if it was up to me, I'd let you go...*
(Willie looks at his fists.)
Willie: *But the lads have a temper, and they've been drinking all day!*
(Willie starts to beat Homer.)
Homer: *Stop pummeling me! It's really painful!*

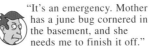

"It's an emergency. Mother has a june bug cornered in the basement, and she needs me to finish it off."

"We've only got nine, maybe ten years tops, when we can giggle in church and, and chew with our mouths open and go days without bathing. We'll never have that freedom again."

THE STUFF YOU MAY HAVE MISSED

At the Try-N-Save, a sign reads, "Catch Back-to-Schooliosis!"

A tanker at the grease-recycling plant reads, "Acne Grease Co."

Inside Lisa's locker are stickers of rainbows, a Happy Little Elf, a sailboat, a flower, and a dolphin.

Homer names his new grease enterprise the "Simpson & Son Grease Co." In 2F07, "Grampa vs. Sexual Inadequacy," he sold a homemade medicine with Grampa called, "Simpson & Son's Patented Revitalizing Tonic."

Lisa visits the Donner's Party Supplies in the mall. A sign in their window reads, "Winter Madness Sale." Dingo Junction is across the way from the party supply store.

Willie crawls though the air ducts of the school in this episode; the last time he did so was in 1F18, "Sweet Seymour Skinner's Baadasssss Song."

At the end of the episode, Milhouse is lying on the gym floor, making a grease angel.

THE DANCE

Episode 5F20
Original Airdate: 8/23/98
Writer: Jane O'Brien
Director: Dominic Polcino
Executive Producer: Mike Scully

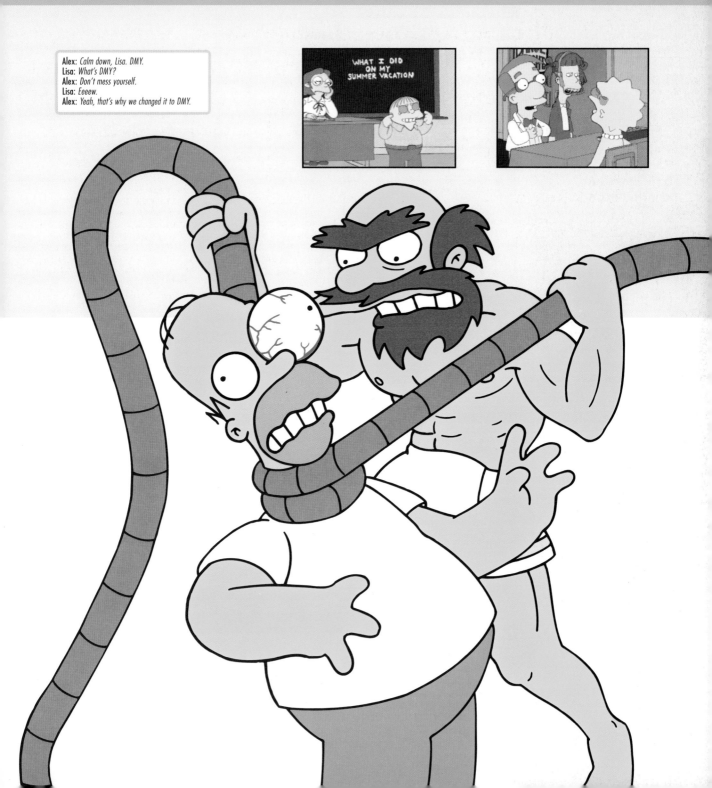

Alex: *Calm down, Lisa. DMY.*
Lisa: *What's DMY?*
Alex: *Don't mess yourself.*
Lisa: *Eeeew.*
Alex: *Yeah, that's why we changed it to DMY.*

Episode 5F21 Original Airdate: 9/20/98 Writer: John Swartzwelder Director: Mark Kirkland Executive Producer: Mike Scully
Guest Voice: William Daniels as K.I.T.T., the "Knight Rider" car

BILL & MARTY

Their station:
KBBL 102.5

The people who laugh hardest at their jokes:
Homer and themselves.

The linchpin of their comedy:
The "boing" sound effect.

Their possible replacement:
The DJ 3000.

Their boldest proposal:
In an effort to curry Bart's favor, they once offered to surgically turn Principal Skinner into some kind of lobsterlike creature.

HOT DOG! WE HAVE A WIENER!

SHOW HIGHLIGHTS

"Oh, honey. Don't eat that— wouldn't you rather have your sugar bag?" Marge, upon catching Homer sadly eating flour.

"They won't let me in the big people library downtown. There was some... unpleasantness. I can never go back."

"I brought you a tuna sandwich. They say it's brain food. I guess because there's so much dolphin in it, and you know how smart they are."

"Homer, you've got it set on 'whore.'" Marge, after being shot in the face with splattering eyeshadow, rouge, and lipstick by Homer's makeup gun.

"Hey Dad, heard you swearin'. Mind if I join in? Crap, boobs, crap." Bart, visiting Homer in the basement.

"Authorities say the phony pope can be recognized by his high-top sneakers and incredibly foul mouth." Kent Brockman, delivering his nightly broadcast.

Film Flub:
Homer: Stupid movie! Who invented these dumb things anyway? Was it you, Bart?
Lisa: It was Thomas Edison, Dad.
Bart: I thought he invented the lightbulb.
Lisa: That, too. He also invented the phonograph, the microphone, and the electric car.
Homer: One man can't do all that. You're a liar, honey, a dirty rotten liar.
Grampa: Finish her! Finish her!
Lisa: It's true. I read it on a place mat at a restaurant.
Homer: Really? A restaurant? Well, now I don't know what to think.

Homer's Edison Epiphany:
Homer: Marge, that's it! That's why I haven't done anything with my life! I need to be more like Thomas Edison!
Marge: Whatever.
Homer: And I'm starting right now! No more damn pajamas!
(Homer gets out of bed, takes off his pajamas, and throws them out the window. Homer stands naked, calling out.)
Homer: From this day forward, I am an inventor!
(A man walking his dog calls up to Homer.)
Man: Do us a favor. Invent yourself some underpants.

THE STUFF YOU MAY HAVE MISSED

A snippet of Yello's "Oh Yeah" is played under Bill and Marty's "Newsflush." It was last used in 4F22, "The People of New York vs. Homer Simpson."

The digital sign on the gate outside Homer's possible cemetery reads, "The Graveyard of the Future." One of the graves there has the name "Tamzarian" on it. Tamzarian is Principal Skinner's real last name, as discovered in 4F23, 'The Principal and the Pauper."

At Homer's funeral, Barney holds four Oscars. He revealed his filmmaking ability in 2F31, "A Star Is Burns."

Also at Homer's funeral are Robot from "Lost in Space," Heckle and Jeckle, Lenny (wearing a presidential sash), and Ned Flanders, who is dressed like a cardinal.

A banner at Homer's surprise party reads, "World's Greatest Accomplisher."

In the footage of Homer in outer space, he eats Beer Paste.

Among the books Homer reads at the library is *A Child's Garden of Edison.*

Leaking barrels of radioactive waste can be seen in the Simpsons' basement.

The Edison Museum sign also reads, "No Gang Colors."

Items in the Edison Museum gift shop include a clock shaped like a lightbulb and a lightbulb snow globe. T-shirts for sale each have pictures of a lightbulb on them and read, "Screw This," "AC DC," and "Don't Mess with Texas." The filament in the lightbulb in the latter shirt is shaped like the Lone Star State.

(Homer sits at a card table in the basement, smoking a cigar, trying to think of inventions.)
Lisa: You started smoking, Dad?
Homer: Yes, Thomas Edison smoked several cigars a day.
(Bart holds up Homer's empty notepad.)
Bart: Yeah, he invented stuff, too.
Homer: Shut up.

I WILL NOT FILE FRIVOLOUS LAWSUITS
I WILL NOT FILE FRIVOLOUS LAWSUITS
I WILL NOT FILE FRIVOLOUS LAWSUITS

After Homer realizes he has lived exactly half the average life expectancy, he falls into a deep depression. The family tries to cheer him up by showing him home movies of his varied accomplishments. When the film breaks, Homer wants to find out who's to blame for inventing movies. Lisa explains that Thomas Edison invented movies, along with lightbulbs and a host of other important products. Homer does a little research, and soon, all he can talk about is Thomas Edison.

He quits his job and starts an inventing career. His first attempts at creating new products fail miserably, and his depression returns. At the dinner table, while leaning back in his chair, Homer nearly falls over backwards. At the last moment, he's caught by the extra legs he hinged onto the back of his chair during his inventing spree. His family tells him that he's finally come up with a great idea.

Telling his inspirational poster of Edison about his successful invention, Homer discovers from the picture that Edison himself is sitting in a six-legged chair. Homer realizes that Edison may not have told anyone about the chair, and he and Bart travel to the Edison Museum to destroy the evidence so he can take the credit. About to smash the chair with one of his failed inventions, an automatic hammer, Homer sees a chart Edison made comparing his achievements to da Vinci's. It's strikingly similar to a chart Homer has in which he compares himself to Edison. Homer realizes that he and Edison are kindred spirits and decides he can't destroy the chair. Later, the automatic hammer Homer left behind and the six-legged chair are discovered in the museum, Edison gets credit for the ideas, and his heirs stand to make a fortune.

BART THE MOTHER

Episode 5F22 Original Airdate: 9/27/98 Writer: David S. Cohen Director: Steven Dean Moore
Executive Producer: Mike Scully Guest Voice: Phil Hartman as Troy McClure (Final Appearance)

The Simpsons take a trip to the Family Fun Center. On the go-kart track, Marge sees Nelson run Milhouse off the road. Later, in the arcade, Bart sees Nelson cash in his prize tickets for a BB gun. He asks Nelson if he can come over and try it out sometime. Marge overhears this and, having witnessed Nelson's earlier behavior, forbids him to do so.

Nevertheless, Bart goes to Nelson's. When he tries out the gun, he accidentally kills a robin. Marge finds out, and instead of handing down a punishment, she simply tells Bart that she is giving up on him. Bart discovers that the robin had eggs in her nest and decides that he can't let them die, too.

When Marge finds out that Bart is trying to save the robin's eggs, she forgives him. When they hatch, the family discovers that the nest actually contained lizard eggs. Marge, Bart, and Lisa take the lizards to the Springfield Birdwatching Society to find an explanation. There, Seymour Skinner informs them that what they have are Bolivian tree lizards, a deadly species that consumes bird eggs without the mother's knowledge and lays their own in the nest. He informs Marge and Bart that the lizards have to be killed. Marge helps Bart escape with the lizards, but the birdwatchers catch up with him. After a struggle, the lizards are accidentally set free. They go on to decimate the town's pigeon population, to the delight of the townspeople.

SHOW HIGHLIGHTS

"Cram it, ma'am." Nelson, to Marge, after Marge chides him for ramming Milhouse into the wall of the go-kart track.

> (Bart cashes in his tickets at the arcade prize counter.)
> **Bart:** Okay, what can I get for twelve, count 'em, twelve prize tickets?
> **Attendant:** Two thumbtacks and a mustache comb or five rubber bands and an ice cube.
> (Nelson walks over and puts down a roll of tickets on the counter.)
> **Nelson:** What can I get for eight thousand tickets?
> **Attendant:** A BB gun or an Easy-Bake Oven.
> **Nelson:** Hmm...hot food is tempting, but I just can't say "no" to a weapon.
> (The attendant hands over the BB gun. Bart gasps in awe.)
> **Bart:** Whoo! Can I try that sometime?
> **Nelson:** Yeah, sure. It never hurts to have a second set of prints on a gun.

"You're an octo-wussy! Oh, look at me, I'm Bart Simpson! I'm scared to use a gun! I want to marry Milhouse! I walk around like this: La, la, la, la, la." Nelson, taunting Bart for not wanting to shoot a bird.

> **Homer:** Oh, I hate folding sheets!
> **Marge:** That's your underwear.
> **Homer:** Well, whatever it is, it's a two-man job. Where's Bart?

"Should we bury it or chuck it into a car full of girls?" Nelson, considering what to do with the bird Bart killed.

"Hi, little eggs. I'm not sure how to tell you this, but, your—your mom was involved in an incident. Mistakes were made." Bart, apologizing to the eggs for killing their mother.

> "Hi, I'm Troy McClure. You may remember me from such nature films as *Earwigs—Eeeew!* and *Man vs. Nature: The Road to Victory.*"

> "This is the most exciting thing I've seen since Halley's Comet collided with the moon."

> (Marge sees Bart up in the treehouse.)
> **Marge:** What do you think he's doing up there?
> **Homer:** I don't know. Drug lab?
> **Marge:** Drug lab?
> **Homer:** Or reading comic books. What am I, Kreskin?

"It's already wiped out the dodo, the cuckoo, and the nene. And it has nasty plans for the booby, the titmouse, the woodcock, and the titpecker." Principal Skinner, on the Bolivian tree lizard.

> **Skinner:** Well, I was wrong. The lizards are a godsend!
> **Lisa:** But isn't that a bit shortsighted? What happens when we're overrun by lizards?
> **Skinner:** No problem. We simply unleash wave after wave of Chinese needle snakes. They'll wipe out the lizards.
> **Lisa:** But aren't the snakes even worse?
> **Skinner:** Yes, but we're prepared for that: We've lined up a fabulous type of gorilla that thrives on snake meat.
> **Lisa:** But then we're stuck with gorillas!
> **Skinner:** No, that's the beautiful part. When wintertime rolls around the gorillas simply freeze to death.

THE STUFF YOU MAY HAVE MISSED

The text under the sign at the Family Fun Center reads, "As seen on *When Disaster Strikes 4*."

Games in the "Family Fun Center" arcade include "Pack Rat Returns" and "Shark Bait." Prizes at their prize counter include: a Happy Little Elf, a football, a camera, a Krusty alarm clock, a beatbox, a banjo, an X-Wing fighter, a Def Leppard mirror, and a framed *Kroon along With Krusty* album. The Elf, the camera, and the Def Leppard mirror were all prizes at the carnival in 5F08, "Bart Carny." *Kroon along With Krusty* was last seen in episode 2F12, "Homie the Clown."

Bart watches the Regional Geographic film, *Birds: Our Fine Feathered Colleagues.* It features Troy McClure and Billy, who was last seen in 4F24, "Lisa the Simpson."

Caring for the eggs, Bart reads *Working Mother.* Its cover features a picture of a female fireman with a baby carrier on her back.

The door to the Springfield Birdwatching Society in the Springfield Municipal Building reads, "Pecking Order Strictly Enforced."

The "Oven-Fresh Donuts—Producto de Bolivia" crate has a picture of a chef feeding donuts to a llama on it.

CHIRPY BOY AND BART JR.

What they aren't:
Robins.

What they are:
Bolivian tree lizards.

Favorite foods:
Birds with humorous sounding names that are currently extinct.

What they'll settle for:
Pigeons.

Special abilities:
Gliding and giving doe-eyed, innocent looks.

Wanted by:
The U.S. Wildlife Department.

HIIISSSS

Opening Sequence:

The words "The Simpsons" float in a dark, stormy sky. We cut to Bart, standing at the blackboard, dipping a paintbrush into a blood-filled jack-o'-lantern. He paints "The Simpsons Halloween Special IX" on the board. The bell rings, and he runs out. As Homer pulls into the driveway, Bart skateboards in from offscreen, bouncing off the roof of the car and heading directly toward the garage. He hits his head on the top of the garage door, collapsing to the ground. Lisa, riding into the driveway on her bike, hits Bart; the impact catapults Lisa from the bike and embeds her into the wall above the garage door. Marge pulls her car into the driveway, and, as usual, Homer tries to outrun her. This time, he fails and is crushed against the back wall of the garage.

Hell Toupee

Snake is caught smoking in the Kwik-E-Mart by the Springfield police, and, due to Springfield's three-strikes law, he is executed. Before the execution, he swears revenge on Apu, Moe, and Bart—the people who witnessed his crime. Shortly after he dies, Snake's body is sent to the hospital where his organs are distributed to worthy donors. Snake's hair is tranplanted onto Homer's head. In the middle of the night, Homer wakes up and kills Apu, his body under the influence of Snake's hair. Homer goes onto kill Moe as well. Finally, when he tries to kill Bart, Homer regains control of himself and rips off Snake's hair. Just as the hair starts attacking Bart, the police bust in and kill the evil coif.

SHOW HIGHLIGHTS

 "Oh god, you smokers disgust me. Hey 'Pu, you got a breakfast cereal for people with syphilis?"

"Tonight on Fox: From the producers of 'When Skirts Fall Off' and 'Secrets of National Security Revealed,' it's 'World's Deadliest Executions!'" Ed McMahon, acting as the announcer of Snake's televised electrocution.

"Homer Simpson, you're under arrest for the murders of Moe Szyslak and Apu Nahasa...pasa...Aw, just Moe. Just Moe."

(Wiggum, sucking on a squishee, is interviewed at the Kwik-E-Mart regarding Apu's murder.)
Wiggum: *I'm afraid we have no leads, but I can safely say, Apu did not suffer.*
(The camera pans to Eddie and Lou snacking by the squishee machine. Apu's legs stick out of the top.)
Lou: *Looks to me like he suffered a lot, Chief.*
Wiggum: *Aw geez, Lou. How long were you gonna let me keep drinking this thing?*
(Wiggum takes another sip of the squishee.)

THE STUFF YOU MAY HAVE MISSED

Among the cigarettes advertised on the wall of the Kwik-E-Mart are Laramie Slims and Laramie Ultra-Tar Kings.

Moe eats Penicill-O's. The box features a doctor holding out a bowl of cereal, with the blurb, "Extra Strength."

The file photo of Moe used on the news features him walking out of an outhouse.

Maggie wears white pajamas in this episode.

Homer's Hair Transplant:
Homer: *This is legal, right?*
Dr. Riviera: *Yeah, sure, whatever.*

HORROR IX

Episode AABF01
Original Airdate: 10/25/98
Writers: Donick Cary, Larry Doyle, David S. Cohen
Director: Steven Dean Moore
Executive Producer: Mike Scully

GUEST VOICES: Ed McMahon, Regis Philbin, Kathie Lee Gifford, and Jerry Springer as Themselves, and Robert Englund as Freddy Krueger

The Terror of Tiny Toon

Marge forbids Bart and Lisa to watch the Itchy & Scratchy Halloween special, taking the batteries out of the remote so that they can't watch. Looking for batteries, Bart finds a piece of plutonium in Homer's toolbox and crams it into the remote control. When he and Lisa use the remote, it beams them into the Itchy & Scratchy cartoon. When they laugh at Itchy & Scratchy's antics, the cat and mouse duo get angry and attack them. Homer sits down to watch TV and immediately gets bored with Itchy & Scratchy trying to kill Bart and Lisa. He changes the channel and the chase continues into the *Regis and Kathie Lee* show. Finally, Bart and Lisa get Homer's attention and get him to push the exit button. Itchy and Scratchy follow them out. Homer puts Itchy in a hamster cage, and Scratchy immediately falls in love with Snowball II. Then Marge decides to have Scratchy neutered.

SHOW HIGHLIGHTS

"Get ready for the violentest, disembowelingest, vomit-inducingest Itchy & Scratchy Halloween special ever!"

"To protect and sever." The Itchy & Scratchy police motto.

"Ooh! How are Bart and Lisa gonna get out of this one?" Homer, watching Bart and Lisa get attacked by Itchy & Scratchy on TV.

"That's it! I'm going home! Dom DeLuise can interview himself!" Kathie Lee Gifford, after having Bart, Lisa, Itchy, and Scratchy drop into the soup she's cooking on-air with Regis.

"Ooh, that is gonna hurt tomorrow." Bart, looking at his skeleton after his body is eaten by piranhas.

"Candle in the Wound":
Scratchy, dressed as a skeleton and carrying a candy bag, rings Itchy's doorbell, saying, "Trick or treat!" Itchy dumps a plate of candy into Scratchy's bag and then uses the plate to decapitate him. Scratchy's bloody head lands on the plate and Itchy cuts off the top of his skull, pulling out his brains. Itchy replaces it with a candle, creating an impromptu jack-o'-lantern.

(Bart and Lisa get beamed into the Itchy & Scratchy short.)
Bart: Hey, Lis! We're characters in a cartoon!
Lisa: How humiliating.

THE STUFF YOU MAY HAVE MISSED

Maggie, dressed as a pirate, uses the parrot on her shoulder as a pacifier.

Bart's egging eggs are labeled, "Lisa, Skinner, Flanders, Dad, Dad, and Dad."

Homer's toolbox is labeled, "Homer's Tulebox."

Itchy has a framed picture of cheese in his house.

A small piece of Scratchy's brain extinguishes the candle in his mouth when he reattaches his head to his body.

Poochie, once again voiced by Homer, makes a brief cameo during this short. He was last seen in 4F12, "The Itchy & Scratchy & Poochie Show."

Starship Poopers

Maggie undergoes a strange transformation: Her first baby tooth is a long white fang and her legs drop off, replaced by green tentacles. Soon, the alien known as Kang shows up at the Simpson house with his sister Kodos, claiming to be Maggie's father. Marge admits that about two years before, she was abducted by Kang and Kodos; there, Kang shot her with an insemination ray. Nine months later, Maggie was born. Kang now wants his daughter to return with him to his homeworld. The Simpsons refuse. To settle the argument, they go on "The Jerry Springer Show." Their appearance on the program doesn't resolve the problem. Kang and Kodos threaten to kill all the politicians in Washington if the Simpsons don't hand over Maggie. Marge challenges them to do so in order to get them to leave.

Kang: *Congratulations! You have been selected for our cross breeding program.*
Kodos: *To put you at ease, we have re-created the most common spawning locations of your species. You may choose either the backseat of a Camaro, an airplane bathroom, a friend's wedding, or the alley behind a porno theater.*
Marge: *I absolutely refuse to go along with this. But since I have no choice... I'll take the alley.*

SHOW HIGHLIGHTS

Kodos: *Commander Kang, receiving transmission from infant pod thirteen.*
Kang: *Holy flurking schnit! What's the message?*
Kodos: *Larval stage completed, standing by for orders, experiencing terrible rash, over.*
Kang: *Ensign Kodos, set coordinates for the obscure T-shirt-producing planet known as Earth! It's time I paid a visit to...my daughter!*

Marge: *I can't believe it. Jerry Springer didn't solve our conflict.*
Lisa: *And now he's dead.*

How Dracula Got His Groove Back:
The film the Simpsons are watching when they are visited by Kang and Kodos.

(Kang and Marge sit on a couch together in the aliens' spaceship.)
Kang: *Oh, you look lovely this evening. Have you decreased in mass?*
Marge: (voice over) *I tried to resist, but they applied powerful mind-confusion techniques.*
Kang: *Look behind you!*
(Marge turns. Kang takes out a device and quickly shoots Marge with a beam of blue light.)
Kang: *Insemination complete!*
Marge: *Really? That seemed awfully quick.*
Kang: *What are you implying?*

THE STUFF YOU MAY HAVE MISSED

When Maggie's baby tooth is shown, she's slobbering like Kang and Kodos.

In the scene after the visit with Dr. Hibbert, Maggie no longer has arms. They can be seen lying in the crib among her toys.

The communication device in Kang and Kodos's ship is shaped like a pacifier. Maggie's pacifier is a communications device as well.

Stitches can be seen in Maggie's altered pajamas.

While on "The Jerry Springer Show", the text under Homer reads, "Wife knocked boots with Space Stud!"

(Dr. Hibbert leaps back and gasps after Maggie chews apart his tongue depressor.)
Homer: *Is there anything you can prescribe, Doctor?*
Hibbert: *Fire, and lots of it!*
Marge: *Oh, that's your cure for everything.*

JUDGE SNYDER

Demeanor:
Stern, no-nonsense.

Known for:
His loud gavel-smacking.

One reason why he hates Lionel Hutz:
Hutz repeatedly ran over the judge's son.

Unexpected behavior:
Occasionally legally transferring the identity of one Springfielder to another; participating in "The Simpson Family Smile-Time Variety Hour."

> I MOVE THAT THE LAST SKETCH BE STRICKEN FROM THE RECORD.

WHEN YOU DISH UPON A STAR

Episode 5F19   Original Airdate: 11/8/99   Writer: Richard Appel   Director: Pete Michels   Executive Producer: Mike Scully
Guest Voices: Alec Baldwin, Kim Basinger, Ron Howard, and Brian Grazer as Themselves

Parasailing with his family, Homer accidentally breaks free from their boat, and floats away. After his parachute is torn by a branch, Homer crashes through the skylight of a fancy, secluded house. Homer is amazed to discover the home is the weekend getaway of Alec Baldwin and Kim Basinger. They tell Homer they stay in Springfield to escape from their celebrity and ask him to keep their presence in town a secret. Homer offers them his services as an assistant, and they accept.

Ron Howard stops by, asking to stay with Baldwin and Basinger while he looks for a home in Springfield. Soon, Homer has earned the trust of the stars. But at Moe's, Homer can't resist an opportunity to brag about his new Hollywood friends. By the next morning, all of Springfield knows about their new celebrity neighbors.

Alec and Kim fire Homer, and in revenge, he opens a mobile Museum of Hollywood Jerks in a Winnebago. It features Alec's and Kim's personal items that he had been keeping in his trunk. When Alec and Kim decide to give Homer another chance, they discover him showing off their underwear. They go after Homer in their Humvee. During the chase, Ron Howard winds up being tossed onto the street. Homer gives up, and after a brief trial, he is forbidden from being within 500 miles of any celebrity, living or dead.

SHOW HIGHLIGHTS

Homer's Dream:
(A Homer-ized Yogi Bear and a Bart-like Boo Boo steal a picnic basket together.)
Homie: I'll handle Ranger Ned. After all, I'm smarter than the a-ver-age bear.
(Ned Flanders, dressed as a ranger, walks out from behind a tree to tap Homie on the back.)
Ranger Ned: Well, hello there, Ho-diddly-omie! Well, I'm afraid I'm going to have to ask you to hand over that pi—
(A suddenly savage Homie Bear leaps over a hedge and starts to growl and viciously claw at a screaming Ranger Ned.)
Bart-Bart: Gee, Homie, it's not very nice to maul Ranger Ned.
(Homie holds up a claw.)
Homie: You want some of this?

(On his off-road detour from the traffic to the lake, the Simpsons pass a huge, fancy, gated-off house.)
Marge: This is such a secluded area. I wonder who lives in that house.
Homer: Well, way out in the sticks like this, it could only be hillbillies.
Bart: (pointing something out) So I suppose that's a hillbilly Jacuzzi?
Homer: Yep. That's where they cook up their vittles.

"That sounds like a wager to me!" Homer, after being told that he can't operate a boat under the influence of alcohol.

Alec Baldwin: Are you sure you don't want to go to the hospital, Mr. Simpson? You had an awful lot of glass in you.
Homer: Oh, I don't want to be a bother.

Kim Basinger: Wow, you got everything, Homer! Even the Oscar polish!
(Kim opens up the polish and starts shining her Oscar. Alec walks over.)
Alec: Honey, why don't you give that thing a rest. You're taking the finish off.
Kim: When you win one, you can take care of it however you want.

"It's the only town in America that'll let me fish with dynamite." Ron Howard, on why he wants to move to Springfield.

(Ron sniffs Homer's breath.)
Ron: Do I smell vodka...and wheatgrass?
Homer: It's called a Lawnmower. I invented it, you want one?
Ron: Yeah, okay.
Kim: And I'll take a rum and zinc.
Ron: Ooh, I'll have one of those, too.

"It's about a killer robot driving instructor who travels back in time for some reason." Homer, describing his movie script, *The Terminizer*—an erotic thriller.

"Alec, Alec, regarding that so-called 'silent propulsion system' in *The Hunt for Red October*: I printed out a list of technical errors which I think you'd enjoy discussing." The Comic Book Guy, with the celebrity-hungry mob outside the Baldwin/Basinger compound.

"Step right up and see the world's greatest mobile collection of Alec-and-Ron-and-Kimorabilia!" Homer, describing his new Museum of Hollywood Jerks.

Barney: We love celebrities!
Homer: Oh yeah? What have they ever done for you? When was the last time Barbra Streisand cleaned out your garage? And when it's time to do the dishes, where's Ray Bolger? I'll tell ya: Ray Bolger is lookin' out for Ray Bolger!

"If celebrities didn't want people pawing through their garbage and saying they're gay, they shouldn't have tried to express themselves creatively."

THE STUFF YOU MAY HAVE MISSED

The "Welcome to Lake Springfield" sign also reads, "Formerly Cess Hole 17A."

People hanging out at Lake Springfield include: Lewis, Apu, Ralph, Rod, Todd, and Ned Flanders, Principal Skinner, Mrs. Krabappel, Cletus, and Wendell.

Homer rents his boat from U-Trawl Boat Rentals.

Marge discovers a copy of *Springfield Variety* in the back pocket of Homer's pants.

The Olmec Indian head, first seen in 7F22, "Blood Feud," can be seen in the background of the basement while Marge does laundry.

As he nears the Baldwin/Basinger compound with the celebrity-hungry mob, Sideshow Mel holds up a sign that says, "You Complete Us."

Posters for *9 1/2 Weeks* and *L.A. Confidential* are seen in the background inside Homer's Museum of Hollywood Jerks.

During Homer's speech in the courtroom, a strange-looking man between Lisa and Dr. Nick Riviera seems to transform into a smiling Bart. (Actually the man is behind a headless Bart, and suddenly Bart's smiling head appears.)

Charlie, last seen being dragged away by the FBI in 5F14, "The Trouble With Trillions," sits in the gallery during Homer's trial.

The producer to whom Ron Howard is pitching ideas at the end of the story is Brian Grazer, his partner in their production company, Imagine Films.

> BUTT.BUTT IS NOT MY E-MAIL ADDRESS
> BUTT.BUTT IS NOT MY E-MAIL ADDRESS
> BUTT.BUTT IS NOT MY E-MAIL ADDRESS

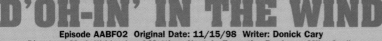

D'OH-IN' IN THE WIND

Episode AABF02   Original Date: 11/15/98   Writer: Donick Cary
Directors: Mark Kirkland and Matthew Nastuk   Executive Producer: Mike Scully

Homer realizes he's never found out what his middle initial "J." stands for. He asks Grampa, who is also stumped. Grampa takes Homer to a farm that used to be a commune where Homer's mother lived. There, Homer finds a mural his mother dedicated to him, with the inscription, "With Love, to My Son Homer Jay Simpson."

Inspired by the mural, Homer decides to become a hippie. He befriends two of his mother's old friends, Seth and Munchie. When he asks them to go on a "freak out" with him, they reveal that they now run a juice business from the farm. Accusing them of selling out, Homer convinces them to go freak out "squares" with him. At the end of the day, they return to the farm, only to discover that Homer's Frisbee has jammed Seth and Munchie's juice machine, destroying their entire shipment of juice.

Trying to make it up to his new friends, Homer sneaks over to the farm at night and makes a whole new batch of juice. When Seth and Munchie wake up in the morning, Homer has already shipped out the new batch. When they ask Homer where he got the extra vegetables, he shows them that he harvested their "private" garden. Soon, all of Springfield is hallucinating from Homer's vegetable juice made from carrots and peyote. The police raid the farm, and Homer tries to share the hippie philosophy of freedom, love, and peace, placing a flower in the barrel of Chief Wiggum's gun. Wiggum shoots Homer, embedding the flower in his forehead.

SHOW HIGHLIGHTS

Fat Guy #3: Bart's suggestion for one of Homer's phony credits on his Screen Actors Guild application.

> **Bart:** Hey, what the heck is your middle name anyway?
> **Homer:** You know, I have no idea. Hey, Dad, what does the "J." stand for?
> **Grampa:** How should I know? It was your mother's job to name ya and love ya and such. I was mainly in it for the spanking.

"Wow, look at this place! There's a pond for skinny dipping, a tire for skinny swinging...I can actually feel the good vibrations." Homer, as he leans his hand into a beehive at the Groovy Grove Natural Farm.

"Boo! Bring on Sha Na Na!" Abe Simpson at Woodstock, during Jimi Hendrix's set.

"Free the Springfield Two, Marge! Free the Springfield Two!" Homer, chanting, after asking Marge to do away with her bra.

> **Seth:** We're just trying to pay the bills, Homer. I mean, we're still hippies at heart.
> **Homer:** Oh yeah? When's the last time you freaked out the establishment? You guys are total sellouts!
> **Munchie:** Wait. Don't you work for a nuclear power plant?
> **Homer:** Look, we can sit here all day and play the blame game, or we can start freaking people out!

> **Homer:** Hi, Marge! We're freaking out squares!
> **Marge:** Oh, lord.
> **Homer:** What's in your brand-new bag, mama?
> **Marge:** Oh, it's that pair of Dockers you wanted. Forty-eight waist with the balloon seat, right?
> (Seth and Munchie laugh.)
> **Homer:** Marge, not in front of the hippies.

TV Moment:
After drinking the bad batch of Garden Blast, Grampa and Jasper sit giggling like Beavis and Butthead.

"The electric yellow has got me by the brain banana!" Lou, feeling the effects of Homer's batch of Garden Blast.

> (Wiggum tastes the tainted Garden Blast.)
> **Wiggum:** My god, it's nothing but carrots and peyote!
> **Eddie:** Damn longhairs never learn, Chief.
> **Wiggum:** It's time for an old-fashioned, hippie ass-whomping!

> **Homer:** We're making a stand! A freaky stand! You can smash this drug barn all you want, but first you'll have to smash our heads open like ripe melons!
> **Munchie:** This man does not represent us.

> **Burns:** Well, let's see what I packed for myself today. One bouillon cube, one Concord grape, one Philly cheesesteak, and a jar of garlic pickles.
> (Mr. Burns laughs, trying to open the jar.)
> **Burns:** No one will want to kiss me after these, eh, Smithers?
> **Smithers:** It's their loss, sir.

> **Homer:** Homer Simpson does not lie twice on the same form. He never has, and he never will:
> **Marge:** You lied dozens of times on our mortgage application.
> **Homer:** Yeah, but they were all part of a single ball of lies.

Movie Poster Moment:
The first shot of Grampa at Woodstock, featuring the couple standing together in the foreground, is a reference to the poster for *Woodstock*.

THE STUFF YOU MAY HAVE MISSED

After Burns's recruitment film ends, the first credit reads, "An Alan Smithee Film." Alan Smithee is a phony name that is often placed on films from which directors have asked to have their names removed.

When Homer becomes a hippie, the two hairs on top of his head curl to reflect his unkempt condition.

Homer watches an old Bob Hope special on video that makes reference to Dean Rusk, the secretary of state for the Kennedy and Johnson administrations. He played a major role in the shaping of the United States's Vietnam policy and was thus reviled by many a hippie.

During their freak out with Homer, Seth and Munchie's car reads, "Hippies on Board." They pass such Springfield stores as Heinrich's Monocle Shop, Yuk-ingham Palace, Neat & Tidy Piano Movers, The Corpulent Cowboy, Painful Memories Party Supply, and Broken Home Chimney Repair.

Ned Flanders's juice-induced hallucinations involve dancing bears and skeletons associated with The Grateful Dead. He also sees walking hammers from Pink Floyd's film *The Wall*, and the lips and tongue "Sticky Fingers" symbol associated with The Rolling Stones.

Songs heard during this episode include, "Incense and Peppermints" by the Strawberry Alarm Clock, "Uptown Girl" by Billy Joel, the theme to the musical *Hair*, the Jimi Hendrix version of "The Star-Spangled Banner," "Time of the Season" by the Zombies, and "White Rabbit" by Jefferson Airplane. The end titles music was performed by Yo La Tengo.

NO ONE CARES WHAT MY DEFINITION OF "IS" IS.
NO ONE CARES WHAT MY DEFINITION OF "IS" IS.
NO ONE CARES WHAT MY DEFINITION OF "IS" IS.

SETH AND MUNCHIE

What they formerly were: Hippies.

What they currently are: Capitalists.

Their place of business: The Groovy Grove Natural Farm.

What they do for fun: Devil sticks, hackey sack, and tending to a garden of illegal plants for personal, private use.

When the sixties died for them: The day they sold their freak bus—December 31, 1969.

Their current vehicle: A Saturn.

How many times Homer hit them with his Frisbee: Twice.

> TIME IS MONEY, MAN.

Guest Voices:
Martin Mull as Seth
George Carlin as Munchie

LISA GETS AN "A"

Episode AABF03 Original Airdate: 11/22/98 Writer: Ian Maxtone-Graham
Director: Bob Anderson Executive Producer: Mike Scully

MR. PINCHY

His favorite foods:
Bacon, eggs, sausage links, and risotto.

What endears him to Homer:
His boylike cowering, his playful water spitting, and how he pinches Marge on the nose.

Demeanor:
Meek.

How Captain McCallister sees him:
Overcoddled.

How Homer ultimately sees him:
Tasty.

SHOW HIGHLIGHTS

Homer: *Cherry Garcia? Honey Bono? Desmond Tutti-Frutti? Lisa, help Daddy find some normal flavors!* (Homer hoists Lisa up to the top shelf of the freezer. She looks at the ice creams.)
Lisa: *Candy Warhol, Xavier Nougat...*
Homer: *Naw, nothin' made of dead guys. What's in the back?* (Homer shoves Lisa farther inside. She starts shivering.)
Homer: *Hurry up! My hands are getting cold!* (Lisa sneezes. Marge rounds the corner, seeing what Homer is doing.)
Marge: *Oh my goodness! Homer, get her out of there!* (Homer pulls Lisa out, and she hands him a pint.)
Homer: *Eh, Sherbet Hoover.*

"Aw, it just turned up in the course of my daily rummaging. By the way, I oiled the hinge on your diary." Marge, telling Lisa how she found her A+++ test.

"Now, now, leave the money out of this. It's not the money's fault you cheated." Skinner, rejecting Lisa's idea to refuse the state grant on the basis that she cheated.

Using the Oscar Mayer Periodic Table:

Krabappel: *Now, who can tell me the atomic weight of Bolognium?*
Martin: *Oooh! Delicious?*
Krabappel: *Correct. I would also accept snacktacular.*

"Hey, you don't have to take that from no punk-ass crab!" Homer, scolding Pinchy for not standing up to a hermit crab.

Lisa: *I know this giant check is very important to everyone here. But what's even more important is the truth.* (The crowd murmurs, Skinner gives Lisa the "cut it out" sign.)
Lisa: *Because after all, education is the search for truth.*
Skinner: *No, no, it isn't! Don't listen to her, she's out of her mind!*

Coming Home from Church:

Bart: *I'm starving! Mom, can we go Catholic, so we can get communion wafers and booze?*
Marge: *No, no one's going Catholic! Three children is enough, thank you.*

Video Game Moment:

Dash Dingo lampoons Sony's popular *Crash Bandicoot* video game series.

Lisa: *Bart, shouldn't you be in class?*
Bart: *I am.* (Bart gestures to a nearby classroom where he apparently sits, reading a book.)
Bart: *It's a little something I whipped up in shop. Mostly latex.*

Nelson: *Lisa, check it out, tomorrow's fraction quiz. I'll give you the numerators free, but the denominators are gonna cost ya.*
Lisa: *I don't want your dirty denominators!*
Nelson: *Well la-dee-da, Lady Cheaterly!*

Lisa: *I cheated! Cheated, cheated, cheated, cheated, cheated!*
Skinner: *Lisa, what are you trying to say?*
Lisa: *I cheated!*
(Skinner gasps.)

THE STUFF YOU MAY HAVE MISSED

The Simpsons brunch at Eatie Gourmet's, a Place for Groceries.

A sign in the Natural Foods section of Eatie Gourmet's reads, "Say It Isn't Soy." Cereals in their cereal section include, Bran Munch, Alfalfa Bits, Raisin Chunks, Wheat Taste, Apple Snacks, Healthly Charms, Nature Rice, Fiber Bites, and Count Caroba. In their ice cream section, Homer looks at Ken & Harry's Milli Vanilla ice cream.

Nelson is Salesman of the Month in his bathroom-office.

In an early scene, Wendell walks through the hall with brown hair.

Gil sells the school a Coleco computer. Coleco was a home video game manufacturer during the early eighties.

Gil last appeared in 5F18, "Natural Born Kissers."

After phony State Comptroller Atkins asks the crowd "Who among you can honestly say you've never cheated—on your wives or your husbands?" Kirk Van Houten is seen glaring at Chase (a.k.a. Pyro) and Luann.

After Homer has Lisa rummage through a gourmet grocery store freezer for ice cream, he purchases a small lobster, intending to fatten it up to eat. When they get home, Lisa has developed a cold. Marge makes her stay home from school and has her play Bart's Dash Dingo video game to pass the time.

When she returns to class, Lisa realizes she forgot to do the reading assignment Ralph brought her, just as Miss Hoover distributes a test. Desperate, Lisa fakes ill again. In the hall, Lisa runs into Bart. When she tells him of her predicament, he brings her to Nelson, who offers to sell her the answer sheet. Lisa is hesitant, but decides to buy it. Armed with the answers, Lisa goes on to score an A+++. Meanwhile, Homer balks at boiling up the lobster. Instead, he names it Mr. Pinchy and adopts it as a pet.

Lisa's test score raises Springfield Elementary's average, qualifying the school for a large state grant. Feeling guilty, Lisa tells Skinner she cheated. He and Superintendent Chalmers ask her to tell no one so that the school will still qualify for the money. Lisa agrees, but at the check presentation, she tells the school the truth. She's praised for her honesty and then she leaves. With Lisa gone, Skinner and Chalmers reveal that the ceremony was a sham and then hold the *real* ceremony in which the state comptroller gives them the money. At home, Homer realizes he has accidentally cooked Pinchy by giving him a hot bath. He sadly eats, and thoroughly enjoys, his late friend.

I WILL NOT SCREAM FOR ICE CREAM
I WILL NOT SCREAM FOR ICE CREAM
I WILL NOT SCREAM FOR ICE CREAM

HOMER SIMPSON IN: "KIDNEY TROUBLE"

Episode AABF04 Original Airdate: 12/6/98 Writer: John Swartzwelder Director: Mike B. Anderson Executive Producer: Mike Scully

On the way home from a family trip to Bloodbath Gulch, Homer refuses to stop the car to let Grampa go to the bathroom. Grampa's kidneys subsequently explode, leaving him in dire need of a transplant. Homer agrees to donate one of his kidneys to Grampa.

At Moe's, Moe, Lenny, and Carl tell Homer that he may not survive the operation. Going home, Homer is left with doubts over the safety of the transplant. Just before the surgery begins, Homer bolts from the operating room. He winds up down at the Springfield docks. There, he decides to get a job on a tramp steamer and leave his past behind.

On the ship, Homer meets up with a group of lost souls who are traveling the seas trying to forget their pasts. When Homer tells them of how he left his father waiting for the transplant, they throw him off the ship. He finally musters the courage to go through with the procedure. But in the operating room, he once again bolts. As he runs from the hospital he's hit by a car that falls off a transport truck. When he wakes up, he discovers that he's broken his arms and legs—and that Dr. Hibbert took one of his kidneys for Grampa when he was unconscious.

THE LOST SOULS:

Who they are:
A contemptible lot of cads, bounders, and tiger stabbers.

Examples of bad behavior:
Robbing banks with hard loaves of bread; betraying the trust of their bosses at the car wash; stealing accordions from blind monkeys.

What they do to pass the time:
Smoke, drink, play cards, and throw people whom they find contemptuous overboard.

> MY STORY OF JILTED LOVE IS LONG AND BITTERSWEET. IF ANYONE HAS TO GO TO THE BATHROOM, GO NOW. I DON'T WANT YOU WALKING AROUND DURING MY STORY.

> MY STORY'S BETTER--IT HAS TIGERS!

SHOW HIGHLIGHTS

At the Animatronic Saloon bar:
Homer: Hey, Robot! Get your fat metal ass down here!
(The bartender walks down to Homer.)
Bartender: First of all, I'm not a robot. And second, I got this metal ass in 'Nam, defending this country for lazy jerks like you.

"What is it with you and robots?"
Marge, to Homer, after he causes some animatronic cowboys to shoot at him.

Grampa: Can't get a good sarsaparilla like this back in Springfield. It angries up the blood.
Bartender: You like it, huh?
Grampa: Up yours!

Grampa: Can I go to the bathroom before we leave?
Homer: But we gotta get home. I don't want to miss "Inside the Actor's Studio." Tonight is F. Murray Abraham.
Grampa: But I really need to—
Homer: (stern) F. Murray Abraham!

Grampa: I don't feel so good. Maybe I oughta eat something.
Dr. Hibbert: Oh, I'm afraid your eating days are over.

Grampa: How long do I have to live, Doc?
Hibbert: (laughs) I'm amazed you're alive now.

Gorilla Squadron, Gorilla Island Six,* and *Apes-A-Poppin': Some of Homer's favorite gorilla movies.

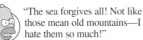
"I'm the luckiest man in the world...now that Lou Gehrig's dead."

Homer: It's not an operation, Moe. The doctor says it's just a procedure.
Moe: No, no, no. Makin' polenta, that's a procedure. You're talking about deadly, life-threatening surgery here.

"Everybody who wants an eyeball or a spine or a vestigial tail will be after you." Lenny, telling Homer about how he'll be on an "Organ Donor Sucker List."

Moe: Listen, I'm just gonna get right to the point here. Can I have your buttocks, I mean, if you die? They look pretty comfortable.
Homer: Yeah, I guess.
Carl: And, uh, are those your original lips?
Homer: Well, actually, I——Hey! Quit harvesting me with your eyes!

"Oh, Homer, that was just a beer can with a whistle glued to it." Marge, on the artificial kidney Homer made.

"Even I wouldn't do that, and I'm America's bad boy!" Bart, commenting on how Homer ran out on the kidney procedure.

Captain McCallister: Welcome aboard the ship of... (dramatic) lost souls!
Homer: The name on the back says Honeybunch.
McCallister: Yar, I've been meaning to paint over that.

Lisa: Dr. Hibbert, I thought you located another kidney for Grampa.
Hibbert: Larry Hagman took it! He's got five of them now. And three hearts. We didn't want to give them to him, but he overpowered us.

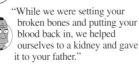
"Try not to move, Dad. You swallowed a lot of motor oil."

"While we were setting your broken bones and putting your blood back in, we helped ourselves to a kidney and gave it to your father."

THE STUFF YOU MAY HAVE MISSED

The brochure for the ghost town features a cactus dressed as a cowboy.

Bloodbath Gulch's slogan reads, "The Friendliest Town in the Old West."

In Bloodbath Gulch, the Simpsons go to Ye Olde Animatronic Saloon. There, an animatronic cowboy chases a showgirl around and around a balcony, much like the pirates chase the women in the Pirates of the Caribbean ride at Disneyland.

In this episode, Grampa says sarsaparilla "angries up the blood." In 4F17, "The Old Man and the Lisa," he says that newspapers "angry up the blood."

The cover of the *TV Guide* features two sumos bumping bellies with the text, "Sumo Babies—200th episode."

"Doc Martens to Podiatry" can be heard over the hospital intercom. Doc Martens are a popular English brand of footwear. Later, another page for "Dr. Bombay" can be heard as well. Dr. Bombay was a character on the sixties TV-sitcom "Bewitched."

The sign on Springfield Hospital reads, "Doctors Carry Less Than $5 Cash."

Down at the docks, Homer passes Barnacle Bill's Anger Management Center and Handsome Pete sitting in front of Davey Jones's Hamper.

The taffy shop at the docks is named Call Me Delish-Mael.

I AM NOT A LICENSED HAIRSTYLIST
I AM NOT A LICENSED HAIRSTYLIST
I AM NOT A LICENSED HAIRSTYLIST

LEAVELLE

Profession:
Professional bodyguard trainer.

Special training aids:
Watermelons, mobile grassy knolls.

Where he yells at his students:
Everywhere, but especially in the "Berating Room."

How he insults his graduates:
He tells them they're not fit to guard a Russian rock band.

How he surprises his graduates:
By singing an impromptu rendition of the theme to *The Bodyguard*.

SHUT YOUR SASS-HOLE, BOY!

Guest Voice:
Mark Hamill as Leavelle

On a trip to Springfield's bimonthly science fiction convention, Homer sees Mayor Quimby and Mark Hamill get surrounded by rioting attendees. Unwilling to stand by and watch them get mobbed, Homer safely escorts them out of the fracas. Mayor Quimby is impressed, and he makes Homer his bodyguard.

Homer begins watching over the mayor. As he accompanies Quimby throughout town, he chooses to look the other way as the mayor receives bribe after bribe. At a meeting in which Quimby grants Fat Tony Springfield Elementary's milk concession, Homer makes a shocking discovery: Fat Tony is supplying the school with rat milk instead of cow milk.

Disgusted, Homer confronts Quimby and accidentally knocks him out the window. Discovering Quimby hanging on the ledge, Homer makes him promise to expose Fat Tony in exchange for pulling him back inside.

Knowing Quimby will be in danger from Fat Tony, Homer vows to protect him. At a production of *Guys and Dolls* starring Mark Hamill, Fat Tony has his henchman, Louie, try to kill the mayor. Louie first gets into a scuffle with Hamill before trying to stab the mayor. Homer grabs Louie just in time, and they fight. With Hamill's help, Homer subdues the gangster. But he soon discovers that while he struggled with Louie, Fat Tony savagely beat Quimby with a baseball bat.

SHOW HIGHLIGHTS

Bi-Mon-Sci-Fi-Con: Springfield's bimonthly science fiction convention.

"This is one small step towards firing your ass!" Neil Armstrong, to his publicist, regarding his lack of popularity at the convention.

Comic Book Guy: *Tell me, how do you feel about forty-five-year-old virgins who still live with their parents?*
Nerdy Young Woman: *Comb the Sweetarts out of your beard, and you're on.*
Comic Book Guy: *Don't try to change me, baby.*

"Welcome futurists, cyberphiles, and the rest of you dateless wonders..." Mayor Quimby's greeting at Bi-Mon-Sci-Fi-Con.

"All right, step away, foolish amateurs, just keep back, keep out of it! The role is mine with the acting and the groupies and the 'Luke, Luke save me' with the light saber and the *Vwhing! Vwhing! Vwhing!*"

"Oh god, can't this town go one day without a riot?"

Quimby: *You call yourselves bodyguards? You're fired!*
Ernie: *Fired, huh? Who else you gonna find to take a bullet for ya?*
Big Tom: *Or have his genitals hooked up to a car battery?*
Quimby: *I'll tell ya who! Him!*
(Quimby points to Homer, standing with his family.)
Homer: *Woo-hoo!*
Marge: *Homer, I don't think you were listening to what he just—*
Homer: *(stern) I said, woo-hoo.*

Leavelle: *As a bodyguard, your only loyalty is to your protectee, not to your family, not to your country, not to Moo-hammed!*
Homer: *Even during Ramadan?*

THE MOB

Episode AABF05
Original Airdate: 12/20/98
Writer: Ron Hauge
Director: Swinton O. Scott III
Executive Producer: Mike Scully

Guest Voices: Mark Hamill as Theater Owner and as Himself, Joe Mantegna as Fat Tony, and Dick Tufeld as Robot from *Lost in Space*

(Leavelle pretends to fire a rifle at a watermelon on a podium. Homer dives in front of the bullet's path.)
Homer: No!
(Homer tumbles to the ground and Leavelle walks over.)
Leavelle: Well, your dive wasn't bad, but I just didn't believe your "Noooo!" You gotta sell it! Remember, your "Nooo!" is what gets you your next job. Now drop and give me twenty.
Homer: NOOOOO!!!
Leavelle: Better.

"THE PRESIDENT DID IT" IS
NOT AN EXCUSE
"THE PRESIDENT DID IT" IS
NOT AN EXCUSE
"THE PRESIDENT DID IT" IS
NOT AN EXCUSE

(Lisa and Bart approach Homer in the kitchen.)
Homer: Hold it, what's your clearance?
Bart: We just want to get a snack.
Homer: Access denied.
Bart: But, Da—
(Homer pinches their shoulders, causing them to pass out.)
Marge: Homer, I don't want you using your new sleeper hold on the children.
Homer: They'll be fine in half an hour.
Marge: That's not the point. And another thing: I asked you to take out the garbage three days ago and you still haven't—
(Homer pinches Marge's shoulder and she passes out. He then looks at his watch.)
Homer: Hmmm. Still half an hour 'til dinner. Oh, well...
(Homer pinches his own shoulder, causing him to fall over and strike his head on the kitchen table.)

"I couldn't be happier with the way that went." Quimby, after asking Homer to honk at a "broad."

"Oh my god, I killed the mayor. All right, stay calm. I'll just use the body to stage an elaborate

farce à la *Weekend at Bernie's...*" Homer, coming up with a plan.

Guys and Dolls: The musical that Homer brings the mayor to, so that he can take his mind off of gangsters.

"Luke be a Jedi tonight! Just be a Jedi tonight! Do it for Yoda while we serve our guests a soda!" Mark Hamill, singing a version of "Luck Be a Lady Tonight."

"I think I saw him in *Rent* or *Stomp* or *Clomp* or some piece of crap." Homer, commenting on Louie's dance solo.

(Homer struggles with Louie, holding a knife. Mark Hamill lies onstage nearby, recovering from a scuffle.)
Mark: Homer, use the for—
Homer: The force?
(Mark points offscreen.)
Mark: The forks! Use the forks!

THE STUFF YOU MAY HAVE MISSED

The Science Fiction Convention sign reads, "Set Phasers on Fun!"

At the convention, Uter wears a "Futurama" shirt. Among the beings signing autographs are Gort, from *The Day the Earth Stood Still*; Doctor Who, from the BBC TV series; and Godzilla.

For Bi-Mon-Sci-Fi-Con, Mrs. Krabappel dresses as Barbarella. Principal Skinner, along with Benjamin, Doug, and Gary from 1F02, "Homer Goes to College," dress as Spock. Other costumes at the con include Chewbacca, Xena, the Terminator, a Borg, the Invisible Man, and Lieutenant Commander Geordi LaForge.

In the background of the convention a booth for *Roswell, Little Green Man* can be seen. *Roswell, Little Green Man* is a comic book published by Matt Groening's *Bongo Comics*.

The Comic Book Guy wears an Alien Biopsy T-shirt featuring an alien head with a Band-Aid on it.

Leavelle's Bodyguard Academy's sign reads, "A Division of Ray-Ban."

The watermelons used to represent protectees are labeled, "Sting," "Madonna," "Al Gore," and "Ann Landers."

The Legitimate Businessman's Social Club was introduced in 8F03, "Bart the Murderer."

The milk cartons at school read "Squeaky Farms Brand Genuine Animal Milk." They features a picture of Fat Tony with a pitchfork.

The maître d' at the dinner theater is patterned after Hal Perry, a regular character actor on "I Love Lucy."

Signs at the Springfield Dinner Theater read, "Mark Hamill IS Nathan Detroit" and "Pepper steak IS the entree."

AMBER AND GINGER

Profession:
Cocktail waitresses at Nero's Palace.

Hobbies:
Smoking, drinking, and marrying drunken customers.

Wear:
A lot of jewelry and even more eye makeup.

Beliefs:
"Letting yourself go" after getting married; getting married with a drink in your hand.

Their new, ill-fated loves:
Ernst and Gunter.

> YOU TWO FELLAS ARE THE NICEST HUSBANDS WE'VE EVER HAD. AND WE'RE NOT GIVING YOU UP WITHOUT A FIGHT.

VIVA NED

After Homer sees Ned Flanders use a senior discount card, he accuses Flanders of being a cheat. Flanders says that he *is* a senior; in fact, he's sixty years old. Flanders says that his ultra-clean living has helped him stay young. But after reflecting on it, Flanders realizes that his clean living has also made him predictable and boring.

He enlists Homer to teach him how to have fun. Homer, in turn, takes Flanders to Las Vegas. There, Homer volunteers for Captain Lance Murdock's attempt to jump over an audience member. Ned is astounded. Homer goes on to teach Flanders how to gamble and even convinces him to drink alcohol.

They wake up the next morning in their trashed hotel suite and discover that during their bender, they both married cocktail waitresses. After trying to find an honorable way to get out of the situation, they both opt to ditch their new wives. The head of security at the casino gets wind of this and does what he can to foil their escape. Homer and Flanders get stopped on their way out of the hotel and are savagely beaten by casino security, Drederick Tatum, the Moody Blues, and Ernst and Gunter. Kicked out of Vegas, Homer and Flanders start their long walk home.

SHOW HIGHLIGHTS

"Gone are such headliners as 'Little Timmy and the Shebangs,' 'The Shebangs,' and 'The New Shebangs, Featuring Big Timmy.'" Kent Brockman, talking about the fall of Mr. Burns's casino.

"Awright young'uns, bath time! Cover up your eyes and drop your britches!" Cletus, about to drive his truck through the car wash with a payload full of his kids.

At the Car Wash Tape Bin:
Marge: *Wow, you can't find this stuff anywhere! Seals and Crofts, Pablo Cruise, Air Supply...Whoa! Loggins and Oates—and it's free.*
Lisa: *I've never heard of these bands, Mom. What kind of music do they play?*
(Bart, looking over a magazine, turns around.)
Bart: *Crap rock?*
Marge: *No...*
Homer: *Wuss rock?*
Marge: *That's it.*

Churchy La Femme: Homer's new nickname for Flanders.

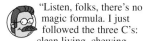

MY MOM IS NOT DATING JERRY SEINFELD
MY MOM IS NOT DATING JERRY SEINFELD
MY MOM IS NOT DATIN JERRY SEINFELD

After Flanders Admits He's Sixty:
Lenny: *What's your secret, Flanders? Goat placenta, monkey sweat?*
Carl: *Some kind of electric hat?*
Moe: *Holy water? It's holy water, right?*
(Moe gets up and splashes holy water in his face.)
Moe: *Ahhhh! It burns!*

"Listen, folks, there's no magic formula. I just followed the three C's: clean living, chewing thoroughly, and a daily dose of vitamin church!"

"You name it, I haven't done it!" Flanders talking about how he resists all the "major urges."

Homer: *Geez, Flanders. You're sixty years old, and you haven't lived a day in your life!*
Carl: *Yeah, even the boy in the bubble had a deck of cards.*

Steady Neddy: Flanders's nickname for himself.

Maude: *Well, you may be a bit cautious, but what's wrong with that? Some people like chunky peanut butter, some like smooth.*
Flanders: *Um-hmm. And some people just steer clear of that whole hornet's nest. I'll stick with just plain white bread, thank you very much. Maybe with a...*
Maude, Todd, and Rod: *Glass of water on the side for dippin'!*

Homer and Ned, on Lance Murdock:
Homer: *He's a daredevil, Ned. He laughs at death.*
Flanders: *When I want to laugh, I'll take Bob Saget, thank you very much.*

Flanders: *You know, this may sound just a teensy bit insane in the ol' membrane, Homer, but I was wondering if you could show me how to have some fun.* (Homer folds his arms and turns to Flanders.)
Homer: *Well, well, well. So flawless Flanders needs help from Stinkypants Simpson.*
Flanders: *Yeah, I—I guess I do.*
Homer: *Welly, welly, welly. Mr. Clean wants to hang with Dirty Dingus McGee.*
Flanders: *How 'bout it Homer? Will you teach me the secret of your intoxicating lust for life?*
Homer: *Wellity, wellity, wellity...*
Flanders: *Stop that! Will you help me or not?*
Homer: *Let's do it.*

"And now, the indestructible Lance Murdock will jump his suicycle over an audience member! And he'll do it while attempting to open a locked safe on his head!" The announcer at Nero's Palace.

The Ring of Fire, the Ring of Ice, the Dog-Doo Stick: Obstacles Murdock gets by to complete his jump.

The Morning After:
Flanders: *(happily excited) I have a pounding headache, my mouth tastes like vomit, and I don't remember a thing!*
Homer: *Welcome to my world.*

"Ned, no! Think of your wives!" Homer, trying to stop Flanders from killing himself over becoming a bigamist.

"Blame me if you must, but don't ever speak ill of the Program! The Program is rock solid! The Program is sound!" Homer, on the Homer Simpson Program.

FLANDERS

Episode AABF06
Original Airdate: 1/10/99
Writer: David M. Stern
Director: Neil Affleck
Executive Producer: Mike Scully

Guest Voices: The Moody Blues
(Graeme Edge, Justin Hayward, John Lodge,
and Ray Thomas) as Themselves

Homer Volunteers for the Stunt:

Homer: *Where do you want me?*
Lance: *On the X!*
(Lance points to a platform in front of his landing ramp. It has a skull and crossbones on it, and it's surrounded with red stains.)
Homer: *You mean the one with the red paint?*
Lance: *Uh, yeah...paint.*

Flanders: *How do you do it, Homer? How do you silence that little voice that says, "Think?"*
Homer: *You mean Lisa?*
Flanders: *Oh no, I mean common sense!*
Homer: *Oh, that. That can be treated with our good friend alcohol. You might want to write that down.*

THE STUFF YOU MAY HAVE MISSED

The Comic Book Guy's bumper stickers read, "The Truth Is in Here," "My Other Car Is a Millennium Falcon," "I Brake for Tribbles," "My Child Is an Honor Student at Starfleet Academy," "Kang Is My Co-Pilot," and "Keep Honking, I'm Charging My Phaser." His license plate is "NCC-1701," the identification number for the *Starship Enterprise.*

When Bart feeds the fire for Homer's chimney barbecue, he's surrounded by such items as a can of paint, a bowling ball, a kite, an umbrella, a stack of papers, a beach ball, a pair of flippers, a can of gas, and a bag of golf clubs.

The surreal duo in the convertible coming back from Vegas look like the illustrations of Hunter S. Thompson and his attorney from *Fear and Loathing in Las Vegas.*

The casinos seen in Las Vegas include Dupes (the marquee reads, "Nudes on Break!"), The Lucky Casino, Nero's Palace, Golddigger's Casino (their marquee reads, "Cirque du Buffet" and "Loosest Craps in Town!"), and "Newark, Newark" (featuring a neon rat on their sign and presenting "Legends of Cleavage" and "Rip Taylor Negron" in the Turnpike Lounge). Other casinos seen are Rivera's (presenting "Okla-Homo!"), the Snowshoe Casino (presenting "Klon-Dykes!" in their Arctic Circle Showroom), the Safari Casino, and Quicksands (their large marquee reads, "The Satin Knights Sing the Moody Blues" with a smaller marquee that reads, "Opening Act: The Moody Blues").

Among the items seen in Homer and Flanders's trashed suite are a keg, a bowling ball, two trophies, an archery target, the Stanley Cup, a barbecue, an oversized cowboy hat bearing the slogan "I ❤ LV", a Rolls Royce—style golf cart, two golf bags, and three watermelons.

The "precious memories" tape reads, "Simpson-Flanders Impulse Wedding."

Among the people at the casino are Gil (last seen in AABF05, "Mayored to the Mob"), Ernst and Gunter (last seen in 5F04, "The Two Mrs. Nahasapeemapetilons"), and Drederick Tatum (4F03, "The Homer They Fall").

"Someone dishonoring their marriage vows? Not in Las Vegas!" Casino Pit Boss, upon seeing Homer and Ned run away from their new wives.

"Las Vegas doesn't care for out-of-towners! Take your money and go someplace else." Casino Pit Boss, to Homer and Flanders.

WILD BARTS CAN'T BE BROKEN

Episode AABF07 Original Airdate: 1/17/99 Writer: Larry Doyle Director: Mark Ervin
Executive Producer: Mike Scully Guest Voice: Cyndi Lauper as Herself

What they are:
Telekinetic, extrasensory, homicidal, proper English school kids.

Their complexion:
Chalky.

Something to keep in mind if confronting them:
Bad things happen after their pupils turn blue.

What they know:
All your secrets.

Pet peeves:
Angry mobs, hypocritical adults.

After the Springfield Isotopes win the league championship, Homer, Barney, Carl, and Lenny go on a bender in which they drunkenly trash Springfield Elementary. The children of Springfield are blamed for the vandalism, and a curfew is put into effect.

When Bart and Lisa see an ad for the film *The Bloodening*, they decide to sneak out with their friends and see it. The film features strange children who read adults' minds, reveal their secrets, and make them hurt one another. When the children of Springfield are busted by Chief Wiggum, they strike upon the idea to reveal the secrets of the adults of Springfield. They broadcast a pirate radio program called "We Know All Your Secrets" and threaten to have a show every night until the curfew is lifted.

The police trace the location of the children's secret broadcasts to their very own billboard. The adults of Springfield face off with the kids of Springfield, each voicing their complaints with one another in a rousing musical number. Soon, the senior citizens of Springfield arrive, breaking up the confrontation. They go on to enact a curfew that keeps everyone under seventy inside after sundown.

SHOW HIGHLIGHTS

"Hurry up and lose so we can get out of here!" Homer, shortly before the first pitch at the Isotopes game.

> *Lisa:* Why do you hate the Isotopes so much, Dad?
> *Homer:* Because I loved them once, and they broke my heart. Let that be a lesson to ya, sweetie. Never love anything.
> *Lisa:* Even you?
> *Homer:* Especially me.

> *Marge:* Like my mother always said, "You've got to stick it out, even if you've picked a loser..."
> (Homer puts his finger in his ear, takes it out, and looks at it.)
> *Homer:* Hmmm...
> *Marge:* "...to the bitter end."

"Yeah, that sniper at the all-star game was a blessing in disguise." Moe, explaining the Isotopes' mid-season comeback.

"There you have it, woo." Kent Brockman, after interviewing "die-hard fan" Homer Simpson.

"Kids! The carnival's in town for one night only! And they've got cotton candy and hats with feathers, and there's no lines because all the stupid kids have curfew, so...Oh right, sorry." Homer, inadvertently taunting Bart and Lisa.

Citizenship, Energy-Shortage Game, Hippo in the House, The Game of Lent: Bart and Lisa's old board games.

"That oughta show little Timmy and Tammy Scumbag who's in charge around here!"

Movie Moment:
The plot of *The Bloodening* loosely resembles the film *Village of the Damned.*

The Perils of Prime Time:
(A young man and a young woman sit on either side of a couch in a coffeehouse.)
Young Man: —robbed me of my manhood!
Young Woman: That's petty theft.
(An unseen audience "wooos." Young Man #2 pops up from sitting on another couch on the other side.)
Young Man #2: Don't go there!
(An unseen audience laughs.)

"And let this be a lesson to you: Kids never learn!" Chief Wiggum, to the Springfield kids he arrested for breaking curfew.

> *Milhouse:* We gotta spread this stuff around! Let's put it on the Internet!
> *Bart:* No—we have to reach people whose opinions actually matter.

"Our Gang" Tribute:
Bart lifts up a plank in a fence and pulls a wagon through. Lisa, Nelson, Martin, and Milhouse follow. Milhouse wears suspenders and sports a cowlick like Alfalfa; a dog with a spot over his eye follows the kids. The scene ends with the familiar music and an iris out as the dog winks at the camera.

> *Homer:* So, Marge, ready for another episode of "Don't Go There"?
> *Marge:* I'm tired of that show. But I've been hearing good things about "Talk to the Hand." Tom Shales says, "the writing snaps, crackles, and pops."
> *Homer:* Okay, whatever takes my mind off my life.

"Brilliant! They transduced amplitude modulation via the concavity of that oversized beverage conveyance. I mean that is some clever voyving."

"Bart, get down here! I'm gonna spank you back to the Stone Age!"

Broadway Moment:
The musical number at the drive-in is a reworking of the song "Kids" from *Bye Bye Birdie.*

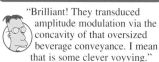

THE STUFF YOU MAY HAVE MISSED

Homer's "Hitler is a jerk!" song is an abbreviated version of a naughty WWII-era playground rhyme.

When Homer drunkenly drives his car through Springfield Elementary, he passes by the trophy case. Inside is a trophy and a ribbon. The empty case had been a source of shame for Principal Skinner and Lisa in 5F20, "Lard of the Dance."

The "Let's All Go to the Lobby" song heard at the Springfield Drive-in was sung by Mr. Burns in 1F16, "Burns Heir."

Luann and Pyro (a.k.a. Chase) can be seen making out at the Springfield Drive-in showing of *The Bloodening.*

When the adults converge on the Springfield kids' pirate radio station, Dr. Hibbert and his wife travel on motorcycles.

Professor Frink's eyes are clearly visible in this episode. Usually they cannot be seen through his thick glasses.

SHERRI DOES NOT "GOT BACK"
SHERRI DOES NOT "GOT BACK"
SHERRI DOES NOT "GOT BACK"
SHERRI DOES NOT "GOT BA
SHERRI DOES NOT "GOT BA
SHERRI DOES NOT "GOT BA

YOU'RE THINKING ABOUT HURTING US.

NOW YOU'RE THINKING, "HOW DID THEY KNOW WHAT I WAS THINKING?"

SUNDAY, CRUDDY SUNDAY

Episode AABF08 Original Airdate: 1/31/99 Writers: Tom Martin, George Meyer, Brian Scully, and Mike Scully
Director: Steven Dean Moore Executive Producer: Mike Scully Guest Voices: Troy Aikman, Rosey Grier, John Madden,
Dan Marino, Rupert Murdoch, Dolly Parton, and Pat Summerall as Themselves

While getting new tires, Homer runs into a former acquaintance, Wally Kogen. Sitting in Moe's together, they see a program on TV about the upcoming Super Bowl. Wally proposes that he and Homer put together a Super Bowl trip. Excited, Homer gathers up a bunch of friends, and they rent a bus to travel to the game.

Meanwhile, Marge and Lisa, looking for something to do, decide to pass the time with "Vincent Price's Egg Magic," one of many craft kits they have received from Patty over the years. Contrary to the packaging, they discover the feet are not included, and Marge calls the company only to get an answering machine message recorded by Vincent Price himself.

At the game, Homer and Wally discover that their tickets are counterfeit. Homer tries to sneak his group into the game, only to get them all thrown into a jail cell in the stadium. Wally sees Dolly Parton walk by the cell, on her way to the half-time show. Having known Dolly for years, Wally has her break them out of the cell. Trying to find some seats, the group stumbles upon a luxury skybox with an elegant buffet. As they gorge themselves on the food, the luxury box's rightful occupant, Rupert Murdoch, arrives. He commands his guards to seize the group.

As they run, they spy an entrance to the field. Determined to catch the end of the game, they go for it. Just as they're about to step onto the field, they're swept back in by the winning team. Homer's group winds up in the team's locker room and celebrates with them. They each receive Super Bowl rings, and Homer takes home the Lombardi trophy.

Sportscasters John Madden and Pat Summerall comment on the plot developments, and then board a bus driven by Vincent Price.

SHOW HIGHLIGHTS

Looking at the Coupon Book:
Marge: *Oooh! Free foot-pain analysis!*
Homer: *Oh, Marge, that's just a trick to get you in there, so they can cure your foot pain!*
Marge: *Oh, I guess.*
(Marge limps away.)

"Me and my Val-U-Qual book are gonna paint the town red—with savings!"

"Wait a minute! These tires won't take a balance!" The Tire Salesman, turning Homer's free wheel balancing into a sale.

"742 Evergreen Terrace, Springfield, oh hi ya, Maude! Come on in!" Marge, greeting Maude Flanders while leaving her address with the manufacturers of "Vincent Price's Egg Magic."

Ticket Taker: *Uhhh, sorry, fellas, but these tickets are counterfeit.*
Wally: *What?*
Homer: *Counterfeit?*
Ticket Taker: *Yeah. See, the hologram's missing, and there's no such team as the Spungos, and finally, these seem to be printed on some sort of cracker.*
(The Ticket Taker takes a bite of the ticket he's holding.)
Homer: *Stop eating our tickets!*

Homer: *Hit the road, Gramps! This is a private skybox!*
Rupert: *I'm Rupert Murdoch, the billionaire tyrant, and this is my skybox.*

"Really? 'Cause I'm a travel agent, and I've heard nothing but bad things." Wally, after one of the winning players says he's going to Disneyland.

Pat Summerall: *Did it strike you as odd that in a Super Bowl show with Dolly Parton we didn't see any football or singing?*
John Madden: *I hadn't thought about it, Pat. But in retrospect, it was kind of a rip-off! What a way to treat the loyal fans who've put up with so much nonsense from this franchise!*

Movie Moment:
Rudy, the short young man who the group doesn't let on the Super Bowl bus, was straight out of the 1993 film, *Rudy.*

I WILL NOT DO THE DIRTY BIRD
I WILL NOT DO THE DIRTY BIRD
I WILL NOT DO THE DIRTY BIRD

Postmaster Bill: *Howdy, partners! Welcome to your post office.*
Bart: *Wow! It's ours?*
(Bart knocks papers off of a shelf and starts writing on the walls.)
Principal Skinner: *Bart!*
Bart: *Be with ya in a minute!*
(Bart keeps writing.)

Wally Kogen: *Hey, you got off easy. I just came in to use the phone, and they got me for the whole Road King package; alignment, shocks, Armor All, stem lube.*
(Homer laughs.)
Homer: *Stem lube! Even I didn't fall for that!*
(concerned) Although winter is coming...

Wally: *I'm sorry, the guys made kind of a mess in your bathroom.*
Bus Driver: *What bathroom?*

Krusty: *You know Dolly Parton?*
Wally: *Yeah, I book a lot of package tours to Dollywood and Euro Dollywood—that's in Alabama.*

The Catholic Church—We've Made a Few...Changes:
A commercial during the Super Bowl that parodies ZZ Top's "Legs" music video.

THE STUFF YOU MAY HAVE MISSED

Ralph's dead-letter selection, the package that makes the drug-sniffing dogs bark, is addressed to "Otto the Bus Driver."

Homer visits "High-Pressure Tire Sales" on his coupon binge.

A plaque featuring a picture of the Tire Salesman holding handfuls of money reads, "Customer Care Specialist."

The group that takes the trip to the Super Bowl includes: the Comic Book Guy, Bumblebee Man, Ned Flanders, Lenny, Carl, Apu, Barney, the Squeaky-Voiced Teen, Reverend Lovejoy, Moe, Krusty, Dr. Nick Riviera, Sideshow Mel, Jasper, Kirk Van Houten, Dr. Hibbert, Captain McCallister, Mr. Burns's lawyer, Charlie, and Chief Wiggum.

The Simpsons have a "Li'l Leonardo" paint-by-numbers set.

At the "Take a Leak with NFL Greats" booth, a kid stands at a urinal beside Jim Plunkett (he was number 16 on the Oakland Raiders) and Ricky Waters (he was number 32 on the San Francisco 49ers).

Wally Kogen's name is strangely similar to that of "The Simpsons" writing team of Wallace Wolodarsky and Jay Kogen.

WALLY KOGEN

His demeanor:
Self-deprecating, yet cheerful.

What he is:
A travel agent who trusts too much.

His travel agency's slogan:
"Now Get Outta Here."

Close personal friend of:
Dolly Parton.

What he calls himself:
A Grade-A sucker.

YOU CAN REALLY GO PLACES IN THE TRAVEL BUSINESS...FEEL FREE TO USE THAT ONE.

Guest Voice:
Fred Willard as Wally Kogen

HOMER SIMPSON, POLICE COP

Rank:
Detective.

Partner:
Lance Kaufman.

Special abilities:
Can turn criminals into explosives; bullet catching; hyper-attractiveness to women.

Financial status:
Millionaire.

Real estate holdings:
A palace in Europe.

Hates:
Crime.

Longevity:
None. He's replaced with a doofus after the first episode.

AND THAT'S THE END OF THAT CHAPTER.

Watching "Police Cops," a mid-season replacement, Homer discovers that its suave lead character bears his name. Homer is thrilled and his friends congratulate him on his newfound celebrity. The next episode of the show portrays Detective Homer Simpson as a fat, bumbling fool, and Homer soon becomes the laughingstock of Springfield.

Homer appeals to the producers of "Police Cops" to change the character back, but they refuse. No longer caring to be the butt of the town's jokes, Homer changes his name to Max Power and adopts a new, impulsive, go-getter attitude. Getting a monogrammed shirt at Costington's, Homer meets Trent Steel, one of Springfield's young

movers and shakers. Impressed with "Max," Trent invites him to a garden party.

At the party, Homer and Marge mingle with the hip, young elite of Springfield. Homer enjoys himself until the entire party travels to a redwood forest in Springfield to protest logging. All of them, including Homer and Marge, chain themselves to trees. When the authorities arrive, Homer gets into a confrontation with the police, and Eddie begins chasing Homer around the tree to which he is chained. The chain cuts through the tree, and its collapse causes a domino effect. Soon, every tree in the forest falls down. Ostracized by Springfield's young elite, "Max Power" changes his name back to Homer Simpson.

THE STUFF YOU MAY HAVE MISSED

The headline on the *Springfield Shopper* reads, "It's War!" Below the headline is a picture of a mushroom cloud.

A banner outside Moe's reads, "TV Sensation Homer Simpson Drinks Here!"

The price tag on Homer's scarf reads, "$."

The Capital City Goofball was last seen in episode 3F18, "22 Short Films About Springfield."

During this episode, Comic Book Guy says, "Worst reading ever." He said a similar phrase, "Worst episode ever," in 4F12, "Itchy & Scratchy & Poochie."

"Police Cops" is produced by "By the Numbers Productions."

When Homer goes to court to change his name, Agnes, Snake, Herman, Otto, and Hans Moleman can be seen sitting in the gallery.

Woody Harrelson is seen at Trent Steel's party dressed in pants made from hemp. He last appeared as his "Cheers" character Woody Boyd in 2F08, "Fear of Flying."

A banner on the side of the bus reads, "We're Pro-Leaf."

Marge wears a special set of pearls to Trent Steel's party.

President Clinton has also appeared in 4F02, "Treehouse of Horror VII," and in AABF08 "Sunday, Cruddy Sunday."

The Larry Davis Experience plays at the garden party.

Both a waiter and a member of the band from the party chain themselves to trees at the protest.

Eddie's bottle of mace reads, "Hippie Strength."

After a falling redwood smashes his cruiser, Wiggum says, "What a tragedy. That car was just two days away from retirement." In 5F18, "Natural Born Kissers," just as one of his police dogs ran off after smelling Homer's underwear, he lamented, "That's a shame. He had one day left 'til retirement."

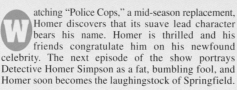

THE MAX

Episode AABF09
Original Airdate: 2/7/99
Writer: John Swartzwelder
Director: Pete Michels
Executive Producer: Mike Scully
Guest Voice: Ed Begley, Jr. as Himself

NO ONE WANTS TO HEAR ABOUT MY SCIATICA
NO ONE WANTS TO HEAR ABOUT MY SCIATICA
NO ONE WANTS TO HE
ABOUT MY SCIATICA

Homer's Mid-season TV Checklist:
(Homer sits in front of the TV with the rest of the family, checking things off on a clipboard.)
Homer: Door?
Marge: Locked.
Homer: Phone?
Lisa: Unplugged.
Homer: Dog, cat?
Bart: Taped and corked.
Homer: Perfect.

SHOW HIGHLIGHTS

"America's Funniest Tornadoes," "Admiral Baby," and "All In the Family 1999": Three of the offerings from Fox's mid-season lineup.

"Look, Marge! I had a scorecard printed up at that all-night scorecard place!" Homer, showing Marge his "Excellent Shows/Very Good Shows" scorecard.

Homer: Networks like animation 'cause they don't have to pay the actors squat!
(Ned pops by the window behind the TV.)
Ned: (in an odd-sounding voice) Plus, they can replace 'em, and no one can tell the diddley-ifference!

"It's hard to believe someone that young could have risen to the rank of admiral." Marge, commenting on "Admiral Baby."

 "Hey, 'Police Cops'! That sounds like a lethal combination!"

":GASP!: He's named like my name!" Homer, upon seeing Homer Simpson on "Police Cops."

"Blood provided by American Red Cross—Give Blood Today!" Message shown at the end of "Police Cops."

Homer: Hey, what's going on? That guy's not Homer Simpson! He's fat and stupid!
Lenny: It looks like they've changed the character into a bumbling sidekick!
Homer: No, no, he can't be! I know, maybe he's just acting stupid to infiltrate a gang of international idiots! Yeah, that's gotta be it!

"The first episode was just a pilot, Dad. Producers fiddle with shows all the time; they change characters, drop others, and push some into the background." Lisa, explaining TV to Homer, as Mr. Largo and the Capital City Goofball walk by outside the window.

"Your character provides the comic relief, like Marlon Brando in *Apocalypse Now*."

Homer Meets with the "Police Cops" producers:
Homer: ...why does the Homer Simpson character have to be so stupid?
Producer #1: Oh, he's not stupid. He's a street-smart fish out of water in a world he never made!

Hercules Rockefeller, Rembrandt Q. Einstein, Handsome B. Wonderful, Max Power: Homer's list of possible new names.

Homer Tells His Family His New Name:
Marge: And what about the tattoo on my you-know-what?
Homer: Oh, honey, they have acids that can burn that off.

 "Nobody snuggles with Max Power. You strap yourself in and feel the G's!"

Trent Steel: So where to eat? You like Thai?
Homer: Thai good, you like shirt?

Marge: Wow, look at this place. The house number is spelled out with letters.
Homer: Get used to it, honey. From now on, we'll be spelling everything with letters.

"I'm talking, of course, about our endangered forests. We have to protect them because trees can't protect themselves. Except, of course, the Mexican fighting trees." Trent Steel, making an appeal to the guests at his garden party.

Chesty LaRue, Busty St. Clair, Hooty McBoob: Homer's list of possible names for Marge.

MANUALA

Hails from:
India.

Marital status:
Married to Apu Nahasapeemapetilon.

Adjectives Apu uses to describe her:
Quick-witted and "smoking."

Her favorite book, movie, and food:
Fried Green Tomatoes.

Dislikes:
Apu's work hours.

Philosophy on pre-arranged marriages:
If they don't work out, you can always get divorced.

Unique ability:
To cook many different dishes using only chickpeas, lentils, and rice.

> YOU ARE TOO KIND, MARGE. I AM SURE YOU HAVE NOTICED THE MANY SMALL IMPERFECTIONS THAT FILL ME WITH SHAME.

Guest Voice:
Jan Hooks as Manjula

Apu gets into trouble with Manjula when she finds out that his eighteen-hour days are not the norm in America, despite his past assertions to the contrary. To show how much he loves her, Apu decides to give Manjula a romantic surprise during the days leading up to Valentine's Day.

When they learn of Apu's romantic gestures, the town's wives become disenchanted with their non-romantic husbands and boyfriends. Homer gathers some Springfield men to help him stop Apu. On Valentine's Day, they trail Apu to the Springfield Airport. They see Elton John there and, thinking Apu has hired him to serenade Manjula, lock him in a dog carrier.

They discover that Apu has actually made plans to have a pilot skywrite a romantic message. Determined to foil Apu's plan, Homer leaps onto the biplane as it takes off. Homer gets into a struggle with the pilot, ruining the skywriting. Maude Flanders, Mrs. Wiggum, and Edna Krabappel each think the altered message is for them. The pilot drags Homer, hanging from the plane, through a rose farm, hoping to injure him with the thorns. Homer winds up falling out of the plane and into the Simpsons backyard covered with roses. The roses fall at Marge's feet, and she kisses Homer, convinced he is romantic. Meanwhile, at Apu's request, Elton John holds a private, Valentine's Day concert for Apu and Manjula.

SHOW HIGHLIGHTS

"And thank you, God, for the bad things adults do, which distract attention from stuff I'm doing." Bart, saying his bedtime prayers.

Papier-mâché mix, pipe cleaners, pig intestines, and sparkle paint: What Marge uses to build Bart's model of the digestive system.

> **Marge:** *You're a lifesaver, Apu! All the other stores are closed!*
> **Apu:** *At eleven-thirty? But this is the peak hour for stoned teenagers buying shiny things.*
> *(Nearby, Jimbo holds up a sheet of tin foil in front of his face.)*
> **Jimbo:** *Whoa! It's a living mirror!*

"You are one Mahat-mama!" Apu, complimenting his wife, Manjula.

"Good rice, good curry, good Gandhi, let's hurry." Apu's pre-meal grace.

"Hmmm. What's an 'eltdown?'" Homer, reading his beeper.

The Guests Who Wouldn't Leave:
> **Marge:** *Maybe we should leave.*
> **Homer:** *Uh-uh, no way. I don't want to miss a word.*
> **Marge:** *You don't know what they're saying!*
> **Homer:** *I'm picking it up. "Sala" seems to mean jerk, and I think 'Manjula' means some kind of spaceship.*

"You're A-peeling—Let's Never Split!" The monkey-themed Valentine that Homer buys.

> **Manjula:** *Until last night, I never knew Apu could be so romantic!*
> **Marge:** *I can't believe it! He covered your whole bed with wildflowers.*
> **Manjula:** *Oh, I'm sure Homer has done that for you.*
> **Marge:** *Well, sometimes I find pickle slices in the sheets.*

"Oh, both my ears are filled with nougat! There's a nut in my eye!" Apu, recovering from being made into a chocolate-covered husband.

"Homer, I've gone through seven years of receipts, and you've spent less on gifts for me than you have on temporary tattoos."

At Moe's, the Apu Backlash:
Principal Skinner: *Edna won't even let me clap her erasers.*
Sideshow Mel: *My Barbara will no longer pleasure me with the French arts!*
Moe: *The gal I'm stalking had me bumped back to two hundred feet.*

Flanders: *Ah, gee. The man's just trying to show his wife he cares for her. How can we sabotage his labor of love?*
Homer: *I don't know, gasoline, axes...I got some stuff in the trunk.*

"Tiffany's, eh? Looks like Smoochy's gonna seal the deal with a diamond the size of a doll's head!"

"Oh, baby—we got him now! There's no escape from the airport!"

APU

CUPID

Episode AABF11
Original Airdate: 2/14/99
Writer: Dan Greaney
Director: Bob Anderson
Executive Producer: Mike Scully
Guest Voice: Elton John as Himself

Apu: *My humble love note is turning into a Valentine's Day massacre!*
Elton John: *You think you've got problems? I just chewed my way out of a dog carrier!*
Apu: *Elton John!*
Elton John: *That's my name! (pause) Well, not really.*

On the Biplane:

Homer: *Hey, you with the scarf! Stop skywriting!*
Fantastic Dan: *I have to deliver a message! It's the skywriter's code!*
Homer: *I am so sick of that damn code!*

Manjula: *I can't believe it; you closed the Kwik-E-Mart just for me.*
Apu: *Well, you and the health inspector.*

"It should get you pretty darn hammered." Apu, describing his Valentine's Day drink, the champagne squishee.

THE STUFF YOU MAY HAVE MISSED

At his dinner party, Apu plays an album entitled "Concert Against Bangladesh."

There is a picture of what appears to be the very first Kwik-E-Mart (seen in 1F10, "Homer and Apu") in the Nahasapeemapetilon apartment.

Apu has a calendar featuring one of the Seven Duffs in a red sports car.

Homer reads a box of Frosty Krusty Flakes in bed.

Fantastic Dan first appeared, living in a Whack-A-Mole game, in 5F08 "Bart Carny."

Apu is changed into a chocolate husband by Baron Von's Munch House.

A very odd-looking Elvis impersonator can be seen at Springfield Airport when Homer points to Elton John's plane.

The biplane pilot's name reads "Fantastic Dan" on the side of the cockpit.

Things Homer's head bashes into while flying upside down in the biplane: a tree, a bridge, a tree with birds in it, a street lamp, and a chimney.

Elton John holds an intimate concert for Apu and Manjula in the Kwik-E-Mart's rooftop garden, where Paul and Linda McCartney also sang for Apu in 3F03, "Lisa the Vegetarian."

The episode ends in a heart-shaped iris out à la "Love, American Style."

LOVES

MANJULA

MARGE SIMPSON IN: "SCREAMING YELLOW HONKERS"

Episode AABF10   Original Airdate: 2/21/99   Writer: David M. Stern   Director: Mark Kirkland
Executive Producer: Mike Scully   Guest Voice: Hank Williams Jr. sings Canyonero jingle

SERGEANT CREW

Demeanor:
No-nonsense, yet weary.

Bad habits:
Slowly reading aloud what she writes on the blackboard.

Believes:
Anger is what makes America great.

Her suggestions for rage channeling:
Fire a weapon at your television screen; pick a fight with someone weaker than you; or write a threatening letter to a celebrity.

SO, WHEN YOU GO OUT FOR A DRIVE, REMEMBER TO LEAVE YOUR MURDEROUS ANGER WHERE IT BELONGS: AT HOME.

Homer sees a Canyonero deftly maneuver through some post–Faculty Talent Show traffic at Springfield Elementary and decides to get one himself. The next day, Homer finds out that his F-Series Canyonero is traditionally thought of as a woman's car and gives it to Marge. Marge is initially wary of the hulking sports-utility vehicle, but it quickly transforms her into a tough, aggressive driver. After illegally cutting around a funeral procession, Marge is sent to traffic school by Chief Wiggum.

Marge's class teaches her how to deal with her road rage. But on her way out of the parking lot, she becomes annoyed with how slowly people are pulling out and decides to bully her way though. Nearly causing an accident, she crashes into a prison fence, allowing an escape. Her license is revoked.

Homer, Bart, and Lisa take a trip to the Wild Animal Kingdom and Homer enables the rhinos to break free. They go on a rampage in the parking lot. Unable to do anything, the police ask Marge to use her Canyonero to round up the rhinos. Marge refuses until she sees Homer, Bart, and Lisa on top of the car surrounded by rhinos. Marge rescues her family using the Canyonero, but winds up destroying the vehicle in the process.

SHOW HIGHLIGHTS

 "I didn't think it was physically possible, but this both sucks and blows."

Chalmers: *Well, Seymour, it seems we've put together a baseball team, and I was wondering—who's on first?*
Skinner: *Yes, not the pronoun but rather a player with the unlikely name of "Who" is on first.*
(Chalmers makes an annoyed sound.)
Chalmers: *Well that's just great, Seymour. We've been out here six seconds; you've already managed to blow the routine.*
(Chalmers stomps off.)
Chalmers: (muttering to himself) *Sexless freak.*

Stan: *Okay, here's how your lease breaks down. This is your down payment, then here's your monthly, and there's your weekly.*
Homer: *And that's it, right?*
Stan: *Yup. Oh, then after your final monthly payment there's the routine CBP or (quietly and quickly) crippling balloon payment.*
Homer: *But that's not for a while, right?*
Stan: *Right.*

Marge: *You cashed in your 401k to buy that stupid Canyonero. Why can't you drive it?*
Homer: *Are you saying I'm gay? Because if that's what you think, then just come right out and say it.*

"Get that corpse off the road! The streets are for the living!" Marge, in her new Canyonero, stuck behind a funeral procession.

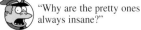 "Why are the pretty ones always insane?"

"In these modern, hectic days of fast food, answering machines, and one night stands, people are getting angrier..." Sergeant Crew, introducing *Road Rage: Death Flips the Finger.*

"I hope you're happy, Simpson! Those prisoners were one day away from being completely rehabilitated!" Wiggum to Marge, after she crashes into a prison fence, causing a mass escape.

"This is Kent Brockman at the scene of a level-three rhino alert..."

"I'm gonna die! Jesus, Allah, Buddha—I love you all!"

The Simpsons Love Stone Phillips:

Homer: *Is there anything that guy doesn't know?*
Australian Gamekeeper: *Well, this Stone Phillips sounds like quite a bloke! What television network is he on?*
Bart: *Why, NBC, of course.*
Lisa: *NBC has lots of great shows, and their news and sports coverage can't be beat.*
Wiggum: *Do you think there's anything great on NBC right now?*
Homer: *Oh, I'm sure of it.*
(Marge turns to camera.)
Marge: *But there's only one way to find out.*

Heard over the End Credits:

Homer: *I'd like to read the following statement, (angry) but I do so under—*
(The sound of a cocking gun is heard.)
Homer: (scared) *—my own free will. It has come to my attention that NBC sucks. I apologize for misleading you and urge you to watch as many Fox shows as possible. So, in summary, NBC bad, Fox good...* (quickly) *CBS great.*
(The gun goes off. Repeatedly.)

GRAMMAR IS NOT A TIME OF WASTE
GRAMMAR IS NOT A TIME OF WASTE
GRAMMAR IS NOT A TIME OF WASTE

THE STUFF YOU MAY HAVE MISSED

A banner outside the school reads, "Faculty Talent Show—Two Milk Minimum."

When Skinner gets off of the human pyramid at the end of the "That's Edu-Tainment!" opening number, Superintendent Chalmers crashes to the ground.

Krusty got his Canyonero in 5F10, "The Last Temptation of Krust."

The Simpsons go auto shopping at The O.K. Car-ral.

Gil last appeared in AABF06, "Viva Ned Flanders."

Evergreen Terrace has its own exit on the freeway.

Among the students in Marge's traffic-school class are Superintendent Chalmers, Agnes Skinner, Moe, Kearney, Apu, and Krusty.

The traffic-school film is presented by Court-Ordered Productions.

Leaving class, Kearney drives a vintage Volkswagen Beetle. In 4F01, "Lisa's Date with Density," he drove a Hyundai.

The motto of the Wild Animal Kingdom is, "Born Free, Then Caged."

MAKE ROOM FOR LISA

Episode AABF12 Original Airdate: 2/28/99 Writer: Brian Scully
Director: Matthew Nastuk Executive Producer: Mike Scully

SHOW HIGHLIGHTS

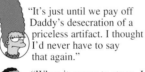

Homer takes Bart and Lisa out on a "special Saturday." It's Lisa's turn to choose what to do, and she decides upon the Smithsonian Traveling Exhibit. There, Homer thoughtlessly defaces the Bill of Rights. OmniTouch, the cell phone company sponsoring the show, strikes a deal with Homer: To pay off the Bill's repairs, he allows the company to put a massive cell phone tower on the roof, with its inner workings in Lisa's room.

Lisa is indignant. Unsympathetic, Homer tells Lisa that she'll have to room with Bart. Soon, Lisa's stomach is hurting from the stress of living with her brother. Homer takes Lisa to Dr. Hibbert, who suggests trying some alternative remedies. When Homer scoffs at this, Lisa reprimands him for his close-mindedness. Realizing Lisa wants to try the remedies, Homer takes her to a New Age store.

There, the saleswoman suggests trying sensory deprivation tanks. During their session, Homer's tank is repossessed. It then falls off the truck and gets buried by Ned Flanders. Meanwhile, Lisa goes through a series of sensory deprivation hallucinations, finally hallucinating that she is Homer and getting a better sense of how much her father loves her. Homer's tank sinks into the ground, winds up in a sewer pipe, and then washes ashore on a beach. Chief Wiggum returns the tank to the store. When Lisa emerges from her tank, she tells Homer that she wants to do something that they'll both enjoy. They end up at the demolition derby.

"That was Men Without Hats...Or as they're known today, Men Without Jobs!" Marty, after playing "Safety Dance" on KBBL.

> Homer, Bart, and Lisa's Special Saturdays:
> **Marge:** *You agreed to spend one Saturday a month doing something with the kids.*
> (Homer groans.)
> **Bart:** *Oh, quit complaining. It's half the work of a divorced dad.*
> **Homer:** *Yeah, but it's twice as much as a deadbeat dad.*

"If it doesn't have Siamese twins in a jar, it's not a fair." Homer, on book fairs.

> "It's just until we pay off Daddy's desecration of a priceless artifact. I thought I'd never have to say that again."

> "When it comes to stress, I believe laughter is the best medicine. You know, before I learned to chuckle mindlessly, I was headed for an early grave myself. Ah, heh, heh, heh!"

"How am I supposed to hallucinate with all these swirling colors distracting me?" Lisa, in the sensory deprivation tank.

"Hey, channel somebody who gives a damn." The Repo Man, to the New Age Saleswoman, as she tries to stop him from taking away all of her merchandise.

"This is the best birthday I ever had." Rod Flanders, after helping his dad bury Homer's sensory deprivation tank, which they believe to be a coffin.

"This inner peace stuff is tough on the ol' coconut!" Homer, bouncing around his sensory deprivation tank as it zooms through the sewers.

"Wow, I've been a cat, a tree, and Cokie Roberts." Lisa, on her sensory deprivation hallucinations.

> I DO NOT HAVE
> DIPLOMATIC IMMUNITY
> I DO NOT HAVE
> DIPLOMATIC IMMUNITY
> I DO NOT HAVE
> DIPLOMATIC IMMUNITY

> (Half awake, Homer listens to the radio at work.)
> **Radio Announcer:** *Okay, FDR is in the White House, an ice cream cone costs a nickel, and a hot new tune by Benny Goodman is hitting the charts. The year is 1939.*
> (Homer snaps awake.)
> **Homer:** *Ninetee— Nineteen thirty-nine! Oh my god! I've gone back in time! I've got to warn everybody about Hitler—and get to the ice cream store!*
> (Lenny and Carl walk in.)
> **Lenny:** *Hey, uh, Homer, what's all the hubbub?*
> **Carl:** *Let me guess...you traveled back in time again?*
> **Homer:** *Shut up! You haven't even been born yet!*

> **Bart:** *Who's Fonzie?*
> **Homer:** *Who's Fonzie? Don't they teach you anything in school? He freed the squares.*

> (The New Age Saleswoman shows Homer and Lisa the sensory deprivation tanks.)
> **Homer:** *Oh, no. No freezing.*
> **New Age Saleswoman:** *No, Mr. Simpson. This is a sensory deprivation tank. It blocks out all the external distractions that bombard our souls.*
> **Homer:** *Can you pee in it?*

THE STUFF YOU MAY HAVE MISSED

When Homer wakes up after his bender, he wears a P. J. O'Harrigan's bumper sticker on his chest.

The Sir Drinks-A-Lot statue features a top-hatted man with a beer belly, drinking a beer.

The ad in the paper for the Smithsonian Traveling Exhibit features the Mercury Space Capsule, The Spirit of St. Louis, and Sammy Davis Jr.'s eye.

Items seen at the Smithsonian Traveling Exhibit include: Lou Gehrig's jersey, The Spirit of St. Louis, the Liberty Bell, and Howdy Doody.

Maggie plays in her crib with a doll of Bongo, the one-eared rabbit from Matt Groening's "Life in Hell."

Marge's notes on the cell phone calls she overhears read, "Otto—drugs?, Mayor Quimby—Interns?, Burns—Greedy?, Krusty—Gay?"

The New Age store Homer takes Lisa to is called Karma-Ceuticals.

Among the items in Karma-Ceuticals is a Stonecutter's symbol. Homer joined the secret brotherhood known as the Stonecutters in 2F09, "Homer the Great." Also seen in the store is a small sculpture of the Hindu god, Ganesh. Apu is seen carrying such a sculpture later in the season in AABF17, "Monty Can't Buy Me Love."

The OmniTouch Representative

Unique ability:
To appear seemingly from out of nowhere and join in on a conversation that had been going on without her.

Demeanor:
Cheerful and businesslike.

What she calls cellular transmitters:
"Keep in Touch Towers."

What she's never seen without:
Her blue OmniTouch blazer and a smile.

UNCLE SAM NEEDS TO SPEND OUR TAX DOLLARS ON THE ESSENTIALS: ANTI-TOBACCO PROGRAMS, PRO-TOBACCO PROGRAMS, KILLING WILD DONKEYS, AND ISRAEL.

SEÑOR DING-DONG

Profession:
Mascot/owner/personnel evaluator at Señor Ding-Dong's Doorbell Fiesta.

Some of the selections at his store:
"Ding-dang-dongs" and "Do-Re-Mis."

Hates:
Chevy vans.

Bad business decisions:
Not carrying jumper cables; hiring Gil.

> IF YOU EVER NEED ME, JUST RRRRING!

At a local steakhouse, Homer feels insulted when a friendly trucker named Red advises him not to try to eat the largest steak on the menu. Homer challenges Red to a steak-eating duel. In the end, Red wins the contest but subsequently dies of beef poisoning. Feeling responsible, Homer decides to take Red's truck and make his last delivery run to Atlanta for him.

Marge goes on an adventure of her own: She and Lisa go to buy a musical doorbell from Señor Ding-Dong's Doorbell Fiesta. After installing the bell, they wait and wait for someone to come to their door and try it. No one comes. Finally, when they try the doorbell themselves, the mechanism jams, and it plays its tune over and over again. On the road, Homer falls asleep while driving and the truck miraculously drives itself to the next truck stop. When Homer relates this story to some other truckers, they show him that all rigs are equipped with auto-drive systems that do the driving for the trucker. They also tell Homer to keep it a secret.

Homer immediately brags to non-truckers about the auto-drive system. The truckers he met find out about Homer's boasting and create a convoy to stop him. Through luck and hapless driving, Homer manages to elude them and make Red's delivery. At home, the Simpson house is surrounded by an angry mob, sick of hearing the family's malfunctioning doorbell. Just before Chief Wiggum shoots it, Señor Ding-Dong arrives, fixing it in the nick of time.

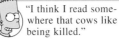

Lisa: *I'm going over to protest this disgusting new restaurant called The Slaughterhouse. It's decorated with hanging steer carcasses and a fountain of blood!*
Marge: *Oooh, I heard about that place on "The Red Grocer."*

"I think I read somewhere that cows like being killed."

Homer: *Wait a minute! Is this the biggest steak you've got? Seventy-two ounces? I thought this was supposed to be a steakhouse, not a little girly underpantsy, pink doily tea party place.*
Waiter: *Well, there is one steak that's only available by special request...We call it "Sir-Loin-A-Lot." It's the size of a boogie board.*
Homer: *Oooh! I'll have that one. And to drink, meatballs.*

"Red Barclay's my name. I'm a trucker and I've eaten steaks from coast to coast with 'taters and toast." Red Barclay, introducing himself to Homer.

Marge: *Is it safe to eat that much food, Dr. Hibbert?*
Hibbert: *You know, I wouldn't have thought so before I bought twelve percent of this restaurant, but now, I feel a balanced diet can include the occasional eating contest.*

(Trucker #1, holding a tire iron, talks to Trucker #2.)
Trucker #1: *Well, we'll have to teach our friend some discretion.*
Trucker #2: *Yeah, just like we did to Jimmy Hoffa.*
Trucker #1: *Hey, shut up!*

"So much steak...lungs filling...sinuses packed with meat!" Homer, during his steak duel with Red Barclay.

"What's happening to me? There's still food, but I don't want to eat it. I've become everything I've ever hated."

"Wannabe" by the Spice Girls: Homer's truck-driving music.

Señor Ding-Dong's Doorbell Fiesta: Where Marge goes to "take a walk on the wild side."

"Awww, great! Look at my shoes! And today's my evaluation with Señor Ding-Dong!" Doorbell salesman Gil, after answering a sample doorbell and stomping out a flaming bag of dog-doo.

"It's time we opened up a can of whup-tushie on this situation!"

"With this baby drivin' your truck for ya, all you gotta do is sit back and feel your ass grow." A trucker on the Navitron Auto-drive System.

"10-4, dead buddy." Homer, to the departed Red.

"All right, Chimey—this time, the bell tolls for thee!" Chief Wiggum, about to shoot the Simpsons' nonstop doorbell.

THE STUFF YOU MAY HAVE MISSED

The Slaughterhouse features a neon sign with a cowboy chainsawing off a smiling cow's head.

The body bag they put Red into reads, "I Died at The Slaughterhouse."

Red's truck, the Red Rascal, has cartoon characters painted on the side of the cab that are reminiscent of Tex Avery's "Wolf & Red."

The tag on Homer's hat reads, "$9.99."

During the episode, Lisa says, "Wow, Dad and Bart have been everywhere! They've eaten submarine sandwiches, grinders, and hoagies!" In episode 2F08, "Fear of Flying," Homer, wanting to travel, says, "I'm sick of eating hoagies! I want a grinder, a sub, a foot-long hero!"

The malfunctioning doorbell plays the tune "Close to You," which was also heard in 7F12, "The Way We Was."

The marquee of Joe's Diner reads, "Now Aware of Camp Value!"

While waiting for someone to ring the doorbell, Marge reads *Vicarious Living*. The cover features a woman standing outside a window, watching a couple inside dining together.

The Monster That Ate Everybody plays at the Stardust Drive-in.

Homer stops at a truck stop called The Gassy Knoll.

The CB codes list reads, 10-33, "Actual bear in air"; 10-34, "Can't unchain wallet"; 10-35, "Hot enough for ya?"; 10-36, "Ghost truck on highway"; 10-37 "Ask me about my grandchildren"; 10-38 "Outsider blabbing about auto-drive system"; 10-39, "I love you, gay buddy"; 10-40, "Taxes due."

Text under the "Welcome to Atlanta" sign reads, "Home of Ted Turner's Mood Swings."

HOMERDRIVE

Episode AABF13
Original Airdate: 3/28/99
Writer: John Swartzwelder
Director: Swinton Scott
Executive Producer: Mike Scully

Homer: *Uh, yeah. I need something that'll keep me awake, alert, and reckless all night long!*
Old Cashier: *Well, Congress is racing back to Washington to outlaw these.*
(The Old Cashier puts down a bottle labeled Stimu-Crank.)
Homer: *Sold!*
(Homer takes off the top and shakes dozens of pills into his mouth.)
Old Cashier: *Hey! You can't take that many pep pills at once!*
Homer: *No problem, I'll balance it out with a bottle of sleeping pills!*

IT DOES NOT SUCK
TO BE YOU
IT DOES NOT SUCK
TO BE YOU
IT DOES NOT SUCK
TO BE YOU

Bart: *Dad, they're trying to kill us!*
Homer: *Oh, why do all my trips end like this?*

Lisa and Marge Meet Señor Ding-Dong:
Lisa: *I thought you were just a marketing gimmick.*
Señor Ding-Dong: *There was a time when that was true, but now, I am so much more.*

SIMPSONS BIBLE

During an especially hot Easter service, the Simpsons begin to doze off and dream about being in Bible stories....

Marge dreams of being Eve in Eden, with Homer as Adam, and Flanders as God. Despite Flanders's warnings, Homer eats the forbidden fruit from the Tree of Knowledge. Marge warns Homer to stop, but winds up eating the fruit herself, after he urges her to. When Flanders catches Marge, he kicks her out. Guilty over not saying anything, Homer tries to sneak her back into Eden, only to get them both cast out.

Lisa dreams of the Exodus from Egypt, casting herself and her classmates as Israelite slaves, Milhouse as Moses, and Principal Skinner as the Pharaoh. After encouraging Milhouse to stand up to Pharaoh Skinner and ask him to let the Israelites go, Lisa and Milhouse are sealed in a pyramid. They escape and lead the other Israelites to the Red Sea. To part it, Lisa has the Israelites flush all of the Egyptians' nearby toilets. The Pharaoh's minions follow the escaping Israelites and are swept away by the rushing water. Free at last, Milhouse and the Israelites begin their long wandering in the desert.

Homer dreams of being King Solomon. He presides over a dispute in which Lenny and Carl, as ancient Israelites, each claim ownership of a pie. Homer reasons that the pie should be cut in two and each man should be sentenced to death. He then eats the pie.

Bart dreams of being King David and battling Goliath's son, Nelson Muntz as Goliath II. During his first battle with Nelson, Bart is knocked far, far away from Israel and his crown is lost to the giant. There, he meets Shepherd Ralph, who takes it upon himself to slay Nelson. Ralph is quickly killed by the giant. Full of rage over Ralph's end, Bart nearly slays Nelson. Ralph, found to actually be alive, finishes the giant off for Bart. Bart is thrown in jail; as it turns out, his subjects feel Nelson was an excellent king.

When the Simpsons wake up, church is over, and everyone is gone. They go outside and discover that the Apocalypse has come. Though Lisa is to be spared, Homer pulls her down from her ascent to heaven, to join her family in hell.

STORIES

Episode AABF14
Original Airdate: 4/4/99
Writers: Tim Long, Larry Doyle, and Matt Selman
Director: Nancy Kruse
Executive Producer: Mike Scully

I CANNOT ABSOLVE SINS
I CANNOT ABSOLVE SINS
I CANNOT ABSOLVE SINS
I CANNOT ABSOLVE SINS
I CANNOT ABSOLVE SINS
I CANNOT ABSOLVE SINS

PIG OF EDEN

Apparent purpose:
To provide a never-ending supply of pork, wisdom, and, when necessary, droll remarks.

Demeanor:
As pleasant and dignified as a walking butcher shop can be.

Exclamation:
"Egad!"

Specialties:
Bacon and "mouth-watering pork ribs."

SHOW HIGHLIGHTS

"Looks like God made you out of my sexiest rib." Homer (Adam), looking over Marge (Eve).

"Oh, there's one more weensy little thing. See that tree over there? I hate to be a bossy Betty, but I have to forbid you to eat its fruit." Flanders (God), laying down his Tree of Knowledge policy to Homer (Adam) and Marge (Eve).

"You're pretty uptight for a naked chick." Homer (Adam) to Marge (Eve), when she scolds him for eating the forbidden fruit.

"Oh, my dear, sweet Eve, I love you even more than the butterscotch pond or the porno bush."

Pig of Eden: *Today I'm featuring mouth-watering pork ribs. Tuck in, then!*
(Homer digs into the pig's side and comes up with a side of ribs. He looks at them.)
Homer (Adam): *Oh, I gave a rib to Eve and now she's gone forever!*
Pig of Eden: *One whole rib and still standing. Oh, aren't you the plucky one, sir.*

"Man, captivity blows."

"Suffering sarcophagus! My tomb!" Pharaoh Skinner, finding his burial place scrawled with the words, "King Butt."

"So long, kids! Give my regards to the British Museum!" Wiggum, sealing Milhouse (Moses) and Lisa in one of the pyramids.

"Eh, slave labor, you get what you pay for." Lisa, commenting on the ineffective booby trap in the pyramid.

"Oy carumba!" Bart, upon seeing the Pharaoh and his minions advancing on the Israelites in front of the Red Sea.

Milhouse (Moses): *So, what's next for the Israelites? Land of milk and honey?*
(Lisa consults a scroll.)
Lisa: *Well, actually it looks like we're in for forty years of wandering the desert.*
Milhouse (Moses): *Forty years? But after that, it's clear sailing for the Jews, right?*
(Lisa looks uneasy as she reads further.)
Lisa: *Uh, more or less. (Causing a distraction) Hey, is that manna?*

Next up in King Solomon's Court: Jesus Christ vs. Checkered Chariot.

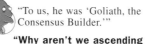

"Now, I'm not saying Jezebel's easy, but before she moved to Sodom, it was known for its pottery!"

"Goliath II is gonna pay—and this time, it's biblical." Bart (King David), on his new battle.

D vs. G2: Stone Cold: The title of the new David/Goliath II bout.

Classic TV Moment:

When Santa's Little Helper talks to Bart (King David), he sounds just like Goliath from the "Davey and Goliath" television show, produced by Art Clokey.

"Jonah! You died the way you lived: inside a whale." Bart (King David), after seeing a skeleton inside Nelson's (Goliath II's) discarded whale-dinner bones.

"To us, he was 'Goliath, the Consensus Builder.'"

"Why aren't we ascending into heaven? Oh, right. The sins." Marge, after seeing the Flanderses lifted up out of the Apocalypse.

THE STUFF YOU MAY HAVE MISSED

The marquee on the First Church of Springfield sign reads, "Christ Dyed Eggs for Your Sins."

A chocolate bunny sits at Lovejoy's pulpit, slowly melting throughout the episode.

A sign near the latrines Bart cleans reads, "Toilets—Egyptians Only."

The Orb of Isis, last seen in 5F17, "Lost Our Lisa," sits on a pedestal inside the pyramid in which Milhouse (Moses) and Lisa are thrown.

When Milhouse (Moses) blows his shofar, Bart is chiseling out a message on the board, with the picture of an eye, a well, a knot, a "D +" and a Pharaoh head. This translates into: "I will not deface."

Ralph's tombstone reads, 975 B.C.— 970 B.C.

The episode ends with AC/DC's "Highway to Hell."

LOVELY DAY IN PARADISE, ISN'T IT?

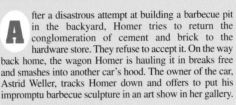

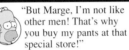

MOM AND

ASTRID WELLER

Profession:
Owner of the "Louvre: American Style" Gallery.

Drives:
Fancy cars and speedboats.

Unique ability:
Staying cool when being greeted by someone with a shotgun.

Sign of sophistication:
She uses a cigarette holder.

> ART ISN'T JUST PRETTY PICTURES. IT'S AN EXPRESSION OF RAW HUMAN EMOTION.

Guest Voice:
Isabella Rossellini as Astrid Weller

After a disastrous attempt at building a barbecue pit in the backyard, Homer tries to return the conglomeration of cement and brick to the hardware store. They refuse to accept it. On the way back home, the wagon Homer is hauling it in breaks free and smashes into another car's hood. The owner of the car, Astrid Weller, tracks Homer down and offers to put his impromptu barbecue sculpture in an art show in her gallery.

Mr. Burns buys Homer's "sculpture," and Homer is officially declared an artist. Having always dreamed of being an artist herself, Marge is uncomfortable with Homer's new art-world notoriety. Homer has another show, and this time, the public does not respond to his failed home improvement projects. To give him inspiration, Marge takes Homer to the Springsonian Museum. Homer is particularly impressed with a Joseph Turner painting of the canals of Venice.

Encouraged by Lisa to try something big, Homer blocks up all of the sewers in town, puts snorkels on all of the animals, and floods the streets of Springfield. Remarkably, the town loves Homer's new "work," but he decides that Marge is the artist in the family.

SHOW HIGHLIGHTS

"But Marge, I'm not like other men! That's why you buy my pants at that special store!"

"You know, installing your own barbecue pit is no harder than adding an aviary or Olympic-sized swimming pool." Doug Vaccaro, on the BBQ Pit Kit infomercial.

"Snapping fingers may not make food appear." The disclaimer heard at the end of the BBQ Pit Kit infomercial.

"Why must life be so hard? Why must I fail in every attempt at masonry?"

"Just go ahead and sue me! Everybody else does! The average settlement is $68,000."

"You squeal on me, I'll kill you." Jasper Johns, after Homer sees him shove dozens of hors d'oeuvres in his pockets.

Astrid: *Your husband's work is what we call "outsider art." It could be by a mental patient or a hillbilly or a chimpanzee.*
Homer: *In high school I was voted most likely to be a mental patient, hillbilly, or chimpanzee.*

"I'm gonna be an outsider artist! That way I can turn all these old baseball cards, Disney memorabilia, and antiques into something valuable!" Homer, sharing his plans with the family.

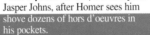

(Homer wears a smock and a beret. He stands before a large lump of clay.)
Homer: *Astrid said the key to my art is anger. But you know me, I'm Mr. Mellow.*
(Bart and Lisa look at each other, making surprised sounds.)
Homer: *So I'm giving you kids permission to get me mad. C'mon, gimme what you got.*
Lisa: *Well, if it'll help...Uhhh, Mom found out her engagement ring is made of rock candy.*
(Homer savagely beats the clay with a stick, grunting with each hit.)
Bart: *Well, I'm flunking math, and the other day, I was a little attracted to Milhouse.*
(Homer screams, beating the clay with fury.)

"I must get back to my hotel and practice my affectations for tomorrow." Homer's Eurotrash admirer Cecil, at Moe's.

Astrid: *Wonderful news, Homer!*
Homer: *Is it about pie?*
Astrid: *Uh, um, no. We're gonna hold a show devoted entirely to you.*
Homer: *Wow! It's like Marge's dream come true, for me! Isn't that great, Marge? For me!*

"You've gone from hip to boring. Why don't you call us when you get to kitsch?" Disaffected Eurotrash Gunter, on Homer's new art.

At the Springsonian Museum:
(Homer and Marge come upon a framed Matt Groening drawing of Akbar and Jeff.)
Homer: *Matt Groening? What's he doing in a museum? He can barely draw!*
(The end of a giant pencil comes into frame, with the eraser rubbing against Homer's head.)
Homer: *Oh, no! I'm being erased!*
(It's revealed that the giant pencil is held by two workmen.)
Workman #1: *Move it, bub! We got an installation to installate!*

POP ART

Episode AABF15
Original Airdate: 4/11/99
Writer: Al Jean
Director: Steven Dean Moore
Executive Producer: Mike Scully
Guest Voice: Jasper Johns as Himself

THE STUFF YOU MAY HAVE MISSED

The note Homer paints to himself on the garage reads, "Start Here Tomorrow 7/17/95."

The sign under Mom & Pop Hardware reads, "A Subsidiary of Global Dynamics, Inc."

Homer puts his shotgun down in Maggie's playpen.

Homer has a bumper sticker that reads, "Single 'N' Sassy." His license plate is 3FJP24.

The banner outside the first show at Astrid's gallery reads, "Inside: Outsider Art." At the second show, it reads, "Solo Show: Homer's Odyssey." Inside that show, there is a sign reading, "No Shoes, No Shirt, No Chardonnay."

Barney's girlfriend, modeled after Yoko Ono, can be seen at the art gallery. She first appeared in 9F21, "Homer's Barbershop Quartet."

When Astrid's black car is seen outside Moe's, it looks as though it's been fixed.

Barney's cocktail napkin drawing is a reproduction of Georges Seurat's *A Sunday Afternoon on the Island of La Grande Jatte.*

Luann and Chase (a.k.a. Pyro) can be seen in the background at Homer's solo show.

The slogan of the Springsonian Museum is "Where the Elite Meet Magritte."

When Smithers and Burns are seen in a swan paddleboat, Smithers is the only one peddling. Lou and Eddie ride by them quickly in a speedboat, pulling Chief Wiggum, waterskiing with his wife, Sarah, on his shoulders.

The Krusty walkie-talkie Milhouse used in 8F04, "Homer Defined," can be seen on the desk in his room.

"You could ride a walrus to work!" Homer, on the Venetian canals.

Homer's Dream:
He wakes up in *The Sleeping Gypsy* by Henri Rousseau; gets beaten up by an anatomical drawing by Leonardo da Vinci; gets shot at by Pablo Picasso's *Three Musicians*; gets drenched by a clock from Salvador Dali's *The Persistence of Memory*; and is pelted by cans of soup thrown at him by Andy Warhol.

Bart: *Are you sure this is art, not vandalism?*
Homer: *That's for the courts to decide, son.*

(Ned looks out the window and sees Springfield is flooded.)
Ned Flanders: *What the flood?! Maude! It's a miracle! The Lord has drowned the wicked and spared the righteous.*
(Maude sees Homer row by on a raft.)
Maude Flanders: *Isn't that Homer Simpson?*
Flanders: (annoyed) *Looks like heaven's easier to get into than Arizona State.*

Marge: *Well, Homer, I have to admit, you created something people really love. You truly are an artist.*
Homer: *No, I'm just a nut who couldn't build a barbecue.*

THE OLD MAN AND THE "C" STUDENT

Episode AABF16 Original Airdate: 4/25/99 Writer: Julie Thacker Director: Mark Kirkland Executive Producer: Mike Scully
Guest Voice: Jack La Lanne as Himself

HANS MOLEMAN

Role in Springfield:
Misfortunate Man about Town.

Name on his driver's license:
Ralph Mellish.

Notable accomplishments:
Directed and starred in the original version of *Man Getting Hit by Football*; taught class on "How to Eat an Orange" at the Adult Education Annex; survived many truck and AMC Gremlin crashes; hosted "Moleman in the Morning" on K-JAZZ radio.

Homer's favorite thing about him:
Giving him a peck on the forehead is "like kissing a peanut."

A POEM BY HANS MOLEMAN. I THINK THAT I SHALL NEVER SEE...MY CATARACTS ARE BLINDING ME.

After Lisa sends a thoughtful letter to the International Olympic Committee, they decide to hold the next Olympics in Springfield. During a ceremony to make the official announcement, Bart offends the officials with an insulting comedy routine. The offer is rescinded. To

teach his students about respect, Principal Skinner make of them perform twenty hours of community se Meanwhile, Homer tries to sell off a thousand springs t purchased to make into Springfield Olympic ma

Bart's community service assignment is the Sprin Retirement Castle. Disapproving of the seniors' hum lifestyle, Bart takes them from the home and gets them take a boat ride together. Soon, Lisa arrives and scolds Ba removing the retirees from the home. Bart shows Lisa v good time they're having, but Lisa reminds them of life home. Meanwhile, back at the house, Marge has told Hom get rid of the springs, and he opts to flush them down the

Mr. Burns's ship accidentally crashes through the seniors boat. As the boat sinks, the seniors blame Bart for misfortune. But Grampa stands up for him, saying tha gave them the best time they have had in twenty years. Th sinks and then bounces back to the surface—as it turns ou keep landing on the mound of springs Homer flushed.

SHOW HIGHLIGHTS

"People, people, please, you are forgetting what the Olympics are all about: giving out medals of beautiful gold, so-so silver, and shameful bronze." The IOC chairman, addressing fellow members.

"It's fun for the whole family and the ends are razor sharp—to protect our nation and its interests." Homer, describing Springy, the Springfield Olympic mascot.

"Now, if you'll excuse me, I'm off to my vacation at Lake Titicaca. Let's see you make a joke out of that, Mr. Smart Guy." Chalmers, to Bart.

The Fireworks, Candy, and Puppy Dog Store: Where Bart briefly believes he'll be serving his community service.

Homer: *My springs! They finally came!*
Marge: *But we lost the Olympics to Shelbyville!*
Homer: *Yeah, but I should have no problem selling a thousand springs.*
Marge: *To who?*
Homer: *Idiots!*
(Homer starts playing with a spring.)
Homer: *Ooh! These are fun!*

"Frankly my dear, I love you—let's remarry." Rhett Butler, in the "Edited for Seniors" version of *Gone with the Wind.*

"You know, the door was open, Chief Break-Everything!" The Old Jewish Man, shouting after Chief breaks through a window and "escapes" à la *One Flew over the Cuckoo's Nest.*

Movie Moment I:
When the seniors escape with Bart and race around Springfield, the sequence mirrors the "Can't Buy Me Love" sequence from *A Hard Day's Night.* The song is performed here by NRBQ.

"I haven't felt this relaxed and carefree since I was watch commander at Pearl Harbor."

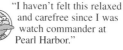

LOOSE TEETH DON'T
NEED MY HELP
LOOSE TEETH DON'T
NEED MY HELP
LOOSE TEETH DON'T
NEED MY HELP

Movie Moment II:
On Mr. Burns's yacht, Smithers sketches Mr. Burns, parodying a scene from *Titanic.*

THE STUFF YOU MAY HAVE MISSED

The International Olympic Committee's sign reads, "Now with Myanmar!" Also on the sign, the symbol of the Olympics is upside-down and none of the rings are linked.

Under the "Town Prepares for Olympics" headline in the *Springfield Shopper* is the smaller headline, "Pickpockets Call Up Reserves."

The Springfield Tire Fire's sign says, "Est. 1989." 1989 was the year "The Simpsons" premiered.

Patty and Selma's proposed mascot, "Ciggy," is a discus thrower made out of cigarettes and ashtrays.

The song "The Children Are Our Future" makes use of the familiar "rolling down the river" riff from "Proud Mary"; the sequence was also choreographed by George Meyer.

The banner on the side of the bus reads, "Junior Volunteers."

Two other episodes that parody *One Flew Over the Cuckoo's Nest* are 7F24, "Stark Raving Dad," and 9F17, "So It's Come to This: A Simpsons Clip Show."

Mr. Burns's boat is called the "Gone Fission II." Its sails have symbols for atomic energy on them.

MONTY CAN'T BUY ME LOVE

Episode AABF17 Original Airdate: 5/2/99 Writer: John Swartzwelder Director: Mark Ervin Executive Producer: Mike Scully
Guest Voice: Michael McKean as Jerry Rude

M r. Burns witnesses charismatic billionaire Arthur Fortune presiding over the grand opening of his Springfield Fortune Megastore. At the opening, Fortune wins the crowd's heart easily, telling them of his extreme sports hobbies and throwing dollar bills out into the audience. Mr. Burns decides he wants that kind of adoration and enlists Homer's help.

Despite their best efforts, they fail at endearing Mr. Burns to Springfield. After learning that Fortune has donated two pandas to the Springfield Zoo, Burns decides to top him by capturing and bringing back the Loch Ness monster.

Mr. Burns, Homer, Willie, and Professor Frink travel to Scotland to find the monster. Discouraged by the progress of the search, Burns has the Loch drained. They find the monster, and Burns has it transported to Springfield. At a press conference, Burns feels he has finally secured the love of Springfield's residents. When he unveils the monster, the flashbulbs that go off disorient Mr. Burns, causing him to knock a lighting tower over, starting a fire. The press conference is ruined. In the end, Burns decides that it's much easier to simply not be loved. No longer needing the Loch Ness monster, he gets the beast a job as a pit boss at a Las Vegas casino.

SHOW HIGHLIGHTS

"At auction, I'd expect this to bring twenty to thirty thousand dollars...Except that on the handle somebody's carved, 'Homer Rocks.'" One of the experts on Antique Appraisal, looking over one of Moe's beer taps.

"I'm doing all my thievin' here!" Nelson, on the Fortune Megastore's shoplifting department.

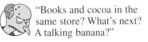 "Books and cocoa in the same store? What's next? A talking banana?"

"Conga like you mean it. Please don't make me shock you!" C. Montgomery Burns, holding his mini-cattle prod, making Smithers dance.

> **Mr. Burns:** *Simpson, I need your help. I want to be loved.*
> **Homer:** *I see. Well, I'll need some beer.*

> (One of the silver dollars Homer and Mr. Burns throw down from a tall building lodges in Lenny's forehead.)
> **Lenny:** *Owwww! Ow! Take it out, take it out!*
> (Carl pulls it out. Blood starts spurting from the wound.)
> **Lenny:** *Oh! Ooooh! Put it back! Put it back!*
> (The bleeding stops.)
> **Lenny:** *That was a close one. Wanna go bowling?*
> **Carl:** *Maybe you should see a doctor about that coin in your brain.*
> **Lenny:** *Maybe you should mind your own business.*
> (A woman walks by and Lenny bows to her, removing the coin from his forehead like taking off a hat.)
> **Lenny:** *Afternoon, miss.*
> (Once again, blood spurts out of his forehead. The woman screams.)

"I can't believe it! I'm still not among the hundred most popular billionaires! I'm behind Adam Sandler, for god's sake!" Mr. Burns, reading *Billionaire Beat*.

"Now, Mr. Rude, I just want you to know I'm a good sport. If you want to make fun of my legendary love of cashews, you have at it." Mr. Burns, appearing on *Jerry Rude and the Bathroom Bunch*, a Howard Stern–style, shock jock radio show.

> **Homer:** *Do you really think you can capture the Loch Ness monster? I mean, he's eluded Leonard Nimoy and Peter Graves.*
> **Mr. Burns:** (scoffs) *Peter Graves couldn't find ugly at a Radcliffe mixer.*

"Well, mistakes have been made." Burns, on whether he's murdered anyone.

The DeLochinator: Mr. Burns's loch-draining device.

"I was a little worried when he swallowed me, but, well, you know the rest." Mr. Burns, explaining how he overpowered the Loch Ness monster.

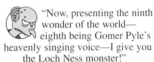 "Now, presenting the ninth wonder of the world—eighth being Gomer Pyle's heavenly singing voice—I give you the Loch Ness monster!"

"You know what? To be loved, you have to be nice to people, every day. But to be hated, you don't have to do squat!"

> **Movie Moment:**
> Mr. Burns's press conference falling apart when all of the flashbulbs go off is reminiscent of *King Kong*.

THE STUFF YOU MAY HAVE MISSED

On line at the "Antique Appraisal" show are: Herman with a German military helmet; Dr. Hibbert with a vase; Miss Hoover with some books; the Comic Book Guy with a copy of *Sad Sack*; Krusty scratching his back with a menorah; Apu with a statue of Ganesh; and Principal Skinner with an old blunderbuss— a bell-shaped musket.

In the Megastore, Homer watches several TVs playing footage of a monkey with a banjo.

Mr. Burns's stuffed Loch Ness monster has a shirt that reads, "Macarena Monster."

At the Loch Ness Pub, Homer plays a Flipper Frenzy pinball machine.

When Homer spins around in his kilt, it's evident that he is not wearing underwear.

Mr. Burns conducts a similarly ill-fated presentation ceremony in 9F04, "Treehouse of Horror III," during the *King Homer* segment.

I HAVE NEITHER BEEN
THERE NOR DONE THAT
I HAVE NEITHER BEEN
THERE NOR DONE THAT
I HAVE NEITHER BEEN
THERE NOR DONE THAT

ARTHUR FORTUNE

Past accomplishments: Boogie-boarding down Mt. Everest; climbing Niagara Falls; knocking out Muhammad Ali; and successfully mating two male pandas.

Notable qualities: His high-energy cheer; his winning smile; his ability to start a successful conga line; how he makes Mr. Burns jealous.

How many Fortune Megastores he currently owns: 112.

What Kent Brockman calls him: A "playful plutocrat."

NOW, I'M AFRAID I'VE GOT SOME BAD NEWS FOR MY ACCOUNTANT TODAY. IT SEEMS THAT I HAVE TOO MUCH MONEY...WHO WANTS A DOLLAR?

LINDSEY NAEGLE

Her company:
Advanced Capital Ventures.

What she produces:
Synergy and books on how to cheat at bridge.

How she used her talents for Springfield:
Synergizing comic books and jury summonses.

Her opinion of Lisa's open letter to Springfield:
Delightfully condescending.

Pet project:
Trying to get a shadow puppet theater in Springfield.

> I CAN'T BELIEVE HOW THEY'RE DUMBING DOWN THE SPRINGFIELD LIBRARY. THEY'VE GOTTEN RID OF THE ENGLISH LITERATURE SECTION AND REPLACED IT WITH A MAKE-YOUR-OWN-SUNDAE BAR.

A fter a riot breaks out during a "How Low Will You Go?" KBBL radio contest, Lisa writes a disgusted letter to the *Springfield Shopper*. Meanwhile, during the melee, Homer runs off with the second prize—a coupon for free boudoir photography. Lisa's letter catches the attention of the Springfield chapter of Mensa, the organization for people with high IQs, and she is accepted as one of them.

Days later, the group finds the gazebo reserved for their Renaissance Faire occupied by surly drunks. Chief Wiggum refuses to help. Eager for gazebo reservation reform, the group storms into the mayor's office. Before they even speak, the mayor flees town, believing that all of his corruption has come to light. The Mensa members look over the town charter and discover that if the mayor abdicates, "a council of learned citizens shall rule in his stead." Reasoning that no one in town is more learned than they, the Mensa members gear up to govern Springfield.

At a press conference to announce their new initiatives, Frink and the Comic Book Guy propose unfair, restrictive rules. The gathered crowd turns on them and Dr. Stephen Hawking suddenly appears, scolding the Mensa members. Lisa is disappointed that her group didn't succeed in their quest to better Springfield. Dr. Hawking tells her not to feel bad, that people each have their own different vision for a perfect world.

SHOW HIGHLIGHTS

Ethnic Mismatch Comedy #644: A sitcom that the Simpsons watch, featuring an Italian man and an English woman. It is canceled mid-broadcast.

"The lowfat pudding that's approved for sale by the government!" The slogan for Grandma Plopwell's Pudding.

> (Hibbert tends to a shaking Carl, holding a Grandma Plopwell's pudding cup.)
> **Hibbert:** *Do you suffer from diabetes?*
> **Carl:** *No.*
> **Hibbert:** *Well, you do now.*
> (Dr. Hibbert breaks into laughter.)

"Please, no more spark plugs." Bart, as the "Human Garbage Disposal," swallowing whatever people throw into a large funnel that he holds up to his mouth while on stage at the "How Low Will You Go" contest.

"But it's me, Moe, wearing a sailor suit! Moe, with a lolly! It's so out of character! Ain't that worth nothin'?" Moe, reacting to the "boos" of the contest audience.

"We are a town of lowbrows, no-brows, and ignorami. We have eight malls, but no symphony. Thirty-two bars but no alternative theater. Thirteen stores that begin with 'Le Sex.'" From Lisa's open letter to the people of Springfield.

"Pudding Spree Not Enjoyed by All": The headline atop Lisa's letter.

 "I don't need to be told what to think—by anyone living."

Homer Calls the Boudoir Photographer:
Homer: *Uh, you're not gonna ask me to pose nude, are ya?*
Photographer: *Well, yes. Unless you have some issues with revealing your body.*
Homer: *Well, I don't, but the block association seems to.* (with contempt) *They wanted a "traditional" Santa Claus.*

Lisa: *With our superior intellects, we could rebuild this city on a foundation of reason and enlightenment. We could turn Springfield into a Utopia.*
Skinner: *A new Athens.*
Lindsey: *Or Walden Two.*
Chief Wiggum: *Yeah, a real Candyland.*
(The Mensa members glare at Wiggum.)
Wiggum: *Of the mind. The mind.*

LISA'S BRAIN

Episode AABF18
Original Airdate: 5/9/99
Writer: Matt Selman
Director: Pete Michels
Executive Producer: Mike Scully
Guest Voice: Stephen Hawking as Himself

THE STUFF YOU MAY HAVE MISSED

Jimmy the Scumbag (last seen in 5F09, "Trash of the Titans") is featured in the Grandma Plopwell's contest commercial.

Bart wears his Bartman cowl when he appears as the "Human Garbage Disposal."

Madeleine Albright serves as one of the judges at the "How Low Will You Go?" contest.

Burns and Smithers go to the "How Low Can You Go?" contest as a horse. Smithers plays the horse's rear. Apu goes as a cow, Lenny as a urinal, Snake as a ballerina, and Kirk Van Houten attends in a diaper.

Boudoir Photography's slogan is "Discretion Guaranteed." It's printed on a large sign on the side of the company van.

Though he skipped town in an earlier scene, a man closely resembling Mayor Quimby can be seen with two women at the dog track.

Other cities on the list of America's most livable cites were Flint, Michigan (#296); Ebola, Rhode Island (#297); and Dawson's Creek, North Carolina (#298).

NO ONE WANTS TO HEAR
FROM MY ARMPITS
NO ONE WANTS TO HEAR
FROM MY ARMPITS
NO ONE WANTS TO HEAR
FROM MY ARMPITS

Homer: *C'mon, you idiots! We're taking back this town!*
Carl: *Yeah, let's make litter out of these literati!*
Lenny: *That's too clever. You're one of them!*
(Lenny punches Carl, knocking him down.)

The members of the **Springfield Chapter of Mensa:** Professor Frink, Dr. Hibbert, Principal Skinner, Lindsey Naegle, and the Comic Book Guy.

"We are hardly nerds. Would a nerd wear such an irreverent sweatshirt?" The Comic Book Guy, showing off his "C:/DOS, C:/DOS/RUN, RUN/DOS/RUN" sweatshirt.

"Try not to speak, it's making your body ripple." The Boudoir Photographer, taking pictures of Homer.

 "Why do we live in a town where the smartest have no power and the stupidest run everything? Maybe I should just move back to Alabama."

"You have been chosen to join the Justice Squadron, 8 A.M. Monday at the Municipal Fortress of Vengeance." The Bright Pack's comic book–influenced wording on Springfield's new, more enticing jury summonses.

"The world has already taken note of our accomplishments. Springfield has moved up to number 299 on the list of America's 300 most livable cities. Take that, East St. Louis!"

"Light is not your friend." The Boudoir Photographer, telling Homer why she's taking his pictures in the basement.

"Sarcasm detector. Oh, that's a real useful invention!" The Comic Book Guy, causing Frink's sarcasm detector to explode.

"We have some new rules and regulations that you're just gonna go ape-poopy over."

"Inspired by the most logical race in the galaxy, the Vulcans, breeding will be permitted once every seven years. For many of you, this will mean much less breeding. For me, much, much more."

"Larry Flynt is right! You guys stink!" Homer, mistaking the identity of Dr. Stephen Hawking.

"Wow. I can't believe someone I never heard of is hanging out with a guy like me." Homer, having a beer with Dr. Stephen Hawking.

Lisa: *Oh, Dr. Hawking, we had such a beautiful dream. What went wrong?*
Dr. Hawking: *Don't feel bad, Lisa. Sometimes the smartest of us can be the most childish.*
Lisa: *Even you?*
Dr. Hawking: *No. Not me. Never.*

CHUCK GARABEDIAN

What he believes are the good things in life:
Family vacations, jet packs, and "Solid Gold" dancers.

What he teaches:
Save money by buying used, unwanted, soiled, and/or mediocre goods.

His arsenal:
The twelve savings secrets.

His archenemies:
Those Wall Street fat cats.

How he likes to relax:
Hanging out on his yacht that smells like cat pee; with beautiful women who used to be men.

LET'S START WITH MEGASECRET NUMBER ONE. YA GOTTA SQUEEZE EVERY PENNY! YOU SEE THIS TUX? I GOT IT CHEAP 'CAUSE ROY COHN DIED IN IT!

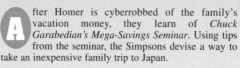

After Homer is cyberrobbed of the family's vacation money, they learn of *Chuck Garabedian's Mega-Savings Seminar*. Using tips from the seminar, the Simpsons devise a way to take an inexpensive family trip to Japan.

In Japan, Bart and Homer attend a Sumo match where Bart smacks a wrestler in the face with a chair and Homer tosses the Japanese emperor in a soiled Sumo thong receptacle. Bart and Homer are thrown in jail. After the family pays their bail, they're left with a single piece of currency, a one-million-yen bill. Homer demonstates for

Lisa the origami he learned in prison by folding it into a "lucky" crane, and the bill flies away in the wind.

The Simpsons get jobs working as fish gutters to earn money for tickets back home. At the factory, they watch a game show on television that grants wishes to families. The next day, the family goes on the show hoping to win plane tickets back to Springfield. They are repeatedly humiliated on the program, but ultimately their wish is granted. Their plane is briefly attacked by Godzilla before they begin the long trip home.

SHOW HIGHLIGHTS

> **Homer Tries the Internet:**
> **Lisa:** *Wow, Dad. You're surfing like a pro.*
> **Homer:** *Oh, yeah. I'm betting on jai alai in the Cayman Islands, I invested in something called News Corp—*
> **Lisa:** *Dad, that's Fox!*
> *(Homer screams and starts pounding a button on the keyboard.)*
> **Homer:** *Undo! Undo!*

"Yoink-dot-adios-backslash-losers!" Snake, after busting into the cybercafe and downloading Homer's bank account at gunpoint.

> **Homer:** *It's just that you and Maude live like royalty in your fancy castle while I got Marge trapped over there like a pig in a mud beehive.*
> **Ned:** *Oh, we're not as well off as you think. We give to eight different churches just to hedge our bets. And the Leftorium's business has gone way downhill since Leftopolis moved in next door.*

"He taught us how to live a Burt Reynolds lifestyle on a Mac Davis income!" Flanders, on Chuck Garabedian and his *Mega-Savings Seminar*.

> **Marge:** *C'mon, Homer. Japan will be fun. You liked Rashomon.*
> **Homer:** *That's not how I remember it.*

"Welcome. I am honored to accept your waste." The talking toilet in the Simpsons' room in Japan.

"Howdy, gangstas! I am average American Joe salaryman waiter!" The Simpsons' waiter at Americatown, introducing himself.

Clobbersaurus: What Homer calls himself, shortly after tossing the Emperor of Japan in a receptacle for soiled Sumo thongs.

Happy Smile Super Challenge Family Wish Show: The Japanese game show on which the Simpsons appear.

"Our categories are: 'Ow, That Hurts!', 'Why Are You Doing This to Me?' and 'Please Let Me Die.'" The Host on "Happy Smile Super Challenge Family Wish Show."

"D'oh! Woo-hoo! Um, that boy ain't right!" Barney, trying to impersonate Homer at Moe's.

 "Game shows aren't about cruelty. They're about greed and wonderful prizes like poorly built catamarans."

"Good-bye, Japan! I'll miss your Kentucky Fried Chicken and your sparkling, whale-free seas."

THE STUFF YOU MAY HAVE MISSED

The copy of *Wired* that Lisa reads features the blurb, "CyberShorts: Virtually Wedgieproof!"

Bart, Lisa, and Homer go to The Java Server. A banner in front of their store reads, "GRAND OPENING—wel.com."

The sign at the *Mega-Savings Seminar* reads, "B.Y.O. Chair."

Products at the 33¢ store include, "Onions?", "Cool Ranch Soda," and orange "That '70s Show" mugs. Also at the store are cases of Skittlebrau, a product that Apu thought Homer dreamed up in 5F03, "Bart Star."

The "In-Flight Movies" pamphlet advertises, "Jim Belushi in KANGA-ROOMMATE!"

The Royal Tokyo Hotel has a banner that reads, "Now with 20% More Bowling!"

A snippet of the Mr. Sparkle commercial, featuring a two-headed cow, can be seen while Bart, Lisa, and Marge are having seizures. The ad was featured in 4F18, "In Marge We Trust."

Americatown features pictures of the Kool-Aid Man, Uncle Sam, and Elvis. It's decorated with other pictures of a star, a gun, a pie, a guitar, a bat, and a baseball. Inside animatronic figures pose and dance: E.T. seems to be pointing up Marilyn Monroe's flying skirt, Abe Lincoln dances with the Statue of Liberty, and a boxer (possibly Muhammad Ali) fights an astronaut.

The Simpsons' waiter at Americatown wears a T-shirt that reads "UCLA Yankee Cola" and a cowboy hat.

A sign hanging in downtown Tokyo has a marquee ticking up from 13,654,747 to 13,654,754. The text above it reads, "Price of a Tokyo Golf Membership."

The fight card at the Sumo stadium reads, "Today: Sakatumi vs. Nakadowna."

The Simpsons work at the "Osaka Seafood Concern."

KTV's sign reads, "Home of the Digital Puppet News Team."

OVER TOKYO

Episode AABF20
Original Airdate: 5/16/99
Writers: Donick Cary and Dan Greaney
Director: Jim Reardon
Executive Producer: Mike Scully
Guest Voices: George Takei as Wink, the game show host

Lisa: *Now can we do something Japanese?*
Homer: *Oh, I'm sick of doin' Japanese stuff! In jail, we had to be in this dumb Kabuki play about the forty-seven Ronin, and I wanted to be Yoshi, but they made me Ori.*
Bart: *Then we had to do two hours of origami followed by flower arranging and meditation.*
(Homer leans down to Bart.)
Homer: *(in Japanese) Should we tell them the secret of inner peace?*
Bart: *(in Japanese) No, they are foreign devils.*

On the show:

Host: *Thank you, thank you. And welcome to our contestants from America, the Simpson family.*
Marge: *You honor us.*
Host: *Don't patronize me.*

Host: *Now, our game shows are a little different from yours. Your shows reward knowledge. We punish ignorance.*
Homer: *Ignor-what?*
(Fire shoots out of Homer's microphone, directly into his face. He screams.)

A TRIBUTE TO TROY McCLURE

Musicals:
Stop the Planet of the Apes, I Want to Get Off! (3F15)

The Educational Films/Filmstrips:

Lead Paint: Delicious But Deadly (8F22)
Here Comes the Metric System! (8F22)
Fuzzy Bunny's Guide to You Know What (8F22)
Sixty Minutes of Car Crash Victims (9F14)
Alice's Adventures through the Windshield Glass (9F14)
The Decapitation of Larry Leadfoot (9F14)
The Meat Council Presents: Meat and You–Partners in Freedom (3F03)
Two Minus Three Equals Negative Fun! (3F03)
Firecrackers: The Silent Killer (3F03)
Designated Drivers: The Life-Saving Nerds (3F07)
Phony Tornado Alarms Reduce Readiness (3F07)
Shoplifters Beware (3F07)
Young Jebediah Springfield (3F13)
Locker Room Towel Fight: The Blinding of Larry Driscoll (3F15)
Someone's in the Kitchen with DNA (4F24)
Alice Doesn't Live Anymore (4F24)
Mommy, What's Wrong with That Man's Face? (4F24)
Birds: Our Fine Feathered Colleagues (5F22)
Earwigs–Eeeew! (5F22)
Man vs. Nature: The Road to Victory (5F22)

The Informational Kiosks/Films:

Ah Fudge! Factory Introductory Film (8F03)
Rancho Relaxo Introductory Film (8F14)
Springfield Knowledgeum Introductory Film (5F13)
Welcome to Springfield Airport (5F13)
Where's Nordstrom? (5F13)

The Telethons:

Out with Gout '88 (1F03)
Let's Save Tony Orlando's House (1F03)
The Springfield Public TV Telethon (1F03)

The Video Classes of the Future:

Pepsi Presents Addition and Subtraction (2F15)

The "I Can't Believe They Invented It!" Products

The Candy Bar That Cleans and Straightens Teeth (7F13)
The Eyeball White Whitener (7F14)
Spiffy, the 21st Century Stain Remover (8F07)
The Juice Loosener (9F20)
Sun & Run: The Suntan Lotion That's Also a Laxative (9F20)

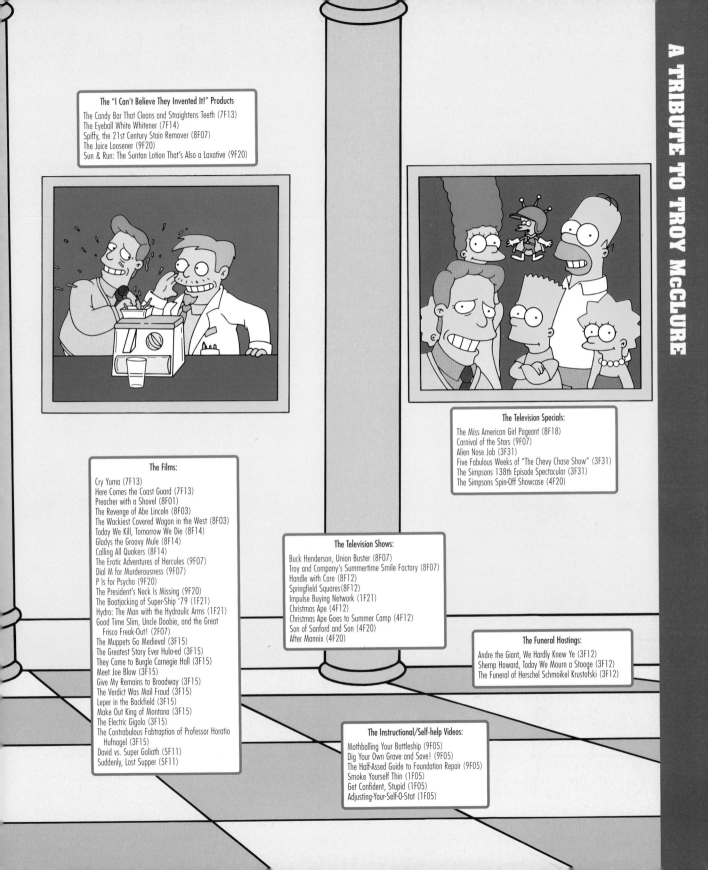

The Television Specials:

The Miss American Girl Pageant (8F18)
Carnival of the Stars (9F07)
Alien Nose Job (3F31)
Five Fabulous Weeks of "The Chevy Chase Show" (3F31)
The Simpsons 138th Episode Spectacular (3F31)
The Simpsons Spin-Off Showcase (4F20)

The Films:

Cry Yuma (7F13)
Here Comes the Coast Guard (7F13)
Preacher with a Shovel (8F01)
The Revenge of Abe Lincoln (8F03)
The Wackiest Covered Wagon in the West (8F03)
Today We Kill, Tomorrow We Die (8F14)
Gladys the Groovy Mule (8F14)
Calling All Quakers (8F14)
The Erotic Adventures of Hercules (9F07)
Dial M for Murderousness (9F07)
P Is for Psycho (9F20)
The President's Neck Is Missing (9F20)
The Boatjacking of Super-Ship '79 (1F21)
Hydro: The Man with the Hydraulic Arms (1F21)
Good Time Slim, Uncle Doobie, and the Great
    Frisco Freak-Out! (2F07)
The Muppets Go Medieval (3F15)
The Greatest Story Ever Hula-ed (3F15)
They Came to Burgle Carnegie Hall (3F15)
Meet Joe Blow (3F15)
Give My Remains to Broadway (3F15)
The Verdict Was Mail Fraud (3F15)
Leper in the Backfield (3F15)
Make Out King of Montana (3F15)
The Electric Gigolo (3F15)
The Contrabulous Fabtraption of Professor Horatio
    Hufnagel (3F15)
David vs. Super Goliath (5F11)
Suddenly, Last Supper (5F11)

The Television Shows:

Buck Henderson, Union Buster (8F07)
Troy and Company's Summertime Smile Factory (8F07)
Handle with Care (8F12)
Springfield Squares(8F12)
Impulse Buying Network (1F21)
Christmas Ape (4F12)
Christmas Ape Goes to Summer Camp (4F12)
Son of Sanford and Son (4F20)
After Mannix (4F20)

The Funeral Hostings:

Andre the Giant, We Hardly Knew Ye (3F12)
Shemp Howard, Today We Mourn a Stooge (3F12)
The Funeral of Herschel Schmoikel Krustofski (3F12)

The Instructional/Self-help Videos:

Mothballing Your Battleship (9F05)
Dig Your Own Grave and Save! (9F05)
The Half-Assed Guide to Foundation Repair (9F05)
Smoke Yourself Thin (1F05)
Get Confident, Stupid (1F05)
Adjusting-Your-Self-O-Stat (1F05)

4F22 - After discovering from the bathroom that his car is being ticketed again.

4F22 - After getting a car boot stuck on his foot.

3G02 - After dropping a saxophone on his foot while asking for an inscription.

3G02 - After finishing the story of Bart's first day of school, Lisa informs him he was supposed to be telling the story of how she got her saxophone.

5F02 - After making the mutated Springfielders attack him by taunting them.

5F01 - After realizing that he's lost his chance to rob the Kwik-E-Mart.

5F03 - After Bart throws something and hits him in the head while he is chased by Homer, who wants to hug him.

5F11 - After learning the company name "Flancrest Enterprises" is already taken.

5F12 - After realizing he shouldn't have stopped Snake from stealing Moe's car.

5F12 - After realizing that he missed the

opportunity to have the 10:15 train smash into Moe's car.

3G04 - After discovering he shot Captain Tenille out of the torpedo tube.

3G04 - After the path of the submarine collides with the directional compass marker on an old-fashioned nautical map.

5F14 - After realizing he has to pay taxes every year.

5F09 - After tripping over a trash can, knocking it over, and realizing he has to take the trash out himself.

5F09 - After the Mayor tells him that the garbagemen won't work for free, when he was counting on them doing just that.

5F16 - After a paperboy hits him in the head with a newspaper while he is jogging.

5F16 - After hitting his head on a rock while sliding down the Murderhorn.

5F16 - After learning he still has four vertical miles left to go on his climb of the Murderhorn.

5F16 - After discovering he left his wallet on top of the Murderhorn.

5F17 - After hitting his head on a traffic light while riding on a runaway cherry picker.

5F17 - After getting his head caught in between two sides of a drawbridge.

5F18 - After a storage compartment opens and hits him on the head in the restaurant Up, Up, and Buffet!

5F18 - After taunting a stadium full of people, while he and Marge stand there naked, by saying sarcastically, "Why don't you take a picture? It'll last longer," and everyone does.

5F22 - After being hit repeatedly by balls in a batting cage.

5F22 - After tripping down the stairs to the basement because there is no lightbulb.

AABF02 - After Chief Wiggum shoots him, embedding a flower in his forehead.

"D'OH..."

AABF07 - After hearing that more of his secrets will be revealed on the "We Know All Your Secrets" radio program.

AABF07 - After it's revealed that he's been practicing medicine without a license.

AABF09 - After walking into a cactus.

AABF09 - After walking into cactus a second time.

AABF12 - After Bart trades his turn for a 'special Saturday' to Lisa for a dessert.

AABF15 - After throwing his own doormat out the window of his moving car.

AABF15 - After being drenched in his dream by a dripping clock from Salvador Dali's *The Persistence of Memory*.

AABF17- After *almost* winning the jackpot at the Vegas Town Casino.

AABF18 - After Dr. Stephen Hawking uses a springing boxer's glove to hit Homer in the face. Homer had been trying to stick him with the bill at Moe's.

AABF20 - After his square watermelon loses its shape, and he drops it.

AABF20-(In Japanese) After the origami swan he folded out of a one million-yen bill blows away in the wind.

AABF20 - After being beaten with sticks by his family while hanging over them encased in a pig piñata on the *Happy Smile Super Challenge Family Wish Show*.

HOMER SAYS, "MMM..."

"Mmm . . . recirculated air."
After stealing Flanders's air conditioner. (3G02)

"Mmm . . . memo."
After tasting a pencil he had stuck in butter. (5F11)

"Mmm . . . me."
After eating an olive used to represent himself. (5F12)

"Mmm . . . donuts."
Just before drooling on the last donut during a break at the power plant. (3G04)

"Mmm . . . loganberry."
After smelling Bart's scented candle. (5F22)

"Mmm . . . hippo."
After seeing a hippo being barbecued in an infomercial. (AABF15)

"Mmm . . . split peas—with ham!"
After seeing one of Andy Warhol's Campbell's Soup paintings. (AABF15)

"Mmm . . . fifty-dollar pretzel."
While eating a pretzel at a Sumo match in Tokyo. (AABF20)

COUCH GAGS

4F22 City of New York vs. Homer Simpson–Dressed up like the Harlem Globetrotters, the Simpsons pass around a basketball as they each sit down. When the ball reaches Maggie, she leaps up and dunks the ball into a hoop above the couch. The ball hits Homer in the head. *4F23 The Principal and the Pauper*–The family, dressed in astronaut suits, sits down on the couch. It then takes off out of frame like a rocket. *3G02 Lisa's Sax*–Homer runs in and stands in front of the couch. The top half of his body pops off and lands on the couch, revealing Marge inside. The top half of her body then pops off and lands on the couch, revealing Bart. The same happens to Bart, revealing Lisa, and it happens once more, finally revealing Maggie. *5F02 Treehouse of Horror VIII*–The family runs to the couch, gets strapped in as if to an electric chair, and is electrocuted.

5F01 The Cartridge Family, 5F10 The Last Temptation of Krust–The seat cushions of the couch have been replaced with a pool of water. The family rushes in, each with their rear end on fire, and immediately sits in the pool, extinguishing the flames. They all sigh in relief. *5F03 Bart Star, 5F12 Dumbbell Indemnity, AABF05 Mayored to the Mob*–The family rushes in and sits on the couch. Suddenly, junkyard car compactors come in horizontally from offscreen, smashing the family together horizontally. Another car compactor comes down from above frame and smashes the family against the couch, making them into a cube. *5F04 The Two Mrs. Nahasapeemapetilons, 5F13 This Little*

Wiggy–Bart pops up from behind the family TV, looks around, runs offscreen, and then runs back onscreen, holding two spraypaint cans. He spraypaints a crude rendering of the family on the couch, signs it "El Barto," laughs, and then runs off. *5F05 Lisa the Skeptic, 5F14 The Trouble with Trillions*–The family rushes in wearing towels, only to find three old men in towels sitting on the couch, in front of a hot rock pit in the center of the floor, like a sauna. The family leaves them. One of the old men ladles some water on the hot rocks, causing them to steam. *5F06 Realty Bites, 5F15 Girly Edition, AABF06 Viva Ned Flanders*–After the family rushes in and takes their places on the couch, a live-action hand reaches into the frame and spins the scene around and around. When it stops, the Simpsons have been altered into a spin art.

5F07 Miracle on Evergreen Terrace, 5F16 King of the Hill–The family rushes in and sits on the couch. Suddenly the entire living room is pulled back to reveal it is inside a snow globe held by two hands. The hands shake the globe, causing it to "snow." We pull back into the living room and the Simpsons look around in wonder at the flurries. *5F24 All Singing, All Dancing*–The family rushes in as the floor moves like a Jetson-esque treadmill away from the couch. Marge, Bart, Lisa, and Maggie each make it to the couch, but Homer stumbles and is dragged away and then around again, shouting, "Marge, stop this crazy thing!" *5F08 Bart Carny, 5F17 Lost Our Lisa, 5F20 Lard of the Dance*–The family rushes in and sits down, only to have the couch pulled out from underneath them. They land on the floor, and Nelson Muntz pops out from behind the couch, points at them, and says, "Ha, ha!" *5F23 The Joy of Sect*–A tiny version of the family rushes in. Too small to make it to the top of the couch, Marge stands on Homer's hands and helps the children onto the cushions. Next, Marge climbs on herself and then helps Homer up. Santa's Little Helper walks in, grabs the tiny Homer in his mouth, and walks off with Homer screaming. *5F11 Das Bus, 5F18 Natural Born Kissers, AABF04 Homer Simpson in: "Kidney Trouble"*–The family rushes in as frogs, except Maggie, who is a tadpole. The living room is full of water and the couch has been replaced by a lily pad, the TV also sits on a lily pad. Homer turns the TV on with his tongue. *4F24 Lisa the Simpson*–A giant vine bursts out of the living room floor and the Simpsons sprout like vegetables; Bart is a strawberry; Homer is a squash; Marge is an asparagus; Maggie is an artichoke; and Lisa is a pineapple. *3G04 Simpson Tide*–The family does not rush in; instead, we see the Simpsons in their own version of "The Rocky & Bullwinkle Show" opening montage. Thunder and lightning reveal the silhouette of the family rushing toward the couch on a cliff, only to have it fall away. We see the Simpsons' outlines float through a mosaic of colors, and then, under a happy sun, they pop out of the ground in a flower patch. Bart spits out a clod of dirt with a flower planted in it. *5F09 Trash of the Titans*–Homer, Marge, Lisa, and Maggie rush in, only to find the living room replaced with a classroom. Bart stands at a board writing "I WILL NOT MESS WITH THE OPENING CREDITS" over and over again. *5F21 Wizard of Evergreen Terrace, AABF16 The Old Man and the "C" Student*–The family rushes in and has to work their way to the couch through movie seats filled by Principal Skinner, Agnes Skinner, Krusty, Sideshow Mel, Apu, Jimbo, Kearney, the Comic Book Guy, Ned and Maude Flanders, Mr. Burns, Smithers, Lenny, Moe, Hans Moleman, Ralph, Rod Flanders, Milhouse, and Willie. Several of the people in the seats have popcorn or sodas. Homer takes a handful of the Comic Book Guy's popcorn. *5F22 Bart the Mother, AABF12 Make Room for Lisa*–Firemen hold up the Simpsons' couch in the living room. Marge, Bart, Lisa, and Maggie fall from above frame onto the couch. A screaming Homer misses the couch and shoots through the floor, leaving a Homer-shaped hole behind him. *AABF01 Treehouse of Horror IX*–Freddy Krueger (from the *Nightmare on Elm Street* films) and Jason Vorhees (from the *Friday the 13th* films) sit on the couch, waiting for the Simpsons. Freddy turns to Jason, saying, "I don't get it, they should be here by now." Jason shrugs, replying, "Eh, what are you gonna do?" *5F19 When You Dish Upon a Star, AABF09 Homer to the Max*–A humming Marge rushes into the living room with a basket of laundry. She takes out what looks to be a sheet, but it turns out to be a flat, wet Homer. She snaps it out and clips it to a clothesline hanging across the living room. She subsequently pulls similar versions of Lisa, Bart, and Maggie out of the laundry basket and clips them to the clothesline as well. *AABF02 D'oh-in' in the Wind, AABF10 Marge Simpson in: "Screaming Yellow Honkers"*– The family rushes in and sits on the couch, which is equipped with a safety bar. The safety bar clicks down in front of the Simpsons, and the couch takes off, flying above the screen. It comes back down quickly, like a rollercoaster, and sweeps below screen as the Simpsons shout with glee. *AABF03 Lisa Gets an "A," AABF11 I'm with Cupid*–The family rushes in and sits on the couch. Suddenly, large hair dryers emerge from the back of the couch and place themselves on the Simpsons' heads. When they are removed, Homer has Maggie's hair, Marge has Bart's, Bart has Lisa's, Lisa has Homer's, and Maggie has Marge's. The weight of Marge's hairdo makes Maggie fall off the couch. *AABF07 Wild Barts Can't Be Broken, AABF15 Mom and Pop Art*–The family rushes in all wearing ten gallon cowboy hats. They leap onto the backrest of the couch, straddling it like a horse, and wave their hats. The endtable falls away, revealing tail fins on the couch. It now appears to be a bomb. The couch drops through the floor. We watch from above as the family hoot and holler as they fall through bombardier doors, plummeting to earth, like Slim Pickens in the film *Dr. Strangelove, or: How I Learned to Stop Worrying and Love the Bomb*. *AABF08 Sunday, Cruddy Sunday, AABF18 They Saved Lisa's Brain*–With the living room floor underwater, the family rushes in and sits on the couch. An iceberg floats by, grazing the couch and causing it to sink, taking the Simpsons and the endtable down with it. Maggie, on a cushion, emerges from the deep with the remote in her hand and changes the channel. *AABF13 Maximum Homerdrive*–The family rushes in and takes their place on the couch. Bart and Lisa are adult-sized, while Homer and Marge are like children. Homer, with a full head of hair and a Maggie doll, takes the remote from Lisa. Lisa takes it back, slapping his hand maternally. *AABF14 Simpsons Bible Stories*–Homer, Marge, Bart, and Lisa rush in, not noticing the five banana peels lying on the floor in front of the couch. They each slip and fly into the air, flipping over and landing on the couch. After they land, Maggie rushes in, slips on the remaining banana peel, flies into the air, and lands on Marge's lap. *AABF17 Monty Can't Buy Me Love, 9F08 Lisa's First Word, 9F13 I Love Lisa, 9F16 The Front, 9F22 Cape Feare, 2F08 $pringfield (Or, How I Learned to Stop Worrying and Love Legalized Gambling), 3F31 The Simpsons 138th Episode Spectacular*–The family rushes in. They dance in a chorus line. Soon, they are joined by high-kicking Rockettes, a variety of circus animals (including trained elephants), jugglers, trapeze artists, fire breathers, magicians, and Santa's Little Helper, who jumps through a hoop as circus music plays. *AABF20 30 Minutes Over Tokyo*–The family rushes to the couch. After sitting down, they are sucked into the cushions like paper into a shredder. Their shredded image slides out from under the cushions.

WHO DOES WHAT VOICE

DAN CASTELLANETA

Homer Simpson
Grampa Abraham Simpson
Barney Gumble
Krusty the Clown
Groundskeeper Willie
Mayor Quimby
Hans Moleman
Sideshow Mel
Itchy
Arnie Pie
Kodos
Louie
Bill
Captain Lance Murdock
Gary
Freddy Quimby
Poochie
Gil
Squeaky-Voiced Teen
Burns's Lawyer
Big Rich Texan
Fantastic Dan
Alfred E. Neuman (4F22)
Jimmy the Carriage Driver (4F22)
Soccer Hooligan (5F01)
Mall Executive (5F05)
Pope (5F05)
Angel (5F05)
Mr. Teeny (5F10)
Photographer Cop (5F12)
President Chimp (5F12)

Great Uncle Chet (4F24)
Stanley (4F24)
Simpson Men (4F24)
Big Donut (3G04)
Roddy McDonut (3G04)
Big Hand Guy (3G04)
Barney's Mother (3G04)
Lenin (3G04)
Janitor (3G04)
Fidel Castro (5F14)
Major Nougat (5F15)
Mojo (5F15)
Commie Nazi (5F16)
Old Curly (AABF04)
British Raj Man
    (Lost Soul) (AABF04)
Man in Dinner Jacket
    (Lost Soul) (AABF04)
Sad-Looking Frenchman
    (Lost Soul) (AABF04)
Ernie (AABF05)
Bloodening Boy (AABF07)
Postmaster Bill (AABF08)
Bill Clinton (AABF08)
Rudy (AABF08)
Vincent Price (AABF08)
Det. Lance Coffman (AABF09)
Australian Gamekeeper (AABF10)
Navitron Auto-Drive (AABF13)
Señor Ding-Dong (AABF13)
Pig of Eden (AABF14)
Cecil (Eurotrash) (AABF15)

Magic Fish (AABF20)
Mr. Pennybags (AABF20)

JULIE KAVNER

Marge Simpson
Patty Bouvier
Selma Bouvier

YEARDLEY SMITH

Lisa Simpson

NANCY CARTWRIGHT

Bart Simpson
Nelson Muntz
Todd Flanders
Ralph Wiggum
Kearney
Database

HANK AZARIA

Apu Nahasapeemapetilon
Moe Szyslak
Chief Clancy Wiggum
Comic Book Guy
Lou
Carl
Dr. Nick Riviera
Snake (Jailbird)
Kirk Van Houten
Captain McCallister (Sea
    Captain)
Bumblebee Man
Superintendent Chalmers

Professor John Frink
Cletus Del Roy
Legs
Drederick Tatum
Doug
Old Jewish Man
Gunter
Luigi
Pyro (a.k.a. Chase)
Duffman (4F22)
Khlav Kalash Vendor (4F22)
Fly-Headed Bart (5F02)
Gun Clerk (5F01)
Eddie Muntz (5F03)
Cornelius Talmadge (5F04)
PR Man (5F05)
Johnny D (5F06)
Nick Callahan (5F06)
Cliff (5F07)
Ad Exec (5F10)
Robbie the Automaton (5F13)
Asian Ensign (3G04)
Agent Miller (5F14)
Animal Assistants Clerk (5F15)
Head Chocobot (5F15)
Sherpa (5F16)
Larry the Bus Driver (5F17)
Farmer (5F18)
"Real" Comptroller
    Atkins (AABF03)
Big Tom (AABF05)
Det. Homer Simpson (AABF09)

Trent Steel (AABF09)
Stan (AABF10)
Red Carson (AABF13)
Doug Vaccaro (AABF15)
Gunter (Eurotrash) (AABF15)
Arthur Fortune (AABF17)
Chuck Garabedian (AABF20)

HARRY SHEARER

C. Montgomery Burns
Waylon Smithers
Ned Flanders
Principal Skinner
Otto the Bus Driver
Reverend Timothy Lovejoy
Dr. Julius Hibbert
Kent Brockman
Jasper
Lenny
Eddie
Rainier Wolfcastle/McBain
Scratchy
Kang
Herman
Marty
Dr. Loren J. Pryor
Benjamin
Judge Snyder
George Bush
Officer Steve Grabowski (4F22)
Armin Tamzarian (4F23)
Fox Censor (5FO2)

French President (5FO2)
Security Salesman (5F01)
Ernst (5F04)
Glen the Recruiter (5F23)
Movementarian Leader (5F23)
Ad Exec (5F10)
General Donut (3G04)
Agent Johnson (5F14)
Harry S Truman (5F14)
Sanjay (5F14)
Sherpa (5F16)
Thomas Edison's Ghost (5F21)
"Comptroller Atkins"
    (Otto) (AABF03)
Caribbean Outcast
    (Lost Soul) (AABF04)
Dennis Conroy (AABF07)
Bill Clinton (AABF09)
Curtis E. Bear (Eddie) (AABF10)
Burning Bush (AABF14)
IOC Chairman (AABF16)

MARCIA WALLACE

Edna Krabappel

RUSSI TAYLOR

Martin Prince
Uter
Sherri/Terri
Lewis
Wendell

PAMELA HAYDEN

Milhouse Van Houten
Rod Flanders
Janey Powell
Jimbo Jones
Malibu Stacy
Chin Ho (3G02)
Patches (5F07)
Jane the Recruiter (5F23)
Female Ensign (3G04)
Amber (AABF06)
Bloodening Girl (AABF07)
Sarah Wiggum (AABF11)

TRESS MACNEILLE

Dolph
Sunday School Teacher
Brandine Del Roy
Agnes Skinner
Gavin
Psychic
Billy
Manjula's Mother (5F04)
Cookie Kwan (5F06)
Poor Violet (5F07)
Humphrey the Camel (5F08)
Spud (5F08)
Dr. Simpson (4F24)
Cat Lady (5F15)
Channel 6 Executive (5F15)
Mother Simpson at
    Commune (AABF02)

Woman in Wedding Dress
    (Lost Soul) (AABF04)
Nerdy Young Woman (AABF05)
Ginger (AABF06)
Bloodening Boy (AABF07)
Nelson's Mother (AABF07)
Bernice Hibbert (AABF11)
Sergeant Crew (AABF10)
OmniTouch Rep (AABF12)
New Age Clerk (AABF12)
Gwen the Waitress (AABF13)
Gary the Unicorn (AABF14)
Lindsey Naegle (AABF18)
Boudoir Photographer (AABF18)

MAGGIE ROSWELL

Maude Flanders
Helen Lovejoy
Miss Hoover
Luann Van Houten
Princess Kashmir
Shary Bobbins
Kindergarten Teacher (3G02)
Bloodening Girl (AABF07)
F-Series Canyonero (AABF10)

DORIS GRAU

Lunchlady Doris

Songs Sung Simpson!

Included here are song lyrics and musical number descriptions from seasons nine and ten of *The Simpsons*, along with others from seasons one through eight that were not included in *The Simpsons: A Complete Guide To Our Favorite Family.*

The "Cut Every Corner" Song
(sung to a tune resembling "A Spoonful of Sugar")

(Shary Bobbins, Bart, and Lisa stand in Bart's extremely messy room.)

Shary Bobbins: *If there's a task that must be done,*
don't turn your tail and run!
Don't pout! Don't sob!
Just do a half-assed job!
(Shary takes the blanket off Bart's bed and covers up the mess of toys and clothes on his mattress.)
If you cut every corner,
it is really not so bad.
Everybody does it,
even Mom and Dad.
(Shary gestures outside to Homer throwing a broken-down couch into the Flanderses' yard.)
If nobody sees it, then nobody gets mad!
Bart: *It's the American way!*
(Bart sweeps items off of his bureau and crams them into a drawer. Lisa shoves a football, a kickball, and an apple core under the bed. Bart does the same with a box containing toys, a keyboard, and half a sandwich. Lisa shoves toys and Maggie into a toy chest. Bart empties a wastebasket out the window and then tosses the basket out. Shary and Lisa watch Bart throw clothes into the closet.)
Shary Bobbins: *The policeman on the beat needs some time to rest his feet.*
(In a park, Chief Wiggum sits on a bench, fanning a shoeless foot, as Snake robs Hans Moleman in the background.)
Chief Wiggum: *Fighting crime is not my cup of tea!*
(In the Kwik-E-Mart, Apu blows dirt off of a dirty hot dog. Shary Bobbins appears in a picture on back of a milk carton.)
Shary Bobbins: *And the clerk who runs the store can charge a little more for meat!*
Apu: (echoes) *For meat!*
Shary Bobbins: *And milk!*
Apu: (echoes) *And milk!*
Shary Bobbins and Apu: *From 1984!*
(The Simpsons and Shary Bobbins admire Bart's sparkling clean room.)
If you cut every corner, you'll have more time for play!
Shary Bobbins and the Simpsons: *It's the American way!*
(They march out and Homer slams the door. All of the items they shoved away—including Maggie—pop back out. The room is once again a mess.)

(From 3G03, "Simpsoncalifragilisticexpiala(D'oh)cious")

The "Kamp Krusty" Song

(Jimbo, Dolph, and Kearney lead the children—who are sitting on bleachers—in song. Jimbo conducts, Dolph plays guitar.)

Children: *Hail to thee Kamp Krusty*
By the shores of Big Snake Lake.
Though your swings are rusty,
We know they'll never break.
Kearney: *Louder! Faster!*
Children: *From your gleaming mess hall,*
(A frog jumps out of a bowl of gruel Lisa is about to eat.)
To your hallowed baseball field,
(Bart, running and trying to catch a fly ball, falls into an open pit.)
To your spic and span infirmary, where all our wounds are healed.
(An elderly nurse strikes a match on the cast of a red-headed kid with a broken arm, lights her cigarette, and blows smoke in the kid's face.)
Hail to thee Kamp Krusty/Below Mount Avalanche.
(Bart, Lisa, and Milhouse run down a hill followed by several large tumbling boulders.)
We will always love Kamp Krusty,
A registered trademark of the Krusty Corporation.
All rights reserved.
(The bleachers collapse.)

(From 8F24, "Kamp Krusty")

Theme to "You Only Move Twice"
(sung Shirley Bassey-style to a tune resembling "Goldfinger")

Scorpio!
He'll sting you with his dreams of power and wealth!
Beware of Scorpio!
His twisted twin obsessions are his plot to rule the world
And his employees' health!
He'll welcome you into his lair
Like the nobleman welcomes his guest!
With free dental care and a stock plan that helps you invest!
But beware of his generous pensions
Plus three weeks paid vacation each year!
And on Fridays the lunchroom serves hot dogs and burgers and beer!
He loves German beer!

(From 3F23, "You Only Move Twice")

The "Kids/Adults" Song
(sung to the tune of "Kids" from the musical *Bye Bye Birdie*)

(The Springfield adults and kids face off as they begin to sing to one another.)

Kids: *Adults!*
Adults: *Kids!*
Kids: *Adults!*
Adults: *Kids!*
Kids: *Adults!*
Reverend Lovejoy: *Kids, you've had your fun, now we've had our fill!*
Homer: *Yeah, you're only here 'cause Marge forgot her pill!*
(Marge turns around, embarrassed. Nelson spraypaints "OINK" on an oblivious Chief Wiggum's butt.)
Wiggum: *Kids, you're all just scandalizing, vandalizing punks!*
(Krusty walks through the crowd of children.)
Krusty: *Channel hoppin', Ritalin-poppin' monkeys...*
(Krusty leans in to Alison Taylor.)
Krusty: *But please don't quit the fan club!*
Marge: *Kids, I could nag and nag 'til my hair turns blue!*
Mrs. Krabappel: *Kids, you bum my smokes and don't say "Thank you!"*
Rod and Todd Flanders: *Why can't you be like we are?*
(Rod and Todd are splattered with a hail of tomatoes.)
Adults: *Oh, what a bunch of brats!*
Moe: *We oughta drown you just like cats.*
(Snowball II leaps out of his sack he holds up.)
Bart: *Adults! You run our lives like you're Colonel Klink!*
Nelson: *Adults! You strut around like your farts don't stink!*
Lisa: *Adults! You're such a drooling, snoring, boozing, boring bunch! Surly, meany, three-martini lunchers!*
Ralph: *I just ate a thumbtack!*
Milhouse: *Adults! They're always tellin' us to—*
(Grampa yanks Milhouse by the neck with his cane, pulling him close.)
Grampa: *Shut your traps!*
Jasper: *Eh, we're fed-up with all you whipper-snaps!*
(A group of senior citizens converge on the adults and kids.)
Seniors: *We're trying to get some sleep here, it's almost six-fifteen! What's the matter with—*
Adults: *Don't you treat us like—*
Kids: *Can't you just lay off—*
Seniors: *We're sick of all of you!*
All: *Kiiiids tooday!*

(From AABF07, "Wild Barts Can't Be Broken")

"The Garbageman" Song

(The family is visiting Homer in his new office.)

Marge: *I'm really proud of you, Homey. But can the garbageman really do all the things you said?*
Homer: *Oh, the garbageman can, Marge.*
(Homer snaps his fingers and is suddenly dressed in a fancy garbageman uniform.)
Homer: *The garbageman can.*
(Homer snaps his fingers and is suddenly atop a Springfield garbage truck. He points forward and leads a fleet of trucks away. A tune resembling "The Candyman" begins to play.)

Homer: *Who can take your trash out? Stomp it down for you?*
(Atop the truck, Homer passes through a neighborhood as fancy-dressed garbagemen take trashcans to the curb and stomp down their trash.)
Homer: *Shake the plastic bag and do the twisty thingie too? The garbageman!*
(The garbagemen tie up the garbage bags and leap onto the sides of Homer's garbage truck, holding their hats out in a flourish.)
Garbagemen: *Oh, the garbageman can!*
(Krusty is taking out a box labeled, "Used Up Porno" when the garbage truck pulls up. Two smiling garbagemen leap off the truck and toss the box on the heap. Krusty weakly smiles and waves.)
Garbagemen: *The garbageman can, and he does it with a smile and never judges you.*
(In the Simpson kitchen, Marge removes one of Maggie's diapers and turns to Bart and Lisa.)
Marge: *Who can take this diaper?*
(Lisa and Bart hold their noses and wave it away. A garbageman looks in through the kitchen window, taking the diaper.)
Garbageman: *I don't mind at all.*
(Chief Wiggum, in a tuxedo, eats a hot dog in his bedroom. He has a huge mustard stain on his shirt.)
Wiggum: *Who can clean me up before the big policeman's ball? The garbageman!*
(Two garbagemen race in and scrub Wiggum's shirt.)
Garbageman: *Yes, the garbageman can!*
(At Moe's, U2 sits at the bar, holding up their beer mugs and swaying.)
U2: *The sanitation folks are jolly, friendly blokes, courteous and easygoing!*
(A garbageman walks across the bar, mopping up, as another garbageman whispers something to Bono.)
The Edge: *They mop up when you're overflowing!*
(We see another shot of U2 sitting on their barstools, revealing that their rears are exposed. Each member of the band pulls up their pants.)
Bono: *And tell you when your ass is showing!*
(Garbagemen parade through Springfield, holding trashcans. Apu pops up out of one, followed by Sideshow Mel, Ned Flanders, and Oscar the Grouch.)
Apu: *Who can...*
Sideshow Mel: *Who can...*
Ned: *Who can...*
Oscar: *Who can...*
(Homer leads a procession of garbagemen playing trash lids like cymbals and cans like drums, followed by trucks.)
Homer: *The garbageman can!*
(Lisa and Bart rush in to march with him.)
Lisa and Bart: *'Cause he's Homer Simpson, man!*
Everyone: *He cleans the world for you!*
(As the parade marches into the city dump, the townspeople cheer.)

(From 5F09, "Trash of the Titans")

"Checkin' In" from the musical "Kickin' It: A Musical Journey through the Betty Ford Center"

(Onstage, a hiply dressed young celebrity stands before a judge and jury.)
Judge: *How do you find the defendant?*
Jury Foreman: *He's guilty of mayhem, exposure indecent.*
Jurist #1: *Freaked-out behavior both chronic and recent.*
Jury: *Drinking and driving, narcotics possession.*
Jurist #2: *And that's just page one of his ten page confession!*
Judge: *I should put you away where you can't kill or maim us, but this is LA and you're rich and famous!*
(The courtroom set revolves around into a set depicting the Betty Ford Center.)
Young Celebrity: *I'm checkin' in!*
(Doctors stand around a hockey player and a starlet, each in hospital beds.)
Doctors and Patients: *He's checkin' in!*
Young Celebrity: *I'm checkin' in!*
Doctors and Patients: *Checkin', checkin' in!*
Young Celebrity: *No more pills or alcohol, no more pot or Demorol, no more stinking fun at all! I'm checkin' in!*
(The doctors start pushing beds all around the Young Celebrity as they sing.)
Doctors and Patients: *He's checkin' in! He's checkin' in!*
Doctor: *No more looking pale and thin, no more bugs beneath your skin!*
(While aides take away the Young Celebrity's belt and shoelaces, the doctor takes a bottle of pills out of the Young Celebrity's jacket pocket.)
Young Celebrity: *Hey, that's just my aspirin!*
Doctors and Patients: *Chuck it out!*
(The doctor tosses the bottle into a wastebasket held by an aide.)
Doctors and Patients: *You're checkin' in!*

(From 4F23, "The City of New York vs. Homer Simpson")

The "Canyonero" Jingle

Can you name the truck with four-wheel drive,
smells like a steak, and seats thirty-five?
Canyonero! Canyonero!
Well, it goes real slow with the hammer down.
It's the country-fried truck endorsed by a clown.
Canyonero! Canyonero!
Hey, hey!
Twelve yards long, two lanes wide,
sixty-five tons of American pride!
Canyonero! Canyonero!
Top of the line in utility sports,
unexplained fires are a matter for the courts!
Canyonero! Canyonero!
She blinds everybody with her super high-beams.
She's a squirrel-squashin', deer-smackin' drivin' machine.
Canyonero! Canyonero! Canyonero!
Whoa, Canyonero! Whoa!

(From 5F10, "The Last Temptation of Krust")

"Bagged Me a Homer"
(sung by Lurleen Lumpkin)

Oh, the bases were empty on the diamond of my heart,
when the coach called me up to the plate.
I'd been swingin' and missin'
and lovin' and kissin'.
My average was point-double-o-eight.
So I spit on my hands,
knocked the dirt from my spikes,
And pointed right towards center field.
This time I'm hittin' the home run.
This time love is for real.
I'll slide, I'll steal, I'll sacrifice,
a lovin' fly for you.
I've been slumpin' off season,
but now I've found a reason.
I've struck on a love that is true.
I used to play the field.
I used to be a roamer,
But season's turnin' around for me now.
I've finally bagged me a homer.
That's right, I've finally bagged me a homer.

(From 8F19, "Colonel Homer")

The "Chimpan-A to Chimpan-Z" song from the musical, *Stop the Planet of the Apes, I Want to Get Off!*
(sung by Troy McClure as Charlton Heston)

Troy: *I hate every ape I see, from chimpan-A to chimpan-Z.*
No, you'll never make a monkey out of me!
(A destroyed Statue of Liberty rises from the stage.)
Oh my god, I was wrong.
It was Earth, all along.
You finally made a monkey
Ensemble: *Yes, we finally made a monkey*
Troy: *Yes, you finally made a monkey out of me!*
Troy: *I love you, Dr. Zaius!*

(From 3F15, "A Fish Called Selma")

22 Short Films about Springfield, 10–11, 62–63
30 Minutes Over Tokyo, 78–79
33¢ Store, 78–79
401K, 66
9 1/2 Weeks, 52
99 Hilarious Phone Messages, 33

A

Abraham, F. Murray, 55
Acme Piano Wire, 21
Acne Grease Co., 46–47
Ad Execs, **29**
Adam (see also Simpson, Homer), 70–71
Admiral Baby, 62–63
Adult Education Annex, 74
Advanced Capital Ventures, 76–77
Affleck, Neil, 20, 33, 58–59
Ah, Fudge!, 28
Aikman, Troy, 61
air conditioner, 13
air duct, 46–47
Air India, 18–19
Air Supply, 58–59
Airport Refueling Way, 41
Akbar & Jeff, 72–73
Albright, Madeleine, 76–77
Alec–and–Ron–and–Kimorabilia, 52
Alfalfa Bits, 54
Ali, Muhammad, 75, 78–79
Alice Doesn't Live Anymore, 32
Alien Biopsy, 56–57
"All in the Family 1999," 62–63
All Pets Great and Cheap, 29
Allah, 66
Allen, Woody, 10–11
alternative medicine, 67
Amber, **58**–59
"America's Funniest Tornadoes," 62–63
America's Most Livable Cities, 76–77
America's Trash Hole, 38–39
American Gladiators, The, 12
American Red Cross, 62–63
Americatown Restaurant, 78–79
Anderson, Bob, 22–23, 54, 64–65
Anderson, Mike B., 29, 55
Angel Skeleton, **20**
angel, grease, 46–47
Animal Assistants, 37
Another Simpsons Clip Show, 24
"Antiques Appraisal," 75
anus, hog, 46–47
ape–poopy, 76–77
Apes–A–Poppin', 55
Apocalypse Now, 62–63
Appel, Richard, 18–19, 52
Apple Pick, 46–47
applesauce–cicity, 40
Apu's Mother, **18**–19
Aquaman, 14–15
Arf Bag, 42–43
Arizona State, 72–73
Arlen, Texas, 17
Army Proving Ground, 41
arts, French, 64–65
ass–whomping, old fashioned, hippie, 53
Atkins, State Comptroller, Phony, 54
Atlanta, 68–69
auction, bachelor, 18–19
Australian Gamekeeper, 66
automatic hammer, 48
Avery, Tex, 68–69
Aztec Theater, 14–15, 42–43

B

Back–to–Schooliosis, 46–47
Baldwin, Alec, 52
Barbara (Sideshow Mel's friend), 64–65
Barbarella, 56–57
Barclay, Red, 68–69
Barnacle Bill's Anger Management Center, 55
Baron Von's Munch House, 64–65
Bart After Dark, 24
Bart Carny, 25, 49
Bart Gets an Elephant, 18–19
Bart Jr., **49**
Bart of Darkness, 13
Bart Sells his Soul, 22–23, 24
Bart Star, 17, 78–79
Bart the Fink, 29
Bart the Genius, 8–9
Bart the Mother, 49
Bart the Murderer, 56–57
Bart's Comet, 12, 33
Bart's Girlfriend, 14–15
Bart's Inner Child, 41

"Bart's People," 37
Bart-Bart, 52
Bart-Headed Fly, 14–15
Bartman, 76–77
baseball bat, 56–57
Basinger, Kim, 52
bastard, magnificent, 26–27
bathroom, stained glass, 32
"Batman Theme, The", 26–27
Baum, Bruce, 29
BB gun, 49
BBQ Pit Kit, 72–73
Beast, Sign of the, 17
Beavis & Butthead, 53
Bee Gees, The, 13
beef poisoning, 68–69
beef stew, 8–9
Beer Paste, 48
Begley, Ed, Jr., 62–63
Belushi, Jim, 78–79
Ben & His Rat Army, 8–9
Ben Hur, 10–11
Benjamin, 26–27, 56–57
Berating Room, 56–57
Berlin Wall, 8–9, 34–35
Bevering, 12
"Bewitched," 55
Bi-Mon-Sci-Fi-Con, 56–57
Big Tom, 56–57
bigamy, 58–59
Bill of Rights, 67
Bill, **48**
Bill, Postmaster, 61
Billionaire Beat, 75
Billy, 32, 49
Billy Beer, 20
Bird, Brad, 8–9
Birds: Our Fine Feathered Colleagues, 49
birthing babies, 41
Blackenstein, 34–35
Blackula, 34–35
Blisstonia, 26–27
Bloated Liver, The, 29
Blood Feud, 52
Bloodbath & Beyond, 16
Bloodbath Gulch, 55
Bloodening, The, 60
Blottos, 29
Blunchblack of Blotre Blame, The, 34–35
blunderbuss, 75
boar, wild, 28
boat show, 44–45
boat:
    glass bottom, 25
    sinking, 74
    tour, 74
Bodyguard, The, 56–57
Bolger, Ray, 52
Bolivian tree lizards, 49
Bolognium, 54
bomb shelter, 14–15
Bombay, Dr., 55
Bongo, 67
Bongo Comics, 56–57
Bono, 38–39
Boo–Boo, 52
booby, 49
boot (parking enforcement device), 10–11
Borgs, 56–57
Boudoir Photography, 76–77
Bouvier, Patty, 8–9, 14–15, 16, 38–39, 61, 74
Bouvier, Selma, 14–15, 16, 17, 38–39, 74
Boy Scoutz-N the Hood, 24
Brad, **40**
Braille Weekly, 37
brainwashing, 26–27
Bran Munch, 54
Brando, Marlon, 62–63
bribes, 56–57
"Brick House," 30–31
Bright Pack, The, 76–77
British Museum, 70–71
Brockman, Kent, 8–9, 16, 20, 22–23, 26–27, 29, 34–35, 48, 58–59, 60, 66, 75
Broken Home Chimney Repair, 53
Brother, Can You Spare Two Dimes?, 28
Buddha, 66
Bumblebee Man, 61
bunny, chocolate, 70–71
Burns Casino, 18–19, 58–59
Burns Heir, 60
Burns, Baby Burns, 21
Burns, C. Montgomery, 8–9, 16, 22–24, 26–27, 33, 36, 53, 58–60 ,67, 72–77
Burns, Larry, 21

burrito, after-dinner, 32
Bush, George, 21
Butler, Rhett, 74
Butt, King (see also Skinner, Principal Seymour), 70–71
butt:
    butt.butt, 52
    metal plate in, 13
    rod up, 12
    rubber, 13
Butterbaby Flapjacks, 40
butterscotch pond, 70–71
By the Numbers Productions, 62–63
Bye Bye Birdie, 60

C

C.H.U.D., 10–11
Call Me Delish–Mael, 55
Calvin Klein's Pretension, 46–47
Camaros, 50–51
"Can't Buy Me Love," 74
"Can't Somebody Else Do It?," 38–39
"Candle in the Wound," 50–51
Candy Warhol, 54
Candyland, 76–77
Canine Mutiny, The, 26–27
Canyonero, 66
Canyonero, F–Series, 66
Capital City, 12
Capital City Goofball, The, 8–9, 62–63
Capitol City, 17
Capture the Flag, 40
car battery, genitals hooked to, 56–57
carbon monoxide, 42–43
Carl, 10–11, 38–39, 41–43, 55, 58–61, 67, 70–71, 75–77
Carlin, George, 53
Cartridge Family, The, 16
Cary, Donick, 29, 50–51, 53, 78–79
Casablanca, 42–43
castrati, 18–19
Castro, Fidel, 36
Cat Fight, 17
Cat Lady, 37
cattle prod, 75
Cayman Islands, 78–79
CB codes, 68–69
CBP (crippling balloon payment), 66
CBS network, 14–15, 66
Cecil (Eurotrash), 72–73
Cellular transmitters:
    (see also Keep in Touch Towers), 67
Central Park, 10–11
Cess Hole 17A:
    (see also Lake Springfield), 52
Chalmers, Superintendant, 12, 54, 66, 74
Channel 6, 32, 37
Charlie, 36, 52, 61
Charlie Brown Christmas, A, 22–23
Chase:
    (see also Pyro), 12, 54, 60, 72–73
Cheaterly, Lady:
    (see also Simpson, Lisa), 54
"Cheers," 62–63
Cherry Garcia, 54
cherry picker, 41
Chevrolet, 68–69
Chewbacca, 56–57
Chez Guevara, 36
Chief Break–Everything, 74
Child's Garden of Edison, A, 48
"Children Are Our Future, The", 74
China, 12
China, Great Wall of, 8–9
Chinatown, 10–11
Chinese needle snakes, 49
Chippos, 28, 41
Chirpy Boy, **49**
choir boy, noodle–armed, 26–27
cholesterol, 17
chopsticks, 28
Christ, Jesus, 22–23, 29, 66, 70–71
Christmas, 22–23
Christmas II, 38–39
Christmas–Hanu–Kwanzaa spend phase, 38–39
Church, the Catholic, 61
chutzpah, 29
cigars, 48
Ciggy, 74
City of New York vs. Homer Simpson, The, 10–11
Clash, The, 42–43
Clayton, Adam, 38–39
clean living, 58–59
Clean, Mr:
    (see also Flanders, Ned), 58–59
Clinton, President Bill, 61–63
Clobbersaurus, 78–79

Clokey, Art, 70–71
Clomp, 56–57
"Close to You," 68–69
Coco, 37
Cohen, David S., 20, 28, 49–51
Coleco, 21, 54
Collier's Magazine, 36
Colonel Homer, 20
Columbo, 34–35
Comic Book Guy, The, 14–15, 18–19, 26–27, 40, 52, 56–59, 61–63, 75–77
Commie–nazis, 40
Commodores, The, 30–31
communes, 53
community service, 74
Compu–Global Hyper–Mega Net, 28
Concert Against Bangledesh, 64–65
Continental Soccer Association, 16
conversation hat, 32
Cooder, **25**
Copperfield, David, 10–11
corn, creamed, 37
Corpsy the Clown:
　　(see also Krusty the Clown), 29
Corpulent Cowboy, The, 53
Costington's, 38–39, 62–63
Count Caroba, 54
Court Ordered Productions, 66
Crackton, 41
crap rock, 58–59
crap–tacular, 22–23
crapweeds, 12
Crash Bandicoot, 54
Crawford, Cindy, 34–35
Creepy Bloodening Kids, The, **60**
Cremium, 12
Crepes of Wrath, The, 8–9, 10–11
Crew, Sergeant, 66
Criss, Peter, 28
Cuba, 36
cuckoo, 49
cults, 26–27
curfew, 60
Curious George and the Ebola Virus, 13

D

D vs. G2: Stone Cold, 70–71
D'oh–in' In The Wind, 53
D.J. Jazzy Jeff, 44–45
Dalai Lama, 41
Dali, Salvador, 72–73
Dan, Fantastic, 64–65
dance, school, 46–47
Dancers, Solid Gold, 78–79
Dancin' Homer, 20
dancing, irish, 17
dangerous emissions supervisor, 36
Daniels, William, 48
Das Bus, 28
Dash Dingo, 54
Database, 33
dates, pity, 30–31
Davey and Goliath, 70–71
Davey Jones's Hamper, 55
David vs. Super–Goliath, 28
da Vinci, Leonardo, 72–73
Davis, Mac, 78–79
Davis, Sammy, Jr., 67
Day the Earth Stood Still, The, 56–57
Dead Putting Society, 42–43
deductions, 36
Deep Space Homer, 20, 34–35
"Deep, Deep Trouble," **44–45**
Deer Hunter, The, 34–35
Def Leppard, 25, 49
DeLochinator, The, 75
Delroy, Brandine, 41
Delroy, Cletus, 16, 41, 52, 58–59
DeLuise, Dom, 50–51
demolition derby, 67
Denver, Bob, 34–35
deprogramming, 26–27
designated driver, 10–11
Desmond Tutti–Frutti, 54
Detroit, Nathan:
　　(see also Hamill, Mark), 56–57
Devil, 8–9, 44–45
devil sticks, 53
Dietter, Susie, 32
digestive system, model of, 64–65
Digital Puppet News Team, 78–79
Ding–Dong, Señor, 21, **68–**69
Dingo Junction, 46–47
diplomatic immunity, 28, 67
Dirty Bird, 61
"Disco Duck," 13
Disco Stu, 18–19
Discover cards, 46–47
Disneyland, 55, 61
Divorce Specialists, The, 42–43
DJ 3000, 48
DMY (Don't Mess Yourself), 46–47
DNA, 14–15

"Do The Bartman," **8–9**, 34–35
Doc Martens, 55
Dockers, 53
Doctor Who, 56–57
dodo, 49
dog carrier, 64–65
Dog–Doo Stick, The, 58–59
dog–doo, flaming bag of, 68–69
Dollywood, 61
Dolph, 33
domino effect, 62–63
Donner's Party Supplies, 46–47
doowhacky, 14–15
Doris, Lunchlady, 12
DOS, 76–77
Doug, 26–27, 56–57
Doyle, Larry, 37, 50–51, 60, 70–71
drawbridge, 41
Dress Up Plus, 18–19
Duff Cheerleaders, 10–11
Duff Extra Cold, 10–11
Duff Partymobile, 10–11
Duffman, **10–**11
Dumbell Indemnity, 30–31
dune buggies, 36
Dupes Casino, 58–59

E

E.T., 78–79
Earwigs—Eeeew!, 49
East River, 10–11
East St. Louis, 76–77
Easter, 70–71
Easter Island, 18–19
Eastwood, Clint, 24
"Easy Bake Coven," 14–15
Easy–Bake Oven, 49
"Eat my shorts," 13
Eatie Gourmet's, 54
Eddie, 22–23, 50–51, 62–63, 72–73
Eden, 70–71
Edge, Graeme, 58–59
Edge, The, 38–39
Edison Museum, 48
Edison, Thomas, 48
egg, cartoon, 33
eggs, lizard, 49
Egyptians, 8–9
eight track tapes, 13, 42–43
Einstein, Rembrandt Q.:
　　(see also Simpson, Homer), 62–63
electric chair, 33, 44–45
electric hats, 58–59
eldtown, 64–65
emergency room, 41
Emma, 24
emperor, Japanese, 78–79
End of the Line, 41
Energy Shortage, 60
Englund, Robert, 50–51
Enriched Learning Center for Gifted Children, 8–9
Ernie, 56–57
Ernst, 18–19, 58–59
Ervin, Mark, 24, 60, 75
Etern–A–Bond Glue, 41
"Ethnic Mismatch Comedy #644," 76–77
Euro–Dollywood, 61
Eve:
　　(see also Simpson, Marge), 70–71
Ex–Con Security, 16
Executioner Donut, The, 34–35
"Exodus," 70–71
"Exploitation Theater," 34–35
extra–sensory perception, 60
extreme sports, 75

F

facelifts, botched, 37
Faculty Talent Show, 66
Family Fun Center, 49
Farmer Homer's XX Sugar, 20
Farmer, **42–**43
Fartacus, 21
FBI, 36
FCC Educational Programming Requirement, 37
Fear of Flying, 26–27, 62–63
Fiber Bites, 54
fingerprints, 30–31
Finkel, Fyvush, 13
fire truck, remote control, 22–23
Firestone, Roy, 17
Fireworks, Candy and Puppy Dog Store, The, 74
First Aid, 17
First Church of Springfield, 70–71
Fish Called Selma, A, 34–35
fish gutting, 78–79
Five Sleazy Pieces, 10–11
Flanders, Maude, 14–15, 21, 58–59, 61, 64–65, 72–73, 78–79
Flanders, Ned, 13, 16–17, 20–21, 26–27, 29, 34–36, 40, 44–45, 48, 52–53, 58–59, 61–65, 67, 70–73, 76–77, 78–79
　　(see also Clean, Mr.), 58–59
　　(see also God), 70–71

　　(see also La Femme, Churchy), 58–59
　　(see also Neddy, Steady), 58–59
　　age of, 58–59
Flanders, Rod, 17, 29, 40, 52, 58–59, 67
Flanders, Todd, 17, 29, 44–45, 52, 58–59
Fleetwood Mac, 13
Flynt, Larry, 76–77
flower arranging, 78–79
Floyd the Robot:
　　(see also Robbie the Automaton), 33
"Fly vs. Fly," 14–15, 33
Fly–Headed Bart, 14–15
Fonzie, 67
football, pee–wee, 17
Forbidden Closet of Mystery, 33
forbidden fruit, 70–71
Force, The, 56–57
Foreigner, 18–19
forks, the, 56–57
form, "Purpose of Visit," 36
Fortress of Solitude, 40
Fortune Megastores, 75
Fortune, Arthur, **75**
Fourth Grade Dance Recital, 8–9
Fox Censor, 14–15
Fox Network, 32, 50–51, 62–63, 66, 78–79
Foxx, Redd, 29
France, 14–15
Fraser, Brendan, 40
fraud, insurance, 30–31
freak bus, 53
freak–out, 53
freak, sexless, 66
Freak–E–Mart, 32
Fried Green Tomatoes, 64–65
Frink, Professor John, 14–15, 18–19, 26–27, 56–57, 60, 72–73, 75–77
Frisbee, 67
Frostillicus, 32
Frosty Krusty Flakes, 64–65
Fuhreriffic, 25
funeral processions, 66
"Futurama," 56–57

G

Game of Lent, The, 60
Gamera, 78–79
Ganesh, 18–19, 67, 75
Garabedian, Chuck, **78–**79
Garden Blast Juice, 53
garden parties, 62–63
Garofalo, Janeane, 29
Gary, 26–27, 56–57
Gassy Knoll, The, 68–69
Gates, Bill, 28
Gehrig, Lou, 55, 67
genetics, 32
"Gentle Ben," 13
George Thorogood & the Destroyers, 30–31
Geraldine, 33
Gere, Richard, 16
Gifford, Kathy Lee, 50–51
Gil, **21**, 29, 42–43, 54, 58–59, 68–69
Gilded Truffle, The, 30–31, 42–43
Gilligan, 34–35
Ginger, **58–**59
Girly Edition, 37
Glen, **26–**27
Global Dynamics, Inc., 72–73
go–karts, 49
goat placenta, 58–59
God (see also Flanders, Ned), 70–71
Godfather's Parts II, The, 10–11
Godzilla, 56–57, 78–79
Golddigger's Casino, 58–59
Goldreyer, Ned, 32
Goldthwait, Bobcat, 29
Goliath II:
　　(see also Muntz, Nelson), 70–71
Gone Fission II, 74
Gone with the Wind, 74
Goodman, Benny, 67
Goody New Shoes, 29
Gooey, 37
"Gorilla Island Six," 55
"Gorilla Squadron," 55
gorillas, 49
Gort, 56–57
Gould, Stephen J., 20
Grabowski, Officer Steve, 10–11
Grammy Award, 20
Grampa vs. Sexual Inadequacy, 46–47
Grandma Plopwell's Pudding, 76–77
Grateful Dead, The, 53
Graves, Peter, 75
Graveyard of the Future, 48
gravy level, 17
Gray, Milton, 34–35
Grazer, Brian, 52
Greaney, Dan, 21, 33, 64–65, 78–79
grease, retirement, 46–47
Grier, Rosey, 61
Grimes, Frank "Grimey," 42–43

grinders, 68–69
Groening, Matt, 8–9, 44–45, 56–57, 72–73
groin, kicks to, 17
Groovy Grove Natural Farm, The, 53
Guevara, Che, 36
Gumble, Barney, 8–11, 18–19, 30–31, 34–35, 44–45, 60–61, 72–73, 76–79
Gummi Venus de Milo, 22–23
Gun Salesman, **16**
Gunter, 18–19, 58–59
Gunter (Eurotrash), 72–73
Gutter Room, The, 29
Guys and Dolls, 56–57

H

hackey sack, 53
Hagman, Larry, 55
Hail to the Chimp, 30–31
Hair, 53
Hairy Shearers, 18–19
Hall of Wonders, 33
Hall, Klay, 42–43
Halley's Comet, 49
hallucinations, 53, 67
Ham, 33
Hamill, Mark:
    (see also Detroit, Nathan), 56–57
Happy Little Elves, 25, 46–47, 49
"Happy Smile Super Challenge Family Wish Show," 78–79
Hard Day's Night, A, 74
Harrelson, Woody, 62–63
Hartman, Phil, 49
harvest, lima bean, 26–27
Hauge, Ron, 22–23, 30–31, 56–57
Haunted Cash Machine, 32
Hawaii, 30–31
Hawking, Stephen, 76–77
Hayward, Justin, 58–59
HDTV, 36
health inspector, 64–65
Healthy Charms, 54
Heavenly Hills Mall, 20
Heckle and Jeckle, 48
Heinrich's Monocle Shop, 53
"Hell Toupee," 50–51
hemp, 62–63
Her Majesty's Batting Cage, 42–43
Herman, 8–9, 62–63, 75
Hibbert, Dr. Julius, 14–17, 20, 36, 41, 50–51, 55, 60–61, 67–69, 75–77
Hibbert, Mrs. Bernice, 60
"Highway to Hell," 70–71
Hill, Hank, 17
hillbilly Jacuzzi, 52
hippies, 53, 62–63
Hippo in the House, 60
Hitler, Adolph, 25, 42–43, 60, 67
hoagies, 68–69
Hoffa, Jimmy, 68–69
holy water, 58–59
home security, 16
Home Sweet Homediddly-Dum-Doodily, 32
"HΩmega Man, The", 14–15
Homer and Apu, 24, 64–65
Homer Badman, 22–23
Homer Defined, 29, 72–73
Homer Goes to College, 26–27, 56–57
Homer Simpson in: "Kidney Trouble", **55**
Homer Simpson Program, The, 58–59
Homer the Great, 24, 67
Homer They Fall, The, 20, 36, 58–59
Homer to the Max, 62–63
Homer vs. the Eighteenth Amendment, 42–43
Homer's Barbershop Quartet, 20, 24, 72–73
Homer's Enemy, 42–43
Homer's Night Out, 8–9
Homie Bear, 52
Homie the Clown, 49
Honey Bono, 54
Honeybunch:
    (see also Ship of Lost Souls), 55
Hooks, Jan, 18–19, 64–65
Hoover, Miss Elizabeth, 14–15, 32, 46–47, 54, 75
Hope, Bob, 34–35, 53
hot air balloon, 42–43
"Hot Blooded," 18–19
House of Usher, The, 32
How Dracula Got His Groove Back, 50–51
How Low Will You Go?, 76–77
Howard, Ron, 52
Howdy Doody, 67
Hoxha, Adil, 8–9, 10–11
Human Garbage Disposal, The:
    (see also Simpson, Bart)
Humvee, 52
Hunt for Red October, The, 52
Hunt, Helen, 30–31
Hutz, Lionel, 20, 21, 52
Hyundai, 66

I

"I Love Lucy," 56–57
I Married Marge, 42–43

"I'm a Believer," 30–31
I'm with Cupid, **64–65**
ice-blended mochas, 34–35
idiots, international, 62–63
Imagine Films, 52
impostor, 12
In 'n' Out Ear Piercing, 34–35
In Marge We Trust, 20, 78–79
"In the Navy," 34–35
"Incense and Peppermints," 53
Industrial Access Road, 41
Infernobuster 3000, The, 22–23
insemination ray, 50–51
"Inside the Actor's Studio," 55
Intel Inside, 14–15
International Olympic Committee, 74
internet, 60, 78–79
Internet for Dummies, 28
Invisible Man, 56–57
IRS, 36
Israelites, 70–71
It Blows, 13
It's a Wonderful Life, 42–43
Itchy & Scratchy, 8–9, 20, 37, 44–45
Itchy & Scratchy & Marge, 13, 42–43
Itchy & Scratchy & Poochie, 62–63
"Itchy & Scratchy & Poochie Show, The," 50–51
"Itchy & Scratchy Halloween Special," 50–51
Itchy & Scratchy Land, 20

J

J.R.R. Toykins, 33
Jackson, Michael, 8–9, 13
Jacques, 8–9
Jake's Barber Shop, 44–45
Jane, **26**–27
Japan, 78–79
Jasper, 32, 61
Java Server, The, 78–79
Java the Hutt, 29
Jaws, 26–27
Jazz Hole, The, 32
Jean, Al, 13, 34–35
Jedis, 56–57
Jefferson Airplane, 53
"Jeopardy!", 22–23
Jeremiah's Johnson, 10–11
Jerry Rude and the Bathroom Bunch, 75
"Jerry Springer Show, The," 50–51
Jews, 70–71
Jezebel, 70–71
Jimi Hendrix, 53
Joe's Diner, 68–69
Joel, Billy, 53
John, Elton, 64–65
Johnny D., 21
Johns, Jasper, 72–73
Johnson, Agent, 36
Johnson, Arte, 13
Johnson, Lyndon B., 53
Jonah, 70–71
Jones, Indiana, 28
Jones, James Earl, 28
Jones, Jimbo, 21, 33, 64–65
Joy of Sect, The, **26–27**
Judge, Mike, 17
june bugs, 46–47
Junior Skeptic, 34–35
jury summons, 76–77
Just Crichton and King Bookstore, 26–27
Justice Squadron, 76–77

K

K-JAZZ, 74
K.I.T.T., 48
kablingly, 22–23
Kabuki, 78–79
Kamp Krusty, 29
Kang, 50–51, 58–59
    (see also Space Stud), 50–51
KANGA-ROOMMATE, 78–79
kapowza, 37
Karama-Ceuticals, 67
Karl, 8–9, 25
Kashmir, Princess, 8–9, 30–31
Kataffy, Colonel, 37
Kaufman, Lance, 62–63
KBBL (102.5), 48, 67, 76–77
Kearney, 26–27, 33, 66
Keeler, Ken, 12
Keep in Touch Towers:
    (see also cellular transmitters), 67
Kentucky Fried Chicken, 78–79
Khlav Kalash vendor, 41
Khrushchev, Nikita, 28
Kickin' It: A Musical Journey through the Betty Ford Center, 10–11
kidney, artificial, 55
King David:
    (see also Simpson, Bart), 70–71
King Homer, 10–11, 75
King Kong, 75
King of England, 16
King of the Hill, 40

King Solomon:
    (see also Simpson, Homer), 70–71
King Toot's Music Store, 13
kings, damn hell ass, 28
Kirkland, Mark, 17, 25, 53, 74
Kirkland, Mike, 37, 48
Kiss, 28
Kliff's Kar Chalet, 22–23
Klon-Dykes!, 58–59
Knievel, Evel, 14–15
"Knight Rider," 48
Knock Over the Fuzzy Guy, 25
Kodos, 50–51
Kogen, Jay, 61
Kogen, Wally, 61
Kool-Aid Man, 78–79
Krabappel, Edna, 8–9, 12, 14–15, 26–27, 30–32, 44–45, 52, 54, 56–57, 64–65
Kramer, 42–43
Kreskin, 49
Kroon along with Krusty, 49
Krueger, Freddy, 50–51
Kruse, Nancy, 70–71
Krustofsky, Rabbi, 12
Krusty Alarm Clock, 44–45
Krusty Gets Kancelled, 24
Krusty the Clown, 8–9, 13, 16–17, 22–25, 29, 33, 37–39, 50–51, 61, 66–67, 70–71, 75
    (see also Corpsy the Clown), 29
    (see also Prince of Pies), 29
    (see also Sultan of Seltzer), 29
"Krusty the Clown Show, The", 37
"Krusty the Klown Story: Booze, Drugs, Guns, Lies, Blackmail and Laughter, The", 13
Krusty walkie-talkie, 72–73
Krustyburger, 22–23
KTV, 78–79
Kudrow, Lisa, 46–47
Kwik-E-Mart, 17, 18–19, 24, 50–51, 64–65

L

L.A. Confidential, 52
La Femme, Churchy:
    (see also Flanders, Ned), 58–59
La Lanne, Jack, 74
LaForge, Lieutenant Commander Geordi, 56–57
Lake Springfield:
    (see also Cess Hole 17A), 52
Lake Titicaca, 74
Laramie Ultra-Tar Kings, 50–51
Laramie-Slims, 50–51
Lard of the Dance, **46–47**, 60
Largo, Mr. Dewey, 62–63
Larry, 8–9, 44–45, 76–77
Larry Davis Experience, The, 38–39, 62–63
Larry the Bus Driver, **41**
LaRue, Chesty:
    (see also Simpson, Marge), 62–63
Las Vegas, 21, 58–59, 75
Last Temptation of Krust, The, 29, 34–35, 42–43, 66
Lauper, Cyndi, 60
Lawnmower, The, 52
Lawyer, Mr. Burns's, 61
lead paint, protective qualities of, 14–15
Leavelle, **56**–57
Led Zeppelin, 28
Leftopolis, 78–79
Leftorium, 78–79
Legends of Cleavage, 58–59
Legitimate Businessman's Social Club, The, 56–57
Legs, 61
Lenny, 10–11, 16–21, 41–43, 48, 55, 58–63, 67, 70–71, 75–77
Leno, Jay, 29
leprechauns, 33
"Let's All Go to the Lobby," 60
Let's Make a Baby, 33
Lewis, 28, 52
Li'l Bandit, 21, 24
Li'l Bastard Brainwashing Kit, 26–27
Li'l Bastard General Mischief Kit, 26–27
Li'l Leonardo Paint by Numbers Kit, 61
Li'l Lisa Slurry, 25
lice, head, 32
life expectancy, 48
Life in Hell, 8–9, 22–23, 33, 67
light bulb, 48
light sabers, 56–57
Like Father, Like Clown, 12
Lincoln, Abe, 78–79
Lisa Gets an "A," 54
Lisa the Beauty Queen, 25
Lisa the Greek, 42–43
Lisa the Iconoclast, 20
Lisa the Simpson, 32, 49
Lisa the Skeptic, 20
Lisa the Vegetarian, 38–39, 64–65
Lisa vs. Malibu Stacy, 18–19, 36
Lisa's Date with Density, 20, 66
Lisa's Sax, 13
Little Newark, 41
Lobo, Sheriff, 13
lobster, 30–31, 54

Loch Ness Monster, 75
Loch Ness Pub, 75
Lodge, John, 58–59
Logan, Joshua, 24
Loggins and Oates, 58–59
Long, Tim, 70–71
Lord of the Flies, 28
Loren, Bryan, 8–9
Lost in Space, 48, 56–57
Lost Our Lisa, **41**, 70–71
Lost Souls, The, **55**
Lotsa Books, 18–19
Lou, 22–23, 50–51, 72–73
Louie, 56–57
Louvre: American Style Art Gallery, The, 72–73
Love Day, 38–39
Love, American Style, 64–65
Lovejoy, Helen, 8–9, 42–43
Lovejoy, Reverend Timothy, 8–9, 26–27, 40, 44–45, 61
Lovell, Stacy, 18–19
"Luck Be A Lady Tonight," 56–57
Lucy Casino, The, 58–59
Lumpkin, Lurleen, 21

M

Mad magazine, 10–11
Madden, John, 61
Mademoiselle magazine, 10–11
Magic Eight Ball, 25
Magritte, Rene, 72–73
Make Room For Lisa, **67**
make-up gun, 48
Malibu Stacy, 36
malparkage, 10–11
Man Getting Hit by Football, 74
Man vs. Nature: The Road to Victory, 49
Manhattan, 10–11
Mann, Otto, 18–19, 26–27, 28, 30–31, 61, 62–63, 67
manna, 70–71
Mantegna, Joe, 56–57
Marge Be Not Proud, 22–23
Marge in Chains, 13
Marge Simpson in: "Screaming Yellow Honkers," 66
Marge vs. the Monorail, 13, 24
Marine World, 30–31
Marino, Dan, 61
marriage, arranged, 18–19
Martin, Andrea, 18–19
Martin, Steve, 38–39
Martin, Tom, 61
Marty, **48**, 67
Marvin, Lee, 24
"Mattel and Mars Bar Quick Energy Chocobot Hour, The," 37
matter transporter, 14–15
mattress car, 10–11
Maximum Homerdrive, **68–69**
Maxtone-Graham, Ian, 10–11, 36, 38–39, 54
Mayored to the Mob, **56–57**, 58–59
mazzulians, 22–23
McAllister, C.W., 40
McBain, 40
McBoob, Hooty:
　　(see also Simpson, Marge), 62–63
McCallister, Captain, 18–19, 21, 54, 55, 61
McCartney, Linda, 38–39, 64–65
McCartney, Paul, 64–65
McClure, Troy, 17, 28, 32, 33, 49
McGee, Dirty Dingus:
　　(see also Simpson, Homer), 58–59
McKean, Michael, 75
"McLaughlin Group, The," 46–47
McMahon, Ed, 50–51
meditation, 78–79
Mega-Saving Seminar, 78–79
Mel, Sideshow, 16, 17, 20, 42–43, 52, 61, 64–65
Mellish, Ralph:
　　(see also Moleman, Hans), 74
Mellon, Ms., 8–9
Mellow, Mr.:
　　(see also Simpson, Homer), 58–59
Men Without Hats, 67
Mensa, 76–77
Mercury Space Capsule, 67
Merlin's Video Dungeon, 42–43
metal detector, 42–43
Mexican Fighting Trees, 62–63
Meyer, George, 21, 61, 74
Michelangelo's David, 13
Michels, Pete, 16, 28, 41, 52, 62–63, 76–77
Michigan, Flint, 76–77
midseason replacements, 62–63
Milhouse Divided, A, 12
milk, rat, 56–57
Millennium Falcon, 58–59
Milli Vanilla, 54
mines, abandoned, 38–39
mini-adult, 46–47
mini-golf, 42–43
Miracle on Evergreen Terrace, **22–23**, 33
Mirkin, David, 24, 26–27
mob rule, 16
mob, angry, 22–23
Model UN, 17, 28

Moe's Inn, 14–15
Moe's Tavern, 30–31, 42–43, 52, 55, 61–65, 72–73
Mojo the Helper Monkey, **37**
"Moleman in the Morning," 74
Moleman, Hans:
　　(see also Mellish, Ralph), 13, 18–19, 26–27, 62–63, **74**
Mom and Pop Art, **72–73**
Mom–Dad–Grad gift corridor, 38–39
Mommy, What's Wrong with That Man's Face?, 32
Monkees, The, 30–31
monkey sweat, 58–59
Monroe, Marilyn, 78–79
Monster Who Ate Everybody, The, 68–69
Monsters of Poetry, 16
Monty Can't Buy Me Love, 67, **75**
Moo–hammed, 56–57
Moody Blues, The, 58–59
Moon Pie, 32
Moore, Steve, 12
Moore, Steven Dean, 12, 18–19, 26–27, 40, 49–51, 61
Morningwood Penitentiary, 33
mortgage application, 53
mortician, 41
Moses:
　　(see also Van Houten, Milhouse), 70–71
mothballs, 8–9
Mothra, 78–79
motor oil, 55
motor, refrigerator, 42–43
Movementarian Leader, 26–27
Movementarians, The, 26–27
Mr. Bribe, 25
Mr. Pinchy, **54**
Mr. Plow, 20, 22–23
Mr. Sparkle, 20, 78–79
Mt. Everest, 75
Mull, Martin, 53
Mullen, Larry, 38–39
Munchie, **53**
Municipal Fortress of Vengeance, 76–77
Muntz, Nelson, 16–17, 20, 25, 28, 32–33, 44–45, 49, 54, 60, 70–71, 75
　　(see also Goliath II), 70–71
murder house, 21
Murderhorn, The, 40
Murdoch, Rupert, 61
Murdock, Captain Lance, 58–59
Murphy, Bleeding Gums, 8–9
Museum of Hollywood Jerks, 52
Museum of Natural History, 20
mush, kidney, 18–19
music box, 41
mustache combs, 49
My Sister, My Sitter, 38–39
Myanmar, 74

N

Nacho Cheez, 24
Naegle, Lindsey, **76–77**
Nahasapeemapetilon, Apu, 13, 17–19, 24, 26–27, 32, 34–35, 37,
　　40, 50–52, 61, 64–67, 75–79,
Nahasapeemapetilon, Manjula, 18–19, **64–65**
Nakadowna, 78–79
Namath, Joe, 17
Nastuk, Matthew, 53, 67
Natural Born Kissers, **42–43**, 54, 62–63
Nature Rice, 54
Naval Reserve, 34–35
Naval Reserve Tour, 34–35
Navitron Auto–Drive system, 68–69
NBC network, 14–15, 66
neanderthal, 20
Neat & Tidy Piano Movers, 53
Neddy, Steady:
　　(see also Flanders, Ned), 58–59
Negron, Rip Taylor, 58–59
Neil, **40**
Nelson, Frank, 56–57
nene, 49
Nerdy Young Woman, 56–57
Nero's Palace, 58–59
neutron bomb, 14–15
New York Jets, 10–11
Newark, Newark Casino, 58–59
news anchor, 37
Newsflush, 48
Niagara Falls, 75
Nimoy, Leonard, 75
Nintendo, 44–45
Noah, 28
North Carolina, Dawson's Creek, 76–77
nougat, ears filled with, 64–65
Nougat, Major, 37
NRA, 16
NRBQ, 74
Nude–E–Mart, 32

O

O' Hara, Antoine "Tex," 32
O'Brian, Jane, 46–47
O'Donnell, Steve, 24, 26–27

O.K. Car–ral, The, 66
Oakland Raiders, 61
Oakley, Bill, 10–11, 12, 32
Obo–mo–boe, 13
octo–wussy, 49
Officer's Club, 34–35
"Oh, Yeah," 10–11, 48
Okla–Homo!, 58–59
Old Jewish Man, The, 74
Old Man and the "C" Student, The, **74**
Old Man and the Lisa, The, 25, 55
Old Money, 12
Olmec Indian Head, 52
OmniTouch Representative, **67**
"One Bourbon, One Scotch and One Beer," 30–31
One Flew over the Cuckoo's Nest, 74
Ono, Yoko, 72–73
Orb of Isis, 41, 70–71
Organ Donor Sucker List, 55
Ori, 78–79
origami, 78–79
orphans, 12, 22–23
Osaka Seafood Concern, 78–79
Oscar Meyer Periodic Table, 54
Oscars (Academy Awards), 48, 52
Otto Show, The, 20, 42–43
"Our Gang," 60
outsider art, 72–73
overcompensation, 17
ovulation, 33

P

P.J. O'Harrigans, 67
Pack Rat Returns, 49
Painful Memories Party Supply, 53
Paint Your Wagon, 24
pandas, 75
parasailing, 52
Parking Violations Bureau, 10–11
Parton, Dolly, 61
Patches and Poor Violet, **22**–23
Patterson, Ray, 38–39
Pearl Harbor, 55
Penicill–O's, 50–51
Pepper steak, 56–57
Pepsi, homemade, 46–47
Persistance of Memory, The, 72–73
Pete, Handsome, 55
peyote, 53
phasers, 56–57, 58–59
Philbin, Regis, 50–51
Phillips, Stone, 66
Philly Cheesesteak, 53
Picasso, Pablo, 72–73
pickled eggs, 10–11
picnic basket, 52
Pig of Eden, 70–71
pigeons, 49
pills, pink, 18–19
pimps, 10–11
pineapples, 30–31
Pink Floyd, 53
piranhas, 50–51
Pirates of the Caribbean, 55
pistol, beach, 30–31
Pit Boss, 58–59
placemat, 48
Planet of the Apes, 34–35
Planet of the Donuts, 34–35
play date, 33
Playboy Mansion, 10–11
Players Club, 30–31
Plow King, 22–23
Plunkett, Jim, 61
plutonium, 50–51
Polcino, Dominic, 13, 30–31, 46–47
polenta, 55
"Police Cops," 62–63
Police Midnight Charity Cruise, 30–31
police raid, 53
Police–Seized Property Auction, 21
Poochie, 50–51
pope, phony, 48
porn star, 34–35
porno bush, 70–71
Portion Time meals, 32
potato chips, liquid, 18–19
POW camps, 12
powders, 41
Power, Max (see also Simpson, Homer), 62–63
Powers, Ruth, 16
Powersauce, 40
Powersauce Newsbreak, The, 40
prayer, 22–23, 37, 46–47, 64–65
Presley, Elvis, 13, 32, 78–79
Price, Vincent, 61
Prince of Pies:
　　(see also Krusty the Klown), 29
Prince, Martin, 8–9, 12, 20, 28, 32, 34–35, 44–45, 60
Prince, The Artist Formerly Known As, 13
Principal and the Pauper, The, **12**, 33, 48
"Prisoner, The," 26–27

Product Day, 38–39
protective cup, 17
"Proud Mary," 74
Pryor, Dr. J. Loren, 13
Puente, Tito, 36
Pukepail, Joe, 30–31
punk, street, 12
Pyle, Gomer, 75
pyramids, 8–9, 70–71
Pyro:
    (see also Chase), 30–31, 60, 72–73

Q

Quicksands casino, 58–59
Quimby, Freddy, 38–39
Quimby, Mayor Diamond Joe, 14–15, 16, 17, 33, 38–39, 56–57, 67, 76–77
Quint, 26–27

R

racehorse, world's fattest, 32
Radcliffe College, 75
radio, pirate, 60
Raiders of the Lost Ark, 20, 28
Ramadan, 56–57
Ranger Ned, 52
Rashomon, 78–79
Ray–Ban, 56–57
Real Estate Law, 21
Realty Bites, **21**, 29
Reardon, Jim, 10–11, 38–39, 78–79
Red Blazer Realty, 21
Red Rascal, 68–69
"Red Grocer, The," 68–69
Red Sea, 70–71
Redwood Forest, 62–63
Regional Geographic, 49
"Regis and Kathie Lee Show," 50–51
Reiss, Mike, 13, 34–35
Renaissance Faire, 76–77
Renee, **30**–31
Rent, 56–57
Report Card, 12, 33
retirement, 12, 62–63
Reynolds, Burt, 78–79
rhino alert, level three, 66
Rhode Island, Ebola, 76–77
rib, sexiest, 70–71
ribs, pork, 70–71
Richard, 28, 44–45
Ring of Fire, The, 58–59
Ring of Ice, The, 58–59
Ring Toss, 25
riots, 56–57, 76–77
riots, soccer, 16
risks, stupid, 41
Ritz–Carlton Hotel for Transients, The, 12
Rivera's casino, 58–59
Riverdance, 18–19
Riveria, Dr. Nick, 16–17, 32–33, 50–52, 61
Road King package, 61
Road Rage: Death Flips the Finger, 66
Robbie the Automaton:
    (see also Floyd the Robot), **33**
Roberts, Cokie, 67
robin, 49
robots, 32, 52, 55
"Rock the Casbah," 42–43
Rockefeller, Hercules:
    (see also Simpson, Homer), 62–63
Rodan, 78–79
Rolling Stones, The, 53
romance, 30–31, 64–65
Ronin, 78–79
Roosevelt, Franklin Delano, 67
rose farm, 64–65
Rosebud, 13
Rossellini, Isabella, 72–73
Roswell, Little Green Man, 56–57
Rousseau, Henri, 72–73
"Rowan and Martin's Laugh-In," 13
Royal Tokyo Hotel, 78–79
Rubik's Cube, 25
Rude, Jerry, 75
Rudy, 61
Rusk, Dean, 53
Russian district, 41

S

Sabertooth Meadow, 20
Sad Sack, 75
Safari Casino, The, 58–59
"Safety Dance," 67
Saget, Bob, 58–59
"Sailing, Sailing," 30–31
Sakatumi, 78–79
Sam, 44–45, 76–77
Sam, Uncle, 67
Sampson, Homer:
    (see also Simpson, Homer), 42–43
Sampson, Marge:
    (see also Simpson, Marge), 42–43
San Francisco 49ers, 61

Sandler, Adam, 75
sandwich, tuna, 48
sandwiches, submarine, 68–69
"Sanford and Son," 38–39
sanitation commissioner, 38–39
Santa Claus, 22–23, 25, 76–77
Santa's Little Helper, 14–15, 25, 40, 44–45
sarcasm detector, 76–77
sarsaparilla, 55
Saturdays of Thunder, 10–11
Saturn, 53
saxophones, 8–9, 13, 44–45
Say It Isn't Soy, 54
scandals, 34–35
scarlet letter, 14–15
Schlub, Joe, 40
schmutz, 29
Schwimmer, David, 34–35
sciatica, 62–63
Scotland, 75
Scott, Swinton O., III, 21, 36, 56–57, 68–69
Screamatorium of Dr. Frightmarestein, The, 25
Screen Actors Guild, 53
Scully, Brian, 41, 61
Scully, Mike, 16–23, 25–31, 33–43, 46–79
Scumbag, Jimmy the, 20, 38–39, 76–77
Scumbag, Timmy and Tammy, 60
scumdrops, 12
Seals and Crofts, 58–59
Secrets of National Security Revealed, 50–51
Security Salesman, 16
Seinfeld, Jerry, 58–59
seizures, 78–79
Selman, Matt, 42–43, 70–71, 76–77
Señor Ding-Dong's Doorbell Fiesta, 68–69
sensory deprivation tanks, 67
Seth, **53**
Seurat, George, 72–73
Seven Duffs, The, 64–65
sex offenders, 38–39
Sha Na Na, 53
Shark Bait, 49
Shaw, Robert, 26–27
Sheen, Martin, 12
Shelbyville, 74
Shepherd Ralph:
    (see also Wiggum, Ralph), 70–71
Sherbert Hoover, 54
Sherpas, 40
Sherri, **17**, 20, 28, 34–35, 44–45, 46–47, 60
Ship of Lost Souls:
    (see also Honeybunch), 55
shofar, 70–71
sidekicks, bumbling, 62–63
Simmons, Mindy, 36
Simpson & Son Grease Co., 46–47
Simpson & Son's Patented Revitalizing Tonic, 46–47
Simpson and Delilah, 25, 8–9
"Simpson Family Smile–Time Variety Hour, The," 52
Simpson Men, **32**
Simpson Tide, 34–35
Simpson, Abe, 12, 17, 32, 34–35, 40, 42–43, 53, 55, 74
Simpson, Bart, 8–15, 17, 21, 22–31, 33–35, 37, 40–47, 50–52, 54–55,
    60–69, 72–74, 78–79
    community service, 74
    conception of, 42–43
    dreams, 22–23
    homosexual tendencies of, 72–73
    insulting comedy of, 74
    jail time, 78–79
    latex dummy of, 54
    pierced ear, 46–47
    (see also Human Garbage Disposal, The), 76–77
    (see also King David), 70–71
Simpson, Detective Homer, Police Cop, 62–63
Simpson, Homer J., 8–36, 38–51, 53–79
    art of, 72–73
    average settlement against, 60, 72–73
    boudoir photography, 76–77
    defacing Bill of Rights, 67
    dishonorable discharge, 34–35
    football coach, 17
    hippie, 53
    in the gym, 40
    inability to keep secrets, 68–69
    jail time, 30–31, 78–79
    lack of underpants, 48, 75
    masonry failure, 72–73
    middle name, 53
    muscle for hire business, 46–47
    naked, 42–43, 70–71
    on nudity, 76–77
    (see also Adam), 70–71
    (see also Einstein, Rembrandt Q.), 58–59
    (see also King Solomon), 70–71
    (see also McGee, Dirty Dingus), 58–59
    (see also Mellow, Mr.), 72–73
    (see also Power, Max), 58–59
    (see also Rockefeller, Hercules), 62–63

    (see also Sampson, Homer), 42–43
    (see also Simpsons, Stinkypants), 58–59
    (see also Wonderful, Handsome B.), 62–63
    (see also World's Greatest Accomplisher), 48
Simpson, Lisa, 8–15, 20–32, 34–35, 37–39, 41–47, 49–52, 54–55, 58–63, 66–69, 72–74, 76–79
    cheating, 54
    eye color, 25
    open letter to Springfield, 76–77
    response to stress, 67
    taking the bus, 41
    (see also Cheaterly, Lady), 54
Simpson, Maggie, 14–16, 23–24, 44–45, 50–51, 72–73
Simpson, Marge, 8–19, 21–27, 29–31, 33, 36–39, 41–45, 48–51, 54–55,
    61–66, 68–74, 78–79,
    engagement ring, 72–73
    license revoked, 66
    naked, 42–43, 70–71
    on an adventure, 68–69
    on tattoos, 62–65
    (see also Eve), 70–71
    (see also LaRue, Chesty), 62–63
    (see also McBoob, Hooty), 62–63
    (see also Sampson, Marge), 42–43
    (see also St. Clair, Busty), 62–63
    special pearls, 62–63
Simpson, Stinkypants:
    (see also Simpson, Homer), 58–59
Simpsons 138th Episode Spectacular, The, 24
Simpsons Roasting on an Open Fire, 22–23
Sinner, Principal:
    (see also Skinner, Principal Seymour), 13
Sir Drinks–A–Lot, 67
Sir Lovesalot, 38–39
Sir Putt's A Lot Merrie Olde Fun Centre, 42–43
Sir Putt–A–Lot's Merrie Olde Fun Centre, 42–43
Sir–Loin–A–Lot, 68–69
Sit–N–Stare Bus Lines, 10–11
six–legged chair, 48
Skee Ball, 42–43
Skinner, Agnes, 12, 14–16, 62–63, 66
Skinner, Pharaoh:
    (see also Skinner, Principal Seymour), 70–71
Skinner, Principal Seymour, 8–9, 12–16, 20–21, 26–28, 30–31, 34–35,
    37, 44–48, 52, 54, 56–57, 60–61, 64–66, 70–71, 74–77
    (see also Butt, King, 70–71
    (see also Skinner, Pharaoh), 70–71
    (see also Tamzarian, Armin), 12
Skinner, Sergeant Seymour, **12**
Skinner, Principal Seymour:
    (see also Sinner, Principal), 13
Skittlebrau, 17, 78–79
skybox, 61
Skywalker, Luke, 56–57
skywriters code, 64–65
Slaughterhouse Restaurant, 68–69
slaves, 70–71
sleeper hold, 56–57
Sleeping Gypsy, The, 72–73
"Smartline," 20
Smithee, Alan, 54
Smithers, Waylon, 16, 18–19, 36, 53, 72–77
Smithsonian Traveling Exhibit, 67
snacktacular, 54
Snake, 14–16, 21, **24**, 50–51, 62–63, 76–79
Snookums, Mr., 34–35
Snowball, 13
Snowball II, 14–15, 40, 50–51
snowflakes, 30–31
Snowshoe Casino, The, 58–59
Snyder, Judge, 12, 52
So It's Come to This: Another Simpsons Clip Show, 24, 74
soccer, 16
Sodom, 70–71
Someone's in the Kitchen with DNA, 32
Songs to Enrage Bus Drivers, 28
Sony, 54
Space Stud:
    (see also Kang), 50–51
spaghetti, bar of, 40
"Spanish Flea," 42–43
sparkplugs, 76–77
Spendover, 38–39
sperm, cartoon, 33
Spice Girls, The, 68–69
Spinster City Apartments, 16
Spirit of St. Louis, 67
SPLT (Springfield Lawyer Truck), 26–27
Spock, 56–57
Sportacus, 17
Springer, Jerry, 50–51
$pringfield, 18–19
Springfield:
    Birdwatching Society, 49
    Civic Center, 18–19
    Community Church, 14–15
    Dinner Theater, 56–57
    Dog Pound, 8–9
    Drive–In, 60
    Elementary, 8–9, 12, 28, 46–47, 54, 56–57, 60, 66
    Hospital, 55

International Airport, 26–27, 36, 64–65
Isotopes, 60
Knowledgeum, 33
Lawyer House, 26–27
Lawyer Truck:
    (see also SPLT), 26–27
Library, 76–77
Municipal Building, 49
Police, 10–11, 50–51
Police Dept., 20
Retirement Castle, 18–19, 22–23, 42–43, 74
Shopper, 22–23, 38–39, 42–43, 62–63, 74, 76–77
Stadium, 16
Tire Fire, The, 74
Town Charter, 76–77
Variety, 52
Wildcats, 17
Zoo, 75
Springfield, Jebediah, 8–9, 44–45
springs, 74
Springsonian Museum, 41, 72–73
Springy, The Springfield Olympic Mascot, 74
SPRYNGE–FIELDE, 14–15
Spud, **25**
Spungos, 61
squares, 53
Squeaky Farms Brand Genuine Animal Milk, 56–57
Squeaky–Voiced Teen, 12, 61
squishee, 44–45, 50–51, 64–65
St. Clair, Busty (see also Simpson, Marge), 62–63
Stampy the Elephant, 18–19
Stan the car salesman, 66
Stanley Cup, 58–59
Star is Burns, A, 48
"Star Spangled Banner, The," 53
Stardust Drive–In, 68–69
Starfleet Academy, 58–59
Stark Raving Dad, 74
Starship Enteprise (NCC–1701), 58–59
"Starship Poopers," 50–51
state grants, 54
Statue of Liberty, 8–9, 78–79
Steel, Trent, 62–63
Steiger, Rod, 34–35
stenchblossoms, 12
Stern, David M., 17, 58–59
Stern, Howard, 75
Sternin, Joshua, 34–35
Sticky Fingers, 53
Stimu–Crank, 68–69
stinkbags, trash–eating, 38–39
stinkbeetle, 28
Stomp, 56–57
Stonecutters, 67
Strawberry Alarm Clock, The, 53
Streisand, Barbra, 52
Stu's Disco, 30–31
Stupid, Admiral, 34–35
Suddenly Last Supper, 28
Sultan of Seltzer:
    (see also Krusty the Clown), 29
Summer of 4 ft. 2, 25
Summerall, Pat, 61
Sumo Babies, 55
Sumo Stadium, 78–79
sumo wrestling, 78–79
Sunday Afternoon on the Island of La Grande Jatte, A, 72–73
Sunday, Cruddy Sunday, 61, 62–63
Super Bowl, 61
Superfly, 14–15
SuperFriends, The, 12, 33
Superman, 41
Swartzwelder, John, 16, 25, 40, 48, 55, 62–63, 68–69, 75
Sweet Seymour Skinner's Baadasss Song, 46–47
Sweet, Lucius, 36
Sweetarts, 56–57
Swiss Family Robinson, 28
Sycamore Avenue, 41
synergy, 76–77
syphilis, 50–51
Szyslak, Moe, 8–11, 16, 18–20, 26–27, 30–31, 34–35, 38–39,
    42–45, 50–51, 55, 58–61, 64–66, 75–77

T

Takei, George, 78–79
"Talk to the Hand," 60
Talmadge, Cornelius, 18–19
Tamzarian, Armin:
    (see also Skinner, Principal Seymour), 12, 48
tattoos, 24
Tatum, Drederick, 58–59
Team Homer, 12, 20
Tenille, Captain, **34**–35
tentacles, 50–51
Terminator, The, 56–57
Terminizer, The, 52
Terri, **17**, 20, 28, 34–35, 44–47
"Terror of Tiny Toon, The," 50–51
Terwiliger, Sideshow Bob, 8–9, 24, 33, 44–45
Thacker, Julie, 74
Thai food, 62–63
"That '70s Show," 78–79
"That's Edu–Tainment!," 66

The Wall, 53
The Way We Was, 68–69
The Wizard of Evergreen Terrace, 48
They Saved Lisa's Brain, 76–77
This Little Wiggy, **26**–27, 33
Thomas, Ray, 58–59
Thompson, Hunter S., 58–59
thong, 30–31, 78–79
Three Musicians, 72–73
three–strikes law, 50–51
Tiffany's, 64–65
tiger stabbers, 55
"Time of the Season," 53
Tire Salesman, 61
Titanic, 74
titmouse, 49
titpecker, 49
Tobago, 17
toilet chair, 48
toilet, talking, 78–79
Tony, Fat, 56–57
Tooth Chipper, The, 25
torpedo tubes, 34–35
traffic school, 58
transplants, 50–51, 55
Trash of the Titans, **38**–39, 76–77
Travolta, John, 13
Treasures of Isis, 41
Trebek, Alex, 22–23
Tree of Knowledge, 70–71
Treehouse of Horror II, 30–31
Treehouse of Horror III, 10–11, 75
Treehouse of Horror IX, **50**–51
Treehouse of Horror VII, 62–63
Treehouse of Horror VIII, **14**–15, 33
trillion–dollar bill, 36
Trinidad, 17
Trouble with Trillions, The, 25, **36**
truckers, 68–69
Try–N–Save, 22–23, 46–47
Tuba–ma–ba, 13
Tufeld, Dick, 56–57
Tune, Tommy, 10–11
Turner, Joseph, 72–73
Turner, Ted, 68–69
Turnpike Lounge, 58–59
TV–Ratings, 14–15
twins, 17
twins, evil, 17, 46–47
Two Dozen and One Greyhounds, 24
Two Mrs. Nahasapeemapetilons, The, **18**–19, 58–59
tyrants, 61

U

U–Break–It Van Rental, 21
U–Trawl Boat Rentals, 52
U.S. Wildlife Department, 49
U2, 38–39
UCLA Yankee Cola, 78–79
"Ugly Duckling, The," 13
ukulele, 30–31
Ullman, Tracey, 13
Uncle Sam, 78–79
United States Navy, 34–35
Up, Up and Buffet, 42–43
"Uptown Girl," 53
Uter, 56–57
Utopia, 76–77

V

Vaccaro, Doug, 72–73
Val–U–Qual Coupons, 61
Valentine's Day, 12, 64–65
Van Cleef, Lee, 24
Van Houten, Kirk, 17, 18–19, 21, 54, 61, 76–77
Van Houten, Luann, 12, 17, 26–27, 30–31, 54, 60, 72–73
Van Houten, Milhouse, 8–9, 12–13, 16–17, 20, 28–29, 32,
    34–35,
        44–47, 49, 60, 70–73
    (see also Moses), 70–71
Van Houten, Nana, 14–15
Van Houten, Young Milhouse, **13**
Vanzo, Greg, 44–45
Varney, Jim, 25
Venice, canals of, 72–73
Ventimilla, Jeffrey, 34–35
Very Tall Man, The, 10–11
vestigial tail, 55
Veterans of Popular Wars Hall, 37
Veterans of Unpopular Wars Hall, The, 34–35
Vicarious Living, 68–69
Victory City, 17
Vietnam, 12–13, 36, 53, 55
Village of the Damned, 60
Village People, The, 34–35
Villanova University, 10–11
"Vincent Price's Egg Magic," 61
Vio–ma–lin, 13
virgins, 56–57
vitamin church, 58–59
vitamin money, 22–23
Viva Ned Flanders, **58**–59, 66
Volkswagon Beetle, 66

voodoo, 26–27
Vulcans, 76–77
vwhing, 56–57

W

waiting periods, 16
Waiting to Exhale, 24
Walden Two, 76–77
"Wannabe," 68–69
"War," 14–15
Warhol, Andy, 72–73
washcloth, 22–23
Washington D.C., 50–51
water heater, 30–31
watermelon, 56–57
Waters, Ricky, 61
WB Network, The, 13
"We Know All Your Secrets," 60
Weber, Steven, 40
wedding, impulse, 58–59
Weekend at Bernie's, 56–57
Weinstein, Josh, 10–11, 12, 32
Welcome to the Springfield Airport, 33
Weller, Astrid, **72**–73
Wendell, **28**, 44–45, 52, 54
wheatgrass, 52
wheel balancing, 61
Wheel of Misforture, 44–45
"When Buildings Collapse," 32
"When Disaster Strikes 4," 49
"When Skirts Fall Off," 50–51
When You Dish Upon A Star, 52
Where's Nordstrom?, 33
"White Rabbit," 53
Whitney, Alex, **46**–47
Who Shot Mr. Burns (Part Two), 36
"Who's on First?," 66
whore, 48
whup–tushie, 68–69
Wiggle Puppy, 33
Wiggum, Chief Clancy, 14–15, 17, 21–23, 25, 30–31, 33, 38–39,
    42–45, 50–51, 60–63, 66, 67–73, 76–77
Wiggum, Ralph, 12, 28, 32–35, 46–47, 52, 54, 70–71
    (see also Shepherd Ralph), 70–71
Wiggum, Sarah, 64–65, 72–73
"Wild Animal Kingdom," 66
Wild Barts Can't Be Broken, 60
Willard, Fred, 61
Williams, Cindy, 34–35
Williams, Hank, Jr., 29
Willie:
    (see also Shamu), 30–31
Willie, Groundskeeper, 12, 17, 26–27, 30–31, 37, 46–47, 56–57,
    75
Winfield, Paul, 36
Wink, the Game Show Host, 78–79
Winnebago, 52
Winter Madness Sale, 46–47
Winter, Edgar and Johnny, 14–15
Wired magazine, 78–79
witch burnings, 14–15
Withstandinator, The, 14–15
Wolfcastle, Rainier, 26–27, 40
Wolodarsky, Wallace, 61
Wonderful, Handsome B.:
    (see also Simpson, Homer), 62–63
wonders, dateless, 56–57
woodcock, 49
Woodstock, 53
Working Mother Magazine, 49
World Trade Center, 10–11
"World's Deadliest Executions," 50–51
World's Greatest Accomplisher:
    (see also Simpson, Homer), 48
Wright, Steven, 29
Wuhan, 12
wuss rock, 58–59
WWII, 36

X

Xavier Nougat, 54
Xiaoping, Deng, 40

Y

Ye Go Karts, 42–43
Ye Olde Animatronic Saloon, 55
Yello, 10–11, 48
Yo La Tengo, 53
Yoda, 56–57
Yogi Bear, 52
Yoshi, 78–79
Yuk–ingham Palace, 41, 53

Z

zazz, 37
Zebra Girl, 40
zinc, 52
Zombies, The, 53
zork, 37
ZZ Top, 10–11, 61

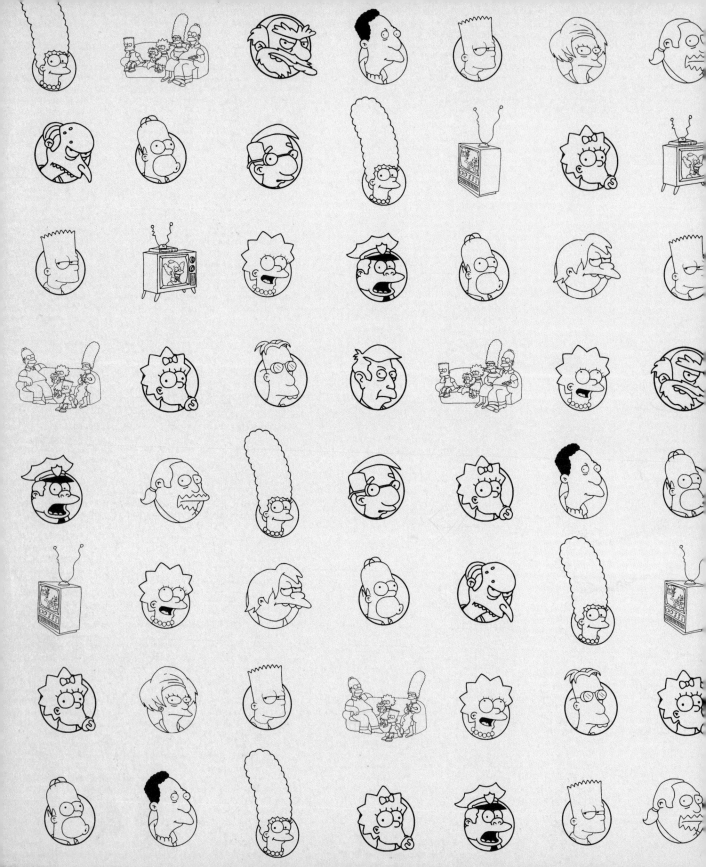